CARNEGIE'S MODEL REPUBLIC

CARNEGIE'S MODEL REPUBLIC

Triumphant Democracy
and the British-American Relationship

A. S. Eisenstadt

STATE UNIVERSITY OF NEW YORK PRESS

Published by
State University of New York Press, Albany

© 2007 State University of New York

All rights reserved

Printed in the United States of America

No part of this book may be used or reproduced
in any manner whatsoever without written permission.
No part of this book may be stored in a retrieval system
or transmitted in any form or by any means including
electronic, electrostatic, magnetic tape, mechanical,
photocopying, recording, or otherwise without the prior
permission in writing of the publisher.

For information, contact State University of New York Press, Albany, NY
www.sunypress.edu

Production by Diane Ganeles
Marketing by Anne M. Valentine

Library of Congress Cataloging in Publication Data

Eisenstadt, Abraham Seldin, 1920-
 Carnegie's model republic : Triumphant democracy and the British-American relationship / A.S. Eisenstadt.
   p. cm.
 Includes bibliographical references.
 ISBN 978-0-7914-7223-1 (hardcover : alk. paper)
 ISBN 978-0-7914-7224-8 (pbk. : alk. paper) 1. Carnegie, Andrew, 1835–1919. Triumphant democracy. 2. Carnegie, Andrew, 1835–1919—Influence. 3. United States—Politics and government—1865–1900. 4. United States—Economic conditions—1865–1918. 5. United States—Social life and customs—1865–1918. 6. National characteristics, American. 7. United States—Relations—Great Britain. 8. Great Britain—Relations—United States. 9. Great Britain—Civilization. 10. National characteristics, British. I. Title.

E661.C2833 2007
973.5--dc22

2007002074

10 9 8 7 6 5 4 3 2 1

Dedicated
in loving memory to my beloved wife Paulette
and my son Jonathan
and with love to my daughters Laura and Elizabeth

Contents

Acknowledgments		ix
Introduction		xi
1	The Road to *Triumphant Democracy*	1
2	Major Themes	15
3	The Antithesis of Models	31
4	Reconciling Ideals	55
5	The British Critique	73
6	Affirming America	95
7	The Pan-Anglian Persuasion	117
8	Conclusion	155
	Notes	179
	A Brief Note on Sources	199
	Index	201

Acknowledgments

MY GREATEST DEBT is to Dean Glenn C. Altschuler, Thomas and Dorothy Litwin Professor of American Studies at Cornell University, whose wise counsel improved two earlier versions of this book. Other drafts were read by Professors Irwin Unger of New York University, Gertrude Himmelfarb of the Graduate Center of the City University of New York, Carnegie's biographer, the late Joseph F. Wall of Grinnell College, and the late Herman Ausubel of Columbia University.

Among the principal libraries I have used in my research are the Manuscripts Division of the Library of Congress, the New York Public Library, the Columbia University Library, the Brooklyn College (City University of New York) Library, the British Museum, the Bodleian Library of Oxford University, the Stirling Library, the Yale University Library, the Baker Library, and the Dartmouth College Library. I was generously helped by their staffs.

My work on this book was aided by grants from the American Philosophical Society and the National Endowment for the Arts.

I am also grateful to two very fine persons who lent me their special skills. Marie Gangemi helped me edit the manuscript and prepare the index. Gregory Magarshak converted a text that had been drafted in one computer language into another.

Introduction

ANDREW CARNEGIE, a world-famous industrialist and philanthropist, was also a highly renowned writer and political activist. Apart from two diaries of his travels that he published, he wrote many essays that arose out of his experience in becoming America's greatest steelmaker and amassing the prodigious wealth that making and selling steel produced. He is best known for his essay on wealth, in which he suggested how men of vast fortunes should disburse their money. While he was still in business, he himself followed several of the routes he suggested; when he left business, he called on the guidance of experts to help him make philanthropy his biggest industry. But in the central decades of his life, particularly in the 1880s, as he was making steel and money, he was also making politics. He did this without any notable prominence in the United States, where he achieved his goals through state agents and business associations, but far more overtly and actively in Britain, where politics was national and London-based and where he tried with greater involvement to shape the course of public affairs. An emigrant from Scotland, he retained his ties with his motherland throughout his life. About his politics he wrote many essays. Yet for all that (apart from a brief biography of James Watt) he wrote only one book, *Triumphant Democracy*, in which he posed the American republic as a model for remaking British political institutions. He considered the book his most important written work.

Triumphant Democracy was part of the larger current of British-American politics and of the dialogue between Britain and the United States about the virtues and deficiencies of their respective nations. The dialogue became intense in the 1760s, flared up in the American Revolution of the 1770s, and proceeded with varying degrees of vitality from the years the United States became independent. To put *Triumphant*

Democracy in its proper context, one has to explore the British-American antithesis out of which it arose and how that antithesis was changing during the years in which Carnegie was formulating his own approach to the two nations. Carnegie's ideas are best understood as part of the transforming politics of the kindred nations, which indeed shaped his particular contribution to the dialogue between them.

The book burst upon the transatlantic scene in mid-April 1886, a massive tome of over five hundred pages, bound in red buckram, its theme boldly announced on its cover. Stamped in gold were two triangles: one of an overturned monarchy, the second of a firmly standing republic. Printed in heavy black were two quotations from the respective leaders of the British Liberal and Conservative parties: William Gladstone's tribute to the American Constitution and the Marquess of Salisbury's tribute to the role of the American Senate. Never was it more clear that here was a book that could be judged by its cover.

Beneath that glittering surface ran the deeper currents of the British-American relationship. Ever since America had declared its independence, there had been an ongoing colloquy between the Americans and the British about the virtues of their respective polities. The colloquy was always intense because it was always self-justificatory, and for the Americans particularly so because it touched the very issue of their identity. The degree of intensity fluctuated from decade to decade, depending on at least two factors, external and domestic: the waters of diplomacy that each polity had to navigate to ensure its own best interest, and the class and ethnicity of groups in both Britain and America that defined their status in their respective societies. To Britain's aristocracy, democratic America represented a model to be questioned and guarded against. For the same reason, to those in Britain who stood outside the governing establishment, America was a model of desirable reform and a beacon of improvement. For Americans, the debate with Britain was less divisively conducted: with a continent to master, the energies of diplomacy and internationalism were largely internalized. The U.S. borders had to be secured. As to domestic pressures, however they expressed themselves, American identity was largely subsumed under a banner of national civism.[1] It hardly covered internal fissures, but it transmuted them into a sentiment of patriotism, the primal element of America's ongoing colloquy with Britain.

The American Civil War brought to a head the antithesis between the ideals of the kindred polities. In the United States, the war was a conflict for the survival of the democratic ideal; for the governing authorities in Britain, it was a chance to challenge the Union's survival and thereby to validate Britain's aristocratic rule. The triumph of the Union ended the antithesis of ideals that had for a century run through the debates between the kindred nations. The new ideas of the postwar decades found many expressions. Most important was the emergence of a Pan-Anglian sodality, a transatlantic group of younger men in both societies who espoused a new policy for conducting British-American relations. This Pan-Anglian persuasion found voice in the newer seats of power and influence both in the United States and Britain.

It found its own unique voice in the writings of Andrew Carnegie. No one was better qualified to express the newer attitude than the Scottish-American who was literally a citizen of both countries. He had been raised in the radical doctrines of Scottish Chartism. His family had arrived and settled in the United States as the conflict of ideals—between the democratic North and the slaveholding South—erupted into war, in which he himself had served in the Union cause. Finding in the North a career open to ambition and talents, of which he had long heard about in Scotland, he soon rose to great enterprise and wealth. Always affiliated to the cause of radical Liberal reform in Britain, he made heavy contributions to the Liberal Party. These soon led him into the company of the party leaders and to a personal meeting with the party's chief, Gladstone. When Carnegie told him about the gigantic productivity of American industry, the Liberal leader's surprised response led Carnegie to spend his next four years writing his only major book, *Triumphant Democracy*. Its preachment to the British was simple: adopt the American model and you will achieve America's productivity. The book naturally evoked strong responses on both sides of the Atlantic, which can best be explored in the many reviews the book evoked. Very much part of the ever-vital British colloquy was the fact that Carnegie was a devout Pan-Anglian. He wished for nothing more than a renewed amity between both branches of the Anglo-American nations. Indeed, he inscribed his book to a revived connection of the United States and Great Britain.

Wishing to understand Carnegie's *Triumphant Democracy* in its multiple aspects—as his comparative assays of the different aspects of life in the kindred nations, as an evolving statement of his views of the disposal of wealth in the new industrial age, and as a product of the British-American relationship—I have accordingly sought to answer the following questions. What was the focus of Andrew Carnegie, particularly in its American and British aspects, that led him to write *Triumphant Democracy*? What were the major themes of the book? Setting the book in its larger historical context, what were the elements of the debate over their respective ideals between the kindred polities up to the Civil War and in the transforming decades after the Civil War? The many book reviews of *Triumphant Democracy*, a fount of materials, offer a significant aspect of the intense colloquy between the intellectual classes of the two nations— and the diverse interests they represented: What did the British reviewers say, and what was the American response? Of supreme importance in the British-American relationship of the late nineteenth century was the Pan-Anglian persuasion: What were its constituent tenets? In what respects did it enter the closer diplomatic affinity of Britain and the United States? And in what ways was *Triumphant Democracy* a major document of the Pan-Anglian persuasion? The concluding chapter indicates how, after his book's publication, Carnegie often reiterated its arguments, and contemplates as well other aspects of Carnegie's life and intellect that further illuminate his very important publication.

From what I have said thus far, it will be clear enough that I have nowhere undertaken a biography of Andrew Carnegie or a study of many of his informing ideas. I have not sought to write a book about the great world of his benefactions, many of which survive and indeed shape our world today. Nor have I attempted to canvass the broad spectrum of the British-American relationship, on which the historical literature is prodigious. Using *Triumphant Democracy* as my point of departure and of analysis, I have delved into as much of Carnegie's life and of the British-American relationship that shaped it as would help understand the book's substance and importance and I have availed myself of as much of the scholarship on both subjects as would enhance my study of Carnegie's book.

Though the literature about Carnegie is considerable, an analysis of *Triumphant Democracy* has entered that literature only marginally or to a very limited degree. Its singularity and importance have hardly received the attention they merit. It was, after all, Carnegie's only book. It adumbrated his almost unstinting investigation for four very busy years. Reflecting his active involvement, it summarized both the Anglo-American relationship and Carnegie's role in that relationship. A major transatlantic document, it throws a revealing light on the critically changed connection between the kindred nations. It foreshadowed and explained the doctrine for which he is best known: the gospel of wealth. It laid out the modes of his philanthropy, those he was already practicing and those he would practice on a vast, indeed entrepreneurial scale when he retired from business. It came, in a way that is inadequately recognized, at a revolutionary time in British politics, offering British leaders a way out of the confusions of their domestic problems. As an inhabitant of both nations, Carnegie was uniquely qualified to offer Britain the teachings of the American republic. Without in any way inflating its significance, *Triumphant Democracy* is in fact a valuable assay in comparative political sociology.

For a man who had climbed to prominence as a writer and publicist, *Triumphant Democracy* was the capstone of Andrew Carnegie's life and work. It distilled all that he had believed and achieved. It was not by chance that the half-century of American progress that was the theme of his book coincided precisely with his own rise and success. It is therefore in a basic respect as much as an autobiography as Carnegie—who wrote up a book of memoirs after he had retired from the business of business and the business of philanthropy—ever got to write. His activities and ideas, apparently simple in some ways, were in fact complex. *Triumphant Democracy* was precisely the point of convergence of those activities and ideas. Whoever would try to understand Carnegie, in his many achievements and ideas, must begin with *Triumphant Democracy*.

The special aim of Carnegie's book and the special role of its author in achieving it were best summed up by Bernard Alderson, a young Englishman from Birmingham whose book on the steel master appeared shortly after Carnegie had sold his company to J. P. Morgan. Carnegie had dedicated *Triumphant Democracy* to the reunited states of Britain and America. This, said Alderson, is

> the political project which is dearer to Mr. Carnegie than anything else, and to accomplish which he would gladly sacrifice his fortune. Mr. Gladstone once described Mr. Carnegie as so interwoven in his interests between America and England that he formed a living link between them. The one supreme desire of Mr. Carnegie is to weave together the interests of the two nations and form them into one vast confederacy. He is an enthusiastic advocate of the federation of the English-speaking peoples. . . . He looks upon this reunion as the one great hope for the peace and progress of the world.[2]

1

The Road to *Triumphant Democracy*

WHEN IT BURST into the British-American world of politics and ideas in mid-April 1886, there could be no mistaking the importance and theme of Andrew Carnegie's *Triumphant Democracy*. Running over five hundred pages, the ornate and massive volume commanded immediate attention. More than the great majority of his fellow captains of industry, Carnegie was conscious and articulate about the role of industry and society. It mattered significantly that Carnegie was enormously wealthy. In 1881, when Carnegie Brothers and Company had been formally organized, and capitalized at $5,000,000, Carnegie held fifty-five percent of the capital. In 1886 America, steel was king, and Carnegie was steel.[1] When Carnegie spoke, people listened.

Carnegie announced the theme of his book with loud, unqualified clarity in the book's title and subtitle: *Fifty Years' March of the Republic*. He had written a comparative analysis of the progress of the two nations to which he was immediately affiliated: the Britain from which his parents had emigrated in 1848 when he was a teenager, and the United States in which he had flourished. His theme was patent enough. In half a century, the United States had become the most productive and affluent nation in the world. The reason why was no less patent: America's basic principle was democracy. The clear contrast he found between American and British productivity he ascribed to what he considered to be the clear contrast between democracy and monarchy. Democracy rested on the political equality of its citizens; monarchy, on their inequality.

The book's theme was sounded clearly and blatantly on the book's cover, a resplendent binding in red buckram, with figures stamped in brilliant gold and quotations imprinted in heavy black letters. There was nothing unmistakable about the meaning of the four gold figures: a solid pyramid representing the "republic" standing firmly on its base; another pyramid representing the "monarchy," capsized and standing insecurely on its apex; a scepter broken in two; and a royal crown turned upside down. The quotations were tributes to the American political system from the two principal British political leaders of the day. William Ewart Gladstone, the head of the Liberal Party, hailed the American Constitution as "the most wonderful work ever struck off at a given time by the brain and purpose of man." The Marquess of Salisbury, the head of the Conservative Party, celebrated central features of that Constitution: "The Americans have a Senate—I wish we could institute it here—marvelous in its strength and efficiency. . . . Their Supreme Court gives a stability to their institutions which under the system of vague and mysterious promises here we look for in vain." The triangle cartoons were a judgment and a wish. The quotations were major testimonials to the republic for which Carnegie's book was itself a prodigious testimonial.

Carnegie's purpose in writing *Triumphant Democracy* represented his long-standing involvement in British politics. The involvement had grown strong when Gladstone became prime minister in April 1880. Bound to the Liberal Party by his own political convictions and emotionally inclined to Gladstone as a fellow Scotsman, Carnegie was gratified to be introduced to the prime minister at a small dinner party in June 1882. He was more than pleased to tell Gladstone all about America's great economic progress and why the United States was rapidly outstripping the mother country.

Impressed by the torrent of industrial statistics that gushed from Carnegie's lips, Gladstone asked: "Why does not some writer take up this subject and present the facts to the world—in a simple and direct way?"[2]

Carnegie had already begun work on *Triumphant Democracy*. Meeting Gladstone was a spur to making it his principal enterprise. He wished to promote the radical Liberal doctrines that coincided with the Chartism to which his family had subscribed. In the early 1880s these doctrines were finding new voices and a propitious moment in British politics. Always in touch with public affairs in the United Kingdom, and especially ambitious to find a vehicle for voicing his ideas and playing an active role in British politics, Carnegie joined with some radical members of the Liberal Party in starting a chain of newspapers that his money helped underwrite and whose doctrines he subscribed to and dictated. The newspapers accepted as dogma that the British aristocracy should be dismantled and that America could serve as a model for how it was to be dismantled.

Triumphant Democracy, so Carnegie argued, was a ready answer for the major crises, indeed the deep constitutional issues, that were at that very moment rending the British body politic: the role of the House of Lords, the status of the aristocracy, the claims of the new enfranchised classes, indeed, the instability of the whole constitutional order. The book was, in this way, a preachment for conversion, a gospel to the heads of the British establishment, a call by the very wealthy "star-spangled Scotchman" (as Carnegie was dubbed) for them to mend their ways and find a ready salvation.

THE STEEL MAGNATE of fifty-one who sounded his paean to American democracy in 1886 was, in considerable measure, reciting the ideas he had learned at his family table in Dunfermline over a half-century earlier. The ancient residence of Scottish kings, near the Firth of Forth and directly across from Edinburgh, Dunfermline long been the center of the Scottish damask trade, in which his father was a prosperous weaver. But handweaving was running into problems brought on by machine production that compelled its being moved from the home loom to the factory. Hard times would very soon force his father to sell his looms and give up his trade. Meanwhile, young Andrew was learning from the teachings of his immediate family—his maternal grandfather Thomas Morrison and his uncle George Lauder, Sr. (his mother's sister's husband)—the principles he would cling to all of his life.[3] A vociferous orator and head of the advanced wing of the radical party in his Dunfermline district, Thomas Morrison was also a friend of William Cobbett, a passionate British reformer of the post-Napoleonic years. Grandfather Morrison was "radical to the core and an admirer of the American Republic."[4]

The 1830s and 1840s were the heady decades of Chartism, a collection of radical movements that expressed the great disaffection of those British classes who had been shut out of the advantages of the great reform bill of 1832. The Chartist program—its famous six points—was immediately political of course, but its goal was economic: to relieve the plight of the working classes. Though its principal centers were in England, Chartism also had a Scottish location and definition. The Scots had been disaffected by the 1707 Act of Union, which subsumed Scotland under

English rule. Thus, Scottish Chartism expressed not merely the working-class distress over the economic troubles of the 1830s and 1840s but, however much aristocratic Scots had long since entered the doors of British government, also a patriotic and political disaffection with the hegemony of England over Scotland. In the company of his family members, young Carnegie heard bitter words. "The denunciations of monarchical and aristocratic government, of privilege in all its forms, the grandeur of the republican system, the superiority of America, a land peopled by our own race, a home for freemen in which every citizen's privilege was every man's right—these were the exciting themes upon which I was nurtured."[5] When at last, in 1848, his father's failing fortune compelled the family to seek a better life in the United States, young Carnegie took these nurturing ideas with him. The question was: How far would they be validated by American realities?

The answer, for the very ambitious, ever-achieving young man, was: very far. And so he kept reiterating to his very close "brother-cousin" Dod (as he called him) in Scotland, George Lauder, Jr. To sharpen their political knowledge and capacity to argue, both cousins had been encouraged by George Lauder, Sr., to debate subjects that engaged their interest. Nothing was more interesting in the years after the "flitting" (as the Scots called emigration) of Andrew Carnegie's family to the United States than whether their hopes in the new land had been realized. In Britain by the early 1850s, the great distress of the earlier decades had abated considerably, so it was fair of cousin Dod to argue the virtues of the British system and to persist in questioning those of the American. Young Carnegie's deservedly famous response, written in 1853 when he was seventeen, bears repeating.

> We have perfect political Equality, every one has a voice in the Gov't. [sic]. . . . It is strange that with your immense army and policy you cannot keep the peace. Look at Ireland, for instance. . . . Here [the Irish] find no Royal Family (increasing with fearful rapidity) to squander their hard made earnings, no aristocracy to support, no established church with its enormous sinecures, no electoral districts made for a class to overrule the majority, no primogeniture and entail to curse the land and stop improvements in the soil. . . . They find the various reforms which they struggled for at home in successful operation here—indeed I can think of no reform which you have that we do not

possess. We have all your good traits, which are many, with few or none of your bad ones which I must say are neither few nor far between. But we go ahead. We now possess what the working classes of Your Country look forward to as constituting their political millennium. *We have the charter* [for] *which you have been fighting for years as the Panacea for all Britain's woes, the bulwark of the liberties of the people.*

The United States, added Carnegie, has had the people's charter "from the very beginning. But we are not at a standstill. We have only begun the great work of reform."[6] Here, rough-hewn, insistently argumentative, reductive, astonishingly precocious, were all the essential elements of Carnegie's creed of American democracy.

Three factors shaped his life during the 1860s, encouraging him to translate his personal creed into a public political activity. First, the creed was tested and affirmed by the Civil War. The young man, playing a significant role in the War Department by helping to direct railroad and telegraph operations from his center in Pittsburgh, thoroughly espoused the cause of democracy and freedom that, in his mind, the Union clearly stood for. Second, he became very wealthy. Driven by ambition and a remarkable ability to invest in burgeoning industries (particularly those linked to railroads), he very early amassed a great fortune. Third, he arduously sustained his Scottish affinity, and with it his strong interest in British politics. Letters and gifts flowed regularly between Allegheny and then Homewood, in nearby Pittsburgh, where the American Carnegies had settled and their Scottish family, the Lauders and the Morrisons, back in Dunfermline. Overwork and ill health during the early months of the Civil War afforded him time for a vacation back in Scotland, where his success and wealth were celebrated and where his ambitions as to how he might use them took on a certain definition. In his letter of June 21, 1863, he wrote his cousin Dod a remarkable statement of his own plans:

Isn't it strange how little ambition most of our Scotch acquaintances have to become independent *and then enjoy the luxuries which wealth can [and should] procure?* For my part, I am determined to expand as my means do and ultimately to own a noble place in the country . . . and be distinguished for taking the deepest interest in all those about my place. The position most to be envied, outside the ring of great men, I think is that of a British gentleman who labors diligently to educate and improve the condition of his dependents and who takes an independent part in National politics, always laboring to correct some ancient abuse—to curtail the privileges of the few and increase those of the many. . . . For my part I sometimes think I would like to return to Scotland and try the character myself.[7]

These ambitions he reformulated five years later, after the Civil War had ended, in his famous memorandum of December 1868. He was then thirty-three. His income for the year was $50,000, an astronomical sum in then current terms. He took stock of his life. What would he do with all his money?

Beyond this never earn [he wrote to himself]—make no effort to increase fortune, but spend the surplus each year for benevolent purposes. Cast aside business forever, except for others. Settle in Oxford and get a thorough education, making the acquaintance of literary men—this will take three years' active work—pay especial attention to speaking in public. Settle then in London and purchase a controlling interest in some newspaper or live review and give the general management of it attention, taking a part in public matters, especially those connected with education and improvement of the poorer classes. Man must have an idol—the amassing of wealth is one of the worst species of idolatry. . . . Whatever I engage in I must push inordinately; therefore should I be careful to choose that life which will be the most elevating in its character.[8]

Burton J. Hendrick, the first of his principal biographers, validly called this memorandum the first edition of Carnegie's "gospel of wealth." But one should not miss the equally important point that, as his wealth accumulated, Carnegie used it to spread his gospel of democracy. Democracy, the creed in which he had been reared, was an idol to which he could wholeheartedly consecrate himself. And, in serving his idol, he spelled out the exact path he meant to follow.

In 1868, he planned to concentrate less on earning and more on learning: to go to the summit of English scholarship, Oxford, rather than to the raucous, internecine markets of American business. But realizing his plan was delayed more than a decade. In the 1870s he built his fortune far beyond his earlier imaginings. His wartime experience on the railroads had impressed upon him that a new American industrial world was rapidly taking shape, that its essential ingredient was steel, and that his own "inordinate pushing" (as he had put it) drove him to making steel and to becoming the steelmaster of America and the world. Yet, although a truly self-educated Scotsman (he had had one year of formal schooling), he did not lose his passion for learning. If he could not go to Oxford in England, he would find its variant form right at home: among the literati of New York City (where he had settled after the war) and among their several circles. Carnegie was invited to join one of the more notable ones, that of Mrs. Anne C. L. Botta, through whom he came to know many of the major authors and journal editors of the day. The sodality of American literati was in fact transatlantic, indeed Anglo-American; inevitably Carnegie came to learn about and often enough to meet some of the foremost contemporary English authors and editors, including, among so many others, Matthew Arnold, James Anthony Froude, Herbert Spencer, and John Morley. That he had met and soon befriended John Morley was to prove important in Carnegie's life. Morley was a radical member of the Liberal Party and editor of the influential *Fortnightly Review* (and of the *Pall Mall Gazette*). Indeed, it had been for the *Fortnightly Review* that Andrew Carnegie wrote his first important transatlantic article, "As Others See Us" (February 1882), in which he derogated British aristocracy and glorified American democracy.[9] So building an empire of steel and gaining a higher education were not mutually exclusive: indeed, they were remarkably mutual.[10]

The year 1881 was a pivotal one for Carnegie. He organized Carnegie Brothers Ltd. at a capitalization of $5,000,000 in which he himself held a safely dominant share of $2,721,000.[11] He could now turn to Britain and his always intense preoccupation with British politics. That year, from mid-June to early August, he conducted the first of several such trips, a remarkable coaching tour of some eight hundred miles from Brighton to Inverness with a company of several American friends, the "Gay Charioteers," as he called them. The group of coachmen might vary from one part of the journey to the next, including some old friends of the rich steelmaster, but also some ultra Liberal members of a government then under the ministry of the presiding Liberal, William Ewart Gladstone. It was a remarkable tour: the tourists traveled in a luxurious coach of the most "brilliant equipage," were well-provisioned, well-housed, well-advertised, and well-received, and they jocularly and boisterously drove through (with prior permission, of course) the vast estates of the aristocracy. Carnegie kept a record of the trip, which he first published for private circulation (1882) and then a year later as *An American Four-in-Hand in Britain*. He interlaced his journal with strong republican sentiments, denunciations of the monarchy and the aristocracy, regrets about the flaws and failures of his mother country, and suggestions that it might well consider the great progress of the American republic. Indeed, it was, in this way, a first edition of *Triumphant Democracy*. Always with a plan of ambition in mind, Carnegie took pains to meet the men with whom he would soon be joining in a grand, obviously well-financed syndicate of radical Liberal newspapers. In effect, this was a journey of fulfillment. The poor Scottish lad who had left with his impoverished family thirty-three years before was now returning with all the self-proclaiming advertisements of his success and wealth. When he met Gladstone in 1882, he was already collecting the materials for his truly major evaluation of the kindred polities. He had promised the great Liberal leader, whom he had long admired and studied, the comparative analysis of America and Britain. And he fulfilled his promise in April 1886, with the publication of *Triumphant Democracy*.[12]

WHAT WERE THE many significances of *Triumphant Democracy*? First, Carnegie's road of success, ambition, wealth, constant interest in British politics, and increasing affiliation with men of prominence in public life and literature had projected him to a position of high recognition in British-American affairs. He had himself anticipated its great impact. Having worked on his manuscript for several years, and particularly arduously in 1885, he wrote to his fiancée, Louise Whitfield, in mid-October that his book was "all right.... It's going to be a stunner!"[13] He was justified in his expectation. When the book appeared, it "made a tremendous sensation." The book went through many printings by its American publisher (Scribner's), bringing sales to 17,000 in merely a few months, a great success in its day. At the same time, several expensive English editions were published, followed directly by a shilling reprint, making the book of democratic doctrine available to the British working classes whose cause it advocated. In short order, the book was translated into several European languages, most significantly into French and German.[14] Carnegie's prediction was right: *Triumphant Democracy* had an immediate and continuing transatlantic resonance.

The book's importance was due to a certain degree to the nature of its subject: a comparative evaluation of two kindred nations. It testified as well to the special role of its author, a great industrialist who was also a conspicuous man of letters. Indeed, he sought the last role as assiduously as he played the first. Andrew Carnegie conjoined both roles, making him virtually unique in American entrepreneurial history. But even more: his book's rare perspective was that of a Scottish-born industrialist who knew intimately the workings of the two polities he inhabited virtually simultaneously and who was, in many respects and paradoxically, an outsider in both. Carnegie understood very well the importance of *Triumphant Democracy*. Of all the books he had written, he "would always regard [it] as his magnum opus, his remarkable book."[15]

Triumphant Democracy marked the highest point of his ambition. It advantaged him to play low in American politics; it glorified him to play high in British politics. His intense interest was British public affairs. In American society where wealth was an equalizer and great wealth the best calling card to high society, and where a career in politics most often a pursuit for men of no esteemed talent, Carnegie's ambition needed no further office. But in British society, where aristocracy and wealth often went together and where both were celebrated by a seat in Parliament, it surely spurred Carnegie's drive for success to get a seat. British high society was parliamentary society. Carnegie did not merely want success; he wanted it with a passion. According to his famous personal memorandum of 1868 he planned, after making his fortune, to settle in London, get a newspaper or review, and take part in public matters. By 1886, he had done all that. He advanced the Liberal doctrines he had already announced in his earlier books and articles. He needed only entrance into the Commons to gratify, more than ever, his zealous drive for acceptance and success. His correspondence shows that many of his friends were urging him to stand for Parliament.[16] He always knew his inner heart and zeal: "Whatever I engage in, I must push inordinately."[17] The lodestar of his inordinate pushing was, it is fair to say, to sit in Parliament. The chronology of Gladstone's second ministry and of Carnegie's hard work on his great book runs a parallel and interactive course. Forging London friendships, writing well-published essays, owning a chain of republican newspapers in England all form a meaningful chronological sequence. Seen in this perspective, *Triumphant Democracy* might well emblazon the road for Carnegie's entrance in Parliament. That was part of its great importance. It was his best-formulated, most resounding political statement. But unanticipated events radically changed the course of his life and the aim of his ambition. Shortly after the book appeared, Gladstone and the Liberals fell from power because of the sundering issue of Irish Home Rule. A few months later, Carnegie's own life was severely battered by the deaths of his mother and his brother and by his own near-fatal illness, and he laid aside his parliamentary interests.

No less impressive than its publishing success were the reviews that *Triumphant Democracy* evoked in the United States and Great Britain. To say that it was widely covered in the presses of both countries misses no small part of its importance. The reviews were frequently strong responses to Carnegie's book of doctrine, and often enough impassioned commentaries on the kindred polities—the British and the American—whose modes of governance he was assaying. They amounted to an Anglo-American dialogue on the success of their respective institutions. But, more than that, the reviewers were commenting on the major problems each nation was facing. Many dramatic changes were taking place in 1886, particularly in Britain, where politics was electric with crises, and where Carnegie's words were almost literally alive with that electricity. His book compelled each nation both to specify the problems they were facing and to ask how far the other political society could offer a model for solving them. *Triumphant Democracy* evoked powerful national sentiments on both sides of the Atlantic. Thus, because it was a book both of espousal and indictment, it stirred its reviewers to deeply felt responses both about their own nation and the kindred nation across the sea. The many reviews, no less than the book itself, constituted a major event in the Anglo-American relationship.

Triumphant Democracy urged a doctrine of political equality; very much part of Carnegie's doctrine of democracy was his doctrine on the uses of wealth. Carnegie is probably best known for what is called his "gospel of wealth." A devoté of Herbert Spencer, he viewed the accumulation of wealth as part of the natural evolution of society. He regarded plans for economic equality as unnatural and therefore specious. The only resolution lay, as he saw it, in opening wide the doors to education and allowing the disadvantaged to rise as high in economic success as their ready educational access would now allow them. The members of aristocratic society, he said in *Triumphant Democracy*, were vain and self-absorbed, and used their wealth only to perpetuate their families; those of democratic society, as the many American examples he cited indicated, regularly used their wealth to endow educational institutions, thereby facilitating the access to success and status of the less advantaged classes. If he was self-made, Carnegie also saw himself as made by the books and libraries of America's democratic society; and he accordingly carried on a lifelong enterprise of building the libraries that he deemed the hallmark of a democratic society. Thus, Carnegie's gospel of wealth was one feature of his gospel of democracy. His famous essay on wealth appeared in 1889. It had been fully anticipated, three years before, in *Triumphant Democracy*. But the fact is that Carnegie had strongly subscribed to the "gospel" throughout his life. This dimension of the great importance of *Triumphant Democracy* had its roots in his Scottish origins and his early years in the United States. His gospel of books and learning gives meaning to his quotation from Confucius at the beginning of his famous chapter on education: "There being education, there will be no distinction of classes."

The scores of reviews of *Triumphant Democracy* made clear that the century-long division between America and Britain remained profound and intense. There had been so much to keep the animus alive. The Civil War, one should recall, had brought the two nations almost to the brink of another recourse to arms, creating problems that were, in the 1870s and 1880s, slowly being resolved. And yet, beneath the surface of the patriotic tensions between them, another current was running. A transatlantic sodality was emerging, a vocal group of political leaders and men of affairs, of editors and educators, of writers and intellectuals. They were reaching out to each other, forming a network of power and ideas, of politics and the press. They spoke from positions of status, influence, wealth. They stressed the community of ideals and institutions the United States shared with the United Kingdom. They shared a common language, a common literature, common parliamentary institutions, a common law, a common history. In that fervent age of nationalism and nation-building, many leaders in Britain and America were almost suddenly aware that they belonged to the English-speaking peoples.

These Pan-Angles knew each other. They met in each other's literary circles, in their respective salons and soirées. Not men of arms, indeed often enough believing in arbitration if not themselves outright pacifists, they surely felt that the pen was mightier than the sword. Their essays and editorials often molded Anglo-American politics. Their books shaped opinion. And here indeed was one of the notable features of what Andrew Carnegie had written. *Triumphant Democracy* was a very important Pan-Anglian book. And its author was a powerful Pan-Angle.

Did Carnegie plan to stand for Parliament? The question surely relates both to the reason for his writing *Triumphant Democracy* and to the importance of his magisterial volume. His life can be seen as tracing a patterned trajectory, rational if not always uninterrupted. His preoccupation with British political leadership began in his childhood, continued through his young adulthood, and was always vitalized by his constant connection with friends and family in Dunfermline and Scotland. One has to go back to his memorandum of 1868, written to himself, to remember that he wished to "settle in London & purchase a controlling interest in some newspaper or live review & give the general management of it attention, taking a part in public matters especially those connected with education & improvement of the poorer classes."[18] By 1885 his private plan had almost entirely been fulfilled. He had entered the inner circles of the Liberal Party, and he had financed a whole chain of advanced Liberal newspapers in England, sounding ideas that were very consistent with those of prominent Liberal leaders such as Joseph Chamberlain, John Morley, Charles Bradlaugh, John Bright, and Charles Dilke. Gladstone's second ministry had taken office in April 1880, with the certainty of five years in power and the possibility of having its mandate renewed. While he was coaching through Britain and spreading his republican doctrines through his newspapers, Carnegie was working assiduously on *Triumphant Democracy*. Meanwhile, he was being courted by Liberal party leaders to stand for Parliament. Several seats were proposed for his possible candidacy.[19] The money he was giving to the party, the newspapers he was financing, the friendships he was cultivating, the trips he was regularly taking, and the great book he was now writing: they all cohere, they belong to the great age of Gladstone's secondary ministry, and they form a meaningful context for *Triumphant Democracy*. It was, in April of 1886, very possibly Carnegie's great campaign statement that he might, indeed could, stand for election.

The immense book dwarfed all other statements Carnegie had made on Britain and America, on the kindred nations, on the two societies to which he belonged, on the Anglo-American connection that invested him with a distinction that no other member of either society could claim.

If Carnegie did indeed plan standing for election in Parliament in that spring of 1886, his plan was badly shattered. The Liberal world he had so wondrously entered came tumbling down around him. The chronology should be noted. Gladstone's second ministry fell in June 1885. There was a distinct prospect that Lord Salisbury's Conservative government could last five years. Carnegie decided immediately to get out of the newspaper business. But the writing of his great Liberal Party manifesto, *Triumphant Democracy*, was well on its way. And it would indeed appear in April 1886, when Gladstone had resumed power and was pushing for Irish Home Rule. His bill would hopelessly splinter the Liberal Party and put beyond any realization whatever ambition Carnegie may have had about standing for Parliament.[20]

2

Major Themes

> The old nations of the earth creep on at a snail's pace; the Republic thunders past with the rush of the express. The United States, the growth of a single century, has already reached the foremost rank among nations, and is destined soon to out-distance all others in the race. In population, in wealth, in annual savings, and in public credit; in freedom from debt, in agriculture, and in manufactures, America already leads the civilized world.

THE OPENING PARAGRAPH of Carnegie's *Triumphant Democracy* arrestingly summed up the theme of his volume. What he laid out in the following twenty chapters was a detailed statistical and analytical support of those opening words. The paragraph was the one virtually all of his reviewers cited—indeed, the one with which they began their reviews. In that way, Carnegie's book immediately took its place in international discourse, and most certainly in the discourse of the two nations that it directly compared: the United States and the United Kingdom.[1]

It was intended to be a book of comparative analysis and a book of edification, designed to afford one nation the principled guidance of another. That was why Carnegie wrote it. It invites comparison, most immediately with James Bryce's *The American Commonwealth* (which appeared two years later, in 1888) and, more distantly, with Alexis de Tocqueville's *Democracy in America* (1835, 1840). In all three books the question was always the same: How far is the American polity a relevant, perhaps even instructive, model for our guidance? Carnegie's words were not high-flown. His sentences were simple. His premises were, it would seem, elementary. But it would be fearfully wrong to misconstrue the simplicity of his language with the sophistication of his ideas. Like the most learned of his contemporaries, James Bryce, Henry Maine, and John Morley, to name a few, he understood the complexity of his subject. And he embraced many complex problems of governance and finance within his compass. But also like them, he was reductive in his premises. Tocqueville, after all, apposed democracy and aristocracy. And Bryce, his very close contemporary, apposed the American democratic commonwealth to the British.

Schooled in ideas no less than in the market, Carnegie had written a powerful book of principled instruction. The principles were, as his reviewers at once understood, well worth listening to and, where helpful, taking under serious advisement. He inhabited two worlds and in a certain sense was a foreign visitor—indeed something of an exile—in both. In a way, he never left the democratic Scotland in which he had been raised. In New York City, where he had taken up residence, he was always abroad at home. And he surely never become habituated to the aristocratic Britain where his vast wealth could buy him property but not status or class. This made his book significantly different from virtually all other books about America written by tourists from other countries, who came to visit but never to stay.

What were the principles he found and preached? The United States was a republic and a democracy. Carnegie used the words interchangeably, never raising the question as to the theoretical or historical differences between the two forms of political society. Indeed, his Scottish legacy as well as the heroes he enshrined—men such as Oliver Cromwell, John Bright, and Abraham Lincoln—suggested the essential identity of both forms. The foundation upon which the whole American political structure rested was "the equality of the citizen. There is not one shred of privilege to be met with anywhere in all the laws. One man's right is every man's right. . . . No ranks, no titles, no hereditary dignities, and therefore no classes. Suffrage is universal, and votes are of equal weight. Representatives are paid, and political life and usefulness thereby thrown open to all. Thus there is brought about a community of interests."[2]

That community of interests was hardly the guiding principle of his native land, Great Britain, where birth and rank overrode the personal characteristics and attainment of its inhabitants.[3] British monarchical and aristocratic institutions divided "the people into classes with separate interests, aims, thoughts, and feelings," which American citizens could understand only with difficulty.[4] Americans were *citizens* of their republic; their British cousins were *subjects* of their monarch and inferior in the royal aristocratic order.

Here indeed was the animating point of *Triumphant Democracy*. If his study was a comparative tabulation of the respective achievements of the two polities, nothing stood out as intensely as his feeling that British society was, for him, a perennial *insult*. He was grateful to the American republic, he said, because it had "removed the stigma of inferiority which his native land saw proper to impress upon him at birth."[5] In the United States, "there is no class so intensely patriotic, *so wildly devoted to the Republic as the naturalized citizen*. . . . Only the man born abroad, like myself, under institutions which insult him at his birth, can know the full meaning of Republicanism."[6] "Difference of position in the State, resulting from birth, would be held to insult the citizen."[7] To the insult of class the system of monarchy and aristocracy added another dimension of inferiority. It *emasculated* its subjects. The word appears frequently enough in *Triumphant Democracy* to encourage the question as to whether this was not in some measure part of the insult to which, as Carnegie saw it, the monarchy subjected its citizens. In his concluding general reflections, he summed it up.

> Monarchical institutions emasculate even educated men, and the ignorant masses in greater degree. There is probably not a man of the rank of Cabinet Minister in Britain, no not one, but would have bowed, and that low and repeatedly . . . to Gesler's cap, and smiled to think he had done himself no injury by so doing. . . . It is not the man we declaim against but the effect of the customs, fit only for serfs, by which the monarchy is surrounded, and which tend to keep men—even Radicals—subservient.[8]

His book centered on the almost exponential growth of America's productivity and wealth during the five decades from 1830 to 1880. Depending heavily on the decennial census reports, he regularly cited statistics that demonstrated U.S. productivity and wealth. But how would he explain that remarkable growth within so brief a period? Answering that question, he said, presented "one of the most interesting problems in the social history of mankind."[9] Granting the complexity of the problem, he suggested three factors as the most important: "the ethnic character of the people, the topographical and climatic conditions under which they developed, and the influence of political institutions founded upon the equality of the citizen."[10]

As part of his ever-continuing and ever-expanding self-education, Carnegie had, over a period of nine months in 1878 and 1879, taken a trip through a few continents, mostly Asia, during which he found many profound questions to ponder about the workings of human society. His diary of that journey, *Round the World*, was published in 1884. While he found many common features and values among the societies he visited, he was also impressed by the great poverty among their masses. Topography, climate, location: these factors entered his estimate of their respective conditions and progress.*

Elsewhere in *Triumphant Democracy* Carnegie cited America's vast natural resources: its rich acres and forests, its mineral abundance, its waterways. These were precisely the reasons for the country's great wealth that most other visitors from Europe, and particularly Great Britain, had earlier stressed. Indeed, said many of the British reviewers of *Triumphant Democracy*, her superabundant agriculture and minerals would have made America rich under any condition; the real question, they said, was whether her free institutions had impeded rather than impelled her growth.

"The ethnic character of the people" stood out in Carnegie's reckoning as a major factor in American growth. One cannot go too far into the pages of his book without being impressed by the importance he attached to ethnicity. In keeping with the vogue and mentality of his age, he used the word interchangeably with race and blood. Of course he did not mean the words to stigmatize or demean or exclude those who did not belong to a particular "race" or carry a certain "blood." (As a staunch defender of the Union in the recently concluded Civil War, he hailed the advances of the freedmen in the American South.) But he surely wished to celebrate the British. "The American of today is certainly more than four-fifths

---

* In its language and sophistication, *Round the World* offers a vast contrast with *Triumphant Democracy*. The diary of his journey discloses a man of studied concentration, intensive ability to get at deep-seated motives in human behavior, and a remarkable ability to master a great number and variety of facts and try to grasp their essences. This reminds one again that the diary he had kept for self-instruction and contemplation was quite different in purpose from the comparative study of the kindred societies, which he had written as a book of information and instruction for his erstwhile countrymen in Great Britain.

British in his ancestry."[11] There could be no question at all as to what had formed "the national character, especially in its political phase; because the language, literature, laws, and institutions are English."[12] "The Briton is stable. What he sets about to do he does, or dies in the attempt." What better evidence of this could one cite than General Ulysses S. Grant, in whose "Scotch blood" came tenacity and a self-contained, stubborn force. "This master trait of the British race," noted Carnegie, "shows resplendently in Lincoln, the greatest political genius of our era."[13] But if America's great political and military leaders were British, especially so were their inventively distinguished industrialists. In evaluating America's economic growth, "the strain of British blood, never excelled if yet equalled, must be credited with more than its due share."[14] But the real point, said Carnegie, was that it was America's democratic laws that had aroused the Briton to his innate potential. To his kinsmen across the Atlantic he offered a clear political message: "See, my countrymen, of what your race is capable when relieved from unjust laws and made the peers of any, under republican institutions."[15]

For Carnegie, the most important factor that explained America's phenomenal growth was "the influence of political institutions founded upon the equality of the citizen."[16] Here was the unifying theme of his whole book. Equality spurred men to work for themselves, without the taxes of a superior aristocracy and the burdens of royal wars, liberated from the stigma of class. "The Republic to-day is, as ever it was, a nation of workers. The idlers are few—much fewer than in any other great nation. . . . The rewards of labor are high; and prizes are to be won in every pursuit."[17] Britain was always the opposing model. "The American works much harder than the Briton. His application is greater; his hours longer; his holidays fewer." What accounted for the difference between the far greater productivity of America than Britain? The British were "born under a king and denied equality at birth," whereas the American is "invested under the Republic with the mantle of sovereignty. The drowsy Briton becomes a force here."[18] The high productivity of Americans had long been a theme of domestic and foreign observers, from John Cotton, and including Franklin, Crevecoeur, Tocqueville, Trollope, Grund, and Chevalier. But no one insisted on explaining it so reductively and simply. Political equality stabilized government. Those who live in a regime of political equality are conservative. This was a particularly important message for men guiding British politics when Carnegie's book appeared. Industrious and contented, Americans were far more conservative than the

British because "it is the equality of the citizen—just and equal laws—republicanism, they are resolved to conserve."[19]

Carnegie prefaced each of the twenty chapters of his book with a relevant, often abstruse quotation from a distinguished authority. The names were very widely known and respected: Milton, Herbert Spencer, Dicey, Confucius, Wendell Phillips. Here is why the quotation opening up Chapter IV, "The Conditions of Life," calls for special notice. Its author was *Eigenrac*. It does not take a particular orthographic acuity to realize that Carnegie was citing himself as an authority but spelling his name backwards. Throughout his masterly volume, Carnegie spoke clearly, simply, directly. Apart from directing the book at the British leadership, he wished also to reach the British working classes he had been editorializing in his newspapers during the four years before *Triumphant Democracy* appeared. The shift in the mode and level of his language in a book centering on the contrasting political premises of the kindred nations invites close attention and surely warrants quotation in its entirety.

> The ideal State is one in which every citizen is content with the laws under which he lives. If any body of men in a State agitate for a change of laws, dissatisfaction is proven to exist, and by this much is the State disordered and unenviable. To produce universal satisfaction is possible only by meting out to every citizen the same measures. The slightest inequality produces disturbance, for only under equality are the parts free from strain, and hence in repose. The State in equilibrium has then reached perfection in the political system.[20]

Here again, as succinctly as he would put it in the rest of his masterpiece, was the difference in principle between America and Britain.

IN THE PREFACE of *Triumphant Democracy*, Carnegie announced his book's central features. He argued the great superiority of the principle of American political equality over that of British aristocracy. He undertook a comprehensive analytical canvassing of virtually every aspect of American and British life. His argument rested on a solid factual basis. He had, said Carnegie, consulted many authorities on the subject, as well as "a pile of reference books, census reports, and statistical works [that] lay around upon tables and shelves." He did more than that.

Although designedly written in as light a style as I am master of, mark me, no liberties have been taken with facts, figures, or calculations. Every statement has been carefully verified and re-verified; every calculation has been gone over and over again. My readers may safely rely upon the correctness of every quantitative reference made. Considered as a book of reference, what is herein stated is under-stated rather than over-stated.[21]

It was this point that caught the attention of most of his reviewers and one that compelled those who differed sharply with him about his premises and conclusions to validate their difference on grounds other than the comprehension and accuracy of his facts. It was this point too—presenting the facts and figures about America and Britain—that had, particularly after his conversation with Gladstone, prompted him to complete his massive volume.

Indeed, virtually all the chapters of *Triumphant Democracy* recited America's prodigious economic growth. Some areas of this growth were probably fairly widely known abroad: cities and towns, agriculture, manufactures, mining, trade and commerce, railways and waterways. And yet as Carnegie noted, even in those Jacksonian days, European visitors found the material condition of most Americans to be considerably higher than that of their European counterparts.[22] The principal spur to this vast economic achievement, in Carnegie's eyes, was, again, the political equality of all Americans.

Here were some of the amazing statistics Carnegie recited—indeed proclaimed—to his readers. In 1880, the U.S. population stood at 56,000,000: native-born Americans had increased by over thirty percent in each of the past several decades; and the annual number of immigrants was, in recent decades, also increasing at a high rate.[23] In the mid-1880s, the annual expenditure on education stood at 18,600,000 pounds sterling in the United States, while the United Kingdom spent 6,685,000.[24] The value of American agricultural and pastoral products in 1880 exceeded $3 billion; those of Great Britain were $1,280,000,000.[25] The farms of America comprised around 840,000 square miles, "an area nearly equal to one-fourth of Europe, and larger than the four greatest European countries put together [Russia excepted]."[26] During the past five decades, the United States had moved, in terms of capital invested, from being an almost entirely agrarian nation to one that was one-fifth industrial.

There had been, in these decades, enormous value advances in America's great industries: flour and gristmills, slaughtering and meatpacking, and iron and steel. On that last product, the source of his still increasing fortune, Carnegie wrote: "In 1870 the United States was much below France or Germany as regards the manufacture of steel; ten years later it produced more than these countries together. America now makes one-fifth of the iron, and one-fourth of the steel of the world, and is second only to Great Britain. In steel, America will probably lead the world in 1890."[27] Carnegie recited with special pride America's gigantic advances in making Bessemer steel, which he had helped introduce to the United States, and the fact that Pennsylvania, where his plant was located, "wears the iron crown."[28] Having risen to prominence on the Pennsylvania railroad, and making his steel for the building of railroads, he resounded his announcement that "*the whole of Europe has not built as many miles of railway as the Republic has during some recent years, and in 1880 the whole world did not build as many.*"[29]

What Carnegie wished particularly to declare was that the American national debt was far lower than that of nearly all of the European states. The United States had no income tax and raised its monies by very mild forms of internal taxation. Even vis-à-vis the mother country, what better proof of the republic's financial stability and appeal could be offered than the higher selling price of its national bonds?[30] Here too, he could find reason for reiterating his vaunting of the republic and denouncing royal governments whose vast debt "have their real source in the rule of monarchs and courts, whose jealousies and domestic ambitions, stimulated by the great military classes always created by them, produce the wars or continual preparation for wars which eat up the people's substance and add to their burdens year after year. A nation with a large standing army and navy is bound to make wars."[31]

But his concern was to draw the attention of his British readers to other aspects of American life, particularly those he considered part and parcel of the American premise of equality. Largely self-educated, but always aided by prominent men in his American community who lent him books and guided his learning, Carnegie celebrated the American public school system. It was free, supported mainly by direct taxation, "and no tax is so willingly paid as 'the school tax.'"[32] "Free education may be trusted to burst every obstruction which stands in the path of the democracy toward its goal, the equality of the citizen."[33] Here was America's lesson to every nation: "Seek ye first the education of the people and all other political blessings will be added unto you. The education of the people is the real underlying work for earnest men who would best serve their country. In this, the most creditable work of all, it cannot be denied that the Republic occupies the first place." Scotland had always prized education, and no one prized it more than Carnegie. Giving his wealth to establish free libraries was an early and lifelong passion. His monies poured into setting up or sustaining universities and other institutions for the promotion of learning.

The American achievement exceeded the material, he insisted. Again, one had merely to contrast the republic of 1830 with that of 1880 to see how far it had marched. "Half a century ago it was the fashion in Europe to decry anything America, and to sneer at even the suggestion of culture in the United States."[34] It was probably true that in 1830 the energy of the republic had gone into more material enterprises. "In the building up of a new country there is little time for art cultivation; the establishment of a political and social system and the development of industrial resources must precede and furnish the foundation which the superstructure of art may rise."[35] But in the half-century since, Americans had developed their own art, built burgeoning museums, theaters, architecture, libraries, and created a very noteworthy literature—one well recognized in Europe.[36] "The material progress of the Republic is not the only progress made during the triumphant march of the Democracy."[37] To cite one important example, said Carnegie: "It is estimated that there are twenty-three thousand school libraries in America, containing forty-five million books—*twelve million more than all the public libraries of Europe combined.*"[38] Art and literature, in sum, are growing in every way. "The monarchist boasts more bayonets, the republican more books."[39] One need hardly remind oneself that Carnegie gave so much of his wealth to the cause of books. And art. And music. Both in the United States and in his native land. The very costly New York City music hall that his money built was, almost against his will, named in his honor, and stands today as a monument to international music.

The principle of American political equality had other implications for power and governance in the kindred polities. If it was true enough that the institutions and style of living in American cities roughly approximated those in Britain in the 1880s, nothing could be more different than their rural districts. In rural Britain, the squires and the parsons held power and managed local affairs to their own liking.[40]

Who held power in the kindred polities was of course among the most important questions Carnegie wished to address. Here again he wished to illuminate corners of American life that he knew his British readers knew little of. If the governance of their cities were roughly similar in both nations, it was quite different in their respective rural districts. In the United States, the democratic principle prevailed in the control of local and county government. In Britain, however, control lay in the hands of the squires and the parsons, as it had done for centuries.[41] Again, Britain's aristocratic principle distinguished the two nations. This was true, in a variant form, in the matter of religion. In the United States, state and church were separate: secular power exercised no control over religious beliefs. But far from this "perfect religious equality" diminishing the exercise of American faith, the separation seemed to enhance it.[42] In Britain, the state controlled the church, and national taxation financed the church. And in an anomaly that Americans could hardly understand because it so contradicted their own insistence on separating church and state, the British queen ruled as a devout Anglican in England and as a devout Presbyterian in Scotland.[43] Carnegie railed again at what struck him as the grievous flaw of a basic British institution.

> The evils of the State Church flow from its parent, the Monarchy, of which it is the legitimate offspring. Its archbishops and bishops residing in palaces and rolling in wealth are the religious aristocracy; the thousands of poor curates who drag out existence upon pittances represent the masses. The revenues of the State Church exceed five millions of pounds sterling. The Church owns all kinds of property and is squeamish about none.[44]

In analyzing the sources of power and governance in the United States and the United Kingdom, Carnegie devoted an important chapter to the nonpolitical activities of American citizens. Here he delved into a feature of U.S. life that other visitors had noted before, particularly Alexis de Tocqueville, who had stressed the great importance of associations in American life as a source of power and authority. Carnegie noted a similar tendency. But his perception and explanation were, in important respects, rather different from Tocqueville's.

> This universal self-dependence is manifest everywhere and in everything. . . . The cause of this self-governing capacity lies in

the fact that from his earliest youth the republican feels himself a man. He is called upon to participate in the management of the local affairs of his township, county, or city, or in his relations with his fellows, in his church, trades-union. . . . Everywhere he is ushered into a democratic system of government in which he stands upon an equal footing with his fellows, and in which he feels himself bound to exercise the rights of a citizen.[45]

Because of the basic premises of their society, Americans were far better trained in the art of government. "The truth is," said Carnegie, "that the monarchical form lacks the vigor and elasticity necessary to cope with the republican in any department of government whatever."

AMONG CARNEGIE'S MOTIVES in writing *Triumphant Democracy,* holding America as a model for British political leaders to contemplate figured prominently. In addition to Gladstone, there were other auditors in the Liberal Party whom Carnegie could hope to address, especially those who belonged to the party's radical contingent—men such as Joseph Chamberlain, John Morley, Samuel Storey, Henry Fowler, and Charles Dilke— as well as men such as his fellow Scotsman, the Earl of Rosebery. Carnegie had already shown his great affinity for the M.P.s of the Liberal Party by sending them regular contributions.[46] He knew that the Radical Liberals shared many of the views he was disseminating in his newspaper chain. He had every reason to believe the ideas he was proposing in *Triumphant Democracy* would find a friendly ear among them.

What could the Liberal leaders of the monarchy learn from the republic? The answer was far from being a simple one. What problems was the British polity then facing? How far could America offer relevant instruction in solving those problems? In fact, there was a third question: In offering the republic as a relevant model, how far was Carnegie's representation of American institutions valid?

During the years from 1884 to 1886, after a relatively quiet period, change burst on the stage of British politics. The franchise was democratized and the House of Commons was yet again reformed. The British governing class continued changing from a landowning aristocracy to one whose wealth came from commerce. Relevantly, the issues of taxation and the basis of governance, which were in effect one issue, were raised. And so too was another related issue: that of social legislation. Centering on these issues was a small contingent in each major party whose program was radical: Joseph Chamberlain led the Liberal Radicals, and Randolph Churchill led the Conservatives. Critical to the whole conduct of British politics was the group of Irish Nationalists, the so-called Third Party, led by Charles Stewart Parnell. They called insistently and constantly for Irish Home Rule, so much so that they became a constant impediment to the conduct of affairs in the Commons.

Truly formidable on the horizon of British politics stood the question of Irish Home Rule. Carnegie offered the American model as a way of handling the problem of home rule. Power in the United States centers in the town; above the town is the county; and above the county is the state. The state is the third and largest circle of home rule. "The American believes in Home Rule down to the smallest divisions, and has shown an admirable dislike of centralization."[47] The United States was best perceived as "a great continent of nations" that was governed "through *the federal or home rule system.*"[48] "All the rights of a sovereign State belong to it, except such as it has expressly delegated in common with sister States to the central authority, the National Government at Washington."[49] Was Carnegie merely explaining the American system or seriously proposing it as a model for Britain? The answer is probably both. There is no question that he believed in the model of federal government that the United States offered. Did he imagine that the unitary jurisdiction that prevailed in Britain could be significantly restructured? Clearly he believed in some form of the devolution of a central authority, for at least two reasons: it would end the system of monarchy and aristocracy, which had concentrated its authority at the center, and it would validate the American system of jurisdiction in which he fervently believed. Clearly he also believed that if British rule were based on the political equality of the citizen, it would not be confronting so sundering and destabilizing an issue as Irish Home Rule.

Nothing served more clearly as a measure of the essential difference between aristocracy and democracy than the way each addressed the issue of education. Indeed, in the workings of the life of a society, because it touched so closely on the workings of his own life, nothing meant so much to Carnegie. He celebrated how universal public schools were in the United States and how committedly Americans levied taxes for the education of their children. In Britain, the issue nowhere engaged a similar concern. "Thus are the ideas and methods of democracy and aristocracy contrasted! The former is ever seeking the education of the masses; the latter from its very nature is ever seeking to restrain education to the few, well knowing that privilege dies as knowledge spreads."[50] British aristocracy, as a class, "is by far the richest in the world."[51] But what did it do with its wealth? "Who can point to a member of the aristocracy who has risen beyond his own family, which is only another name for himself? The vain desire to found or maintain a family or to increase its revenues or estate is the ignoble ambition of a privileged order. What they give or lease as a class, with few exceptions, is 'nothing to nobody.'"[52]

By contrast, the republic offered a highly distinguished list of educational institutions that had been established by the contributions of millionaires. These included the Johns Hopkins University, Cornell, Vanderbilt, Vassar, Wellesley, Smith, Bryn Mawr, and the Stevens Institute.[53] If one is looking for the touchstone of *Triumphant Democracy*, one can find it in his chapter on education and in his vaunting of American democracy and his arraignment of British aristocracy. Here America offered Britain a worthy model, said Carnegie. By 1886, when his book appeared, he had already been practicing what he was now preaching. He had already established several public libraries, which he regarded, and would always continue to regard, as the fountainhead of civic education and the mainspring of a functioning democratic society.

In celebrating the virtues of the republic and decrying the flaws of the monarchy, Carnegie had apparently worked himself into a logical conundrum. He had to face the paradox that he was a devout radical, a latter-day Chartist in Britain and a devout conservative in the United States. But, as Carnegie saw it, preaching the American paradigm in his native land was not really a contradiction. All Britain had to do was to adopt the American principle of the full equality of its citizens. Then Britain would at last achieve the "conservatism" that was a central feature of the American system. Surely, even as he was writing *Triumphant Democracy*, British elections were roiling in riot and turmoil. Indeed, said Carnegie, "An American is surprised and shocked at the rowdyism often shown at public meetings in Britain."[54] In fact, turbulence and uncertainty were destabilizing the whole British political order. The great reform acts of 1884 and 1885 aroused sharp, bitter confrontations both between the Liberals and the Conservatives and within each party. When the House of Lords at first blocked the 1884 bill, a cry went up among the radical Liberals: "the Lords: mend them or end them." And in his "unauthorized program," announced in January 1885, Joseph Chamberlain, the wealthy industrialist M.P. from

Birmingham, proposed political and social changes that sought to radically alter the social and political institutions of Britain.[55] The major political writers of the day—Albert Venn Dicey, James Bryce, Henry Maine, and James Anthony Froude among them—wondered and feared in astonishment about where their apparently rudderless state was heading. Desperate for some respite from the seemingly endless constitutional turbulence, some looked across the Atlantic to the American polity, which was, in many respects, the closest analog to the British, for a remedy. Indeed, the leader of the Conservative Party, Lord Salisbury, declared (so Carnegie happily reported) that the Americans were fortunate to have a Supreme Court. He hailed it as "a magnificent institution" and the subject of his "greatest envy" because it "gives a stability to the institutions of the country which, under the system of vague and mysterious promises here [in Great Britain], we look for in vain."[56] The great instability of British politics and the praise of American institutions by British leaders suggested to Carnegie, the paradoxical radical conservative, how to square the circle: "In this respect, the example of the younger political community might well be followed by the elder. When the people of Britain . . . obtain their full political rights, there will be less exciting questions to discuss than those which now press for solution."[57]

Having rid itself of the evil of slavery, the United States stood on the firm ground of "laws that are satisfactory to all citizens."[58] Indeed, it was Prime Minister Gladstone himself who had hailed the American Constitution as "the most perfect piece of work ever struck off at one time by the mind and purpose of man."[59] Here indeed was the highest testimonial as to how America could serve as a model to her mother country. And, driving his point home, Carnegie insisted that the perfection of American principles guaranteed the conservatism of its politics. Thinking surely of the provisos of Chamberlain's "unauthorized programme," Carnegie reminded his readers that "the capitalist and property owner is more secure in the enjoyment of his property in the new than in the old country." At a time when the tax privileges of the great estates of the British aristocracy were being challenged, Carnegie noted that in the United States "property in land stands, and always has stood, upon the same footing as any other kind of property. Therefore land proprietorship has not been rendered odious by unfair advantages conferred upon it."[60] Because of their laws, Americans were not prone to wild excesses. Indeed, their laws underwrote the conservatism of their polity.

They have developed the United States into one of the most conservative communities in the world; conservative of their powerful government, of their Supreme Court and of their Senate, and of all that makes the security of civil and religious liberty, of the rights of property. . . . Let the student of American institutions direct his attention to this fact, and see whether the Republic be not a very conservative Republic indeed.[61]

Carnegie had squared the circle: the British republican, a reconstructed neo-Chartist, was also an American conservative. The republic, said Carnegie, could serve the monarchy as a worthy model.

3

The Antithesis of Models

"So, my fellow Republicans, the world is coming rapidly to your feet, the American Constitution is being more and more generally regarded as the model for all new nations to adopt and for all old nations to strive for." The words stood out in the concluding paragraphs of *Triumphant Democracy*, a fervid peroration in a chapter that summarized America's incomparable achievement. In that sentence, Carnegie was doing more than congratulating the transatlantic fraternity that had made a political philosophy of what they saw as the irreconcilable conflict between monarchies and republics. He was reiterating the essence of his creed, no less than of the massive volume that enshrined it. He proposed the principles and institutions of American life for all nations, new and old, to emulate. He said all nations, but he meant the United Kingdom.

Triumphant Democracy was the surface glittering of a current that had been running strong between Britain and the United States. The essential element of British-American relations for the century that followed the Declaration of Independence was an antithesis of ideals. But the Declaration was itself the culmination of differences that had been building between the motherland and the colony over the century-and-a-half of their singular relationship. The dialogue of antithesis was, of course, intrinsic to the revolutionary England of the seventeenth century, when the premises of the commonwealth challenged those of the Restoration. After 1688, the dialogue, which had been largely internal, was more widely externalized. The polarity of ideas that had riven English political culture diminished;

it was now translated into a deepening conflict between monarchical-administrative England (the court entourage) and her disaffected intellectuals, both within the homeland and more vociferously in her North American settlements (the country group, as they were called). The issues of conflicts between the two were roughly what they had earlier been between the Crown and its opposition: the sources of sovereignty, the prerogative of the monarchy, and the liberties and conscience of the subject.

The struggle between the monarchy and its radical subjects reached its peak during the years of the Civil Wars, of Cromwell and the Commonwealth. Many books have carefully traced out the struggle, but none more carefully than those of Bernard Bailyn and Gordon Wood. In looking for the antithesis of ideals that would later be carefully spelled out by Carnegie, one could not do better than finding its origins in the eighteenth-century conflict laid out by Bailyn in *The Ideological Origins of the American Revolution.*

> The reformers both in England and America advocated reforms—adult manhood suffrage; elimination of the rotten borough system and the substitution of regular units of representation systemically related to the distribution of population; the binding of representation to their constituencies by residential requirements and by instructions; alteration in the definition of seditious libel as to permit full freedom of the press; and the total withdrawal of government control over the practice of religion. *Their program was political, not social or economic.*[1]

The terms anticipated the Chartists by two centuries, and among the most famous of their progeny was Andrew Carnegie. In effect, during the decades before the thirteen North American colonies broke away from England, the sense was widespread among them and their radical British confreres that England had fallen from an earlier loftiness, that her institutions had been corrupted, that liberty had found a far better sanctuary in the New World, and that "America was a purer and freer England."[2]

In declaring their independence, the Americans undertook a willful, hazardous rejection of authority—indeed, of the international order of power. The Americans appealed to the universal truths that were a growing part of the eighteenth-century Western view of governance and power. The Americans put their case in terms that could appeal to an audience of diplomats and *philosophes* who subscribed, in the same program, to enlightened reform and to limiting British power. Ambivalence ran through the whole American posture—bravura and anxiety, self-proclamation and defensiveness, confidence and uncertainty, an overweening vanity and an overweening need for reassurance.[3]

That the revolutionaries were fighting a kindred polity necessarily shaped their conflict and defined it as a conflict of ideals. However much Britain had been Americanized when it was transplanted, in succeeding generations the two antagonists were after all bound by a common ethnicity, language, history, and set of ideas. In several of the the ties between them, the colonies could not efface the hallmarks of their identity. As the controversy intensified, so too did the elemental words of family relations. In America, the pamphleteers and newspapers invoked an earlier familial amity and often berated a motherland that could not understand the claims of her own children.[4]

In the high councils of governance in Britian (including, among others, the Board of Trade and Plantations, the Privy Council, the Treasury, the head minister, Parliament, and the Crown), particularly with the accession of George III, the colonies were denounced as disobedient children who had to be restricted or punished. That their respective material interests were the shaping forces in the growing breach should not mask the fact that family connections, more than empty metaphors, were being sundered. The American literature of both the revolutionary and early national generations overflowed with expressions of kinship: parents, children, cousins, fatherland, motherland. (This last word was freighted with a native and psychological importance—given his own deep ties with his mother—that underscores the role of kinship in Carnegie's *Triumphant Democracy*.)

The British themselves were, as Linda Colley has emphasized, at that very time forging their own sense of becoming a nation.[5] The Scottish Jacobite uprising of 1745, so brutally repressed, was, in a very distinct sense, one part of that rebellion against the English empire of which the American Revolution was another. Expressing a particular, more personal view of that transforming nation, James Boswell, a scion of the Scottish aristocracy, abjectly offered a lifelong subservience to gain the company and approval of England's notable man of letters, Samuel Johnson.[6] Andrew Carnegie's immediate ancestors grew up in these circumstances of strained and hostile relations between England and her colonies, whether immediately proximate or transatlantic.

The antithesis of ideals between the motherland and the colonies inevitably divided family loyalties in the 1770s, much as they earlier had during the English civil wars of the Cromwellian years. Benjamin Franklin sharply broke off with his highly accomplished son, William, who was royal governor of New Jersey before he joined others in leaving the fractious and rebellious colonial "radicals" for what they deemed the legitimate, legal regime of the English motherland.[7] Among the most notable of the Anglo-Americans who fled to the mother country were Jonathan Boucher, Thomas Hutchinson, the erstwhile royal governor of Massachusetts, and of course Joseph Galloway (whose plan for joint governance might very well have kept the kin under one roof).[8]

The conflict between England and her newly independent colonies, however much it raged as a conflict of politics and power, expressed no less deeply a conflict of material interests. The kindred polities had long been bound by trade. Indeed, long after the United States achieved its political independence, commerce continued to link it to the former governing metropolis, which by now was Europe's leading economic power. Frank Thistlethwaite has shown how, during the period from 1776 to 1850, the two states formed an Atlantic economy, a unitary economic society.[9] And John Bartlet Brebner has shown how, through the Civil War years, Canada served as a coupling pin for the two greater powers, binding them into a diplomacy that they could neither resolve nor escape.[10] Trade joined them while politics divided them. That their political cultures were so antipathetic to each other stood out singularly against the fact they were so closely linked economically and geographically. In a way, their economic interdependence exacerbated their political differences. Indeed, because the early American republic was an essentially agrarian community serving and depending on one that was essentially industrial, the political contest between them, far from being lessened, was enhanced.

In the vision of its founders, the United States was the paradigmatic society. Their progenitors had, after all, consecrated themselves to building a Zion in the New World; they could offer the transatlantic community the ideal of their reformed society. They expressed, as Edmund Burke had put it, "the dissidence of dissent," standing in the vanguard of the radical movements of their day, and they wished to justify their position in the court of European opinion. For them, Britain was the antithetical society. Where, during the colonial period, the mother country had served as an example to consider, if not always to emulate, she now became the embodiment of all that was questionable. As for America, what had earlier been regarded as "disturbing deviations from the model of the mother country now could be regarded as desirable perfections."[11] Indeed, from 1776 on, there grew between the kindred communities a *competition of models*, in which each represented, in the eyes of its presiding groups, a better society than the other, an answer to the other's problems, a redemption from the other's vices. The competition was inevitably phrased in moral terms. But the British part of the exchange was nowhere as high-flown, intense, or self-righteous as the American. A society bound by history could not, after all, speak the same language as a society freed by nature.

The revolutionary generation in America spoke always of the antithesis between their order and the older one across the seas. Gordon Wood has spelled with fine clarity that the American Revolution was not merely one of political forms, but a social reformation as well, and that "it added a moral dimension, a utopian depth, to the political separation from England, a depth that involved the very character of their society."[12] With a purpose that was awesome, if also ingenuous, the men of the 1780s undertook to create a culture that would express uniquely American ideas. Benjamin Rush, Noah Webster, Joel Barlow, David Ramsay, and Philip Freneau were only a few who were expounding a new literature for a new nation.[13] The oft-cited prologue to Royall Tyler's play, *The Contrast* (1787), put the cause simply.

> On native themes his Muse displays her pow'rs;
> If ours the faults, the virtues too are ours.
> Whilst all which aims at splendour and parade
> Must come from Europe, and be ready made.
> Strange! we should thus our native worth disclaim,
> And check the progress of our rising fame.

If a new literature was easier to proclaim than to create, one should not ignore what the act of proclaiming it signified. During the first decades of the republic, English models were consulted, and "American intellect remained, in many ways, in a state of colonization . . . of subservience to the critical opinion of the once mother country."[14] Tocqueville had, much earlier, ventured to explain the subservience. Devoting themselves to the works of the soils, the former colonists, he said, exploited their ready access to Britain's works of the mind, so that "one can truly say that English literature flourishes on their own soil."[15]

At the very time that Tocqueville was proffering his explanation, major American writers—men such as Emerson, Whitman, Melville, and Hawthorne—were striking out on their own and creating a truly native literature, born of the dilemmas and ironies of American experience, for reasons and in ways that F. O. Matthiessen has so very well explored in *The American Renaissance*.[16] But the earlier generation could not so readily invent one, not only because its ties to the older culture were yet too close, but also because British literature afforded them a valid substitute, questioning British institutions as it did, or escaping them into the fantasy of a distant, noble, and simple past. Washington Irving, for example, brought his art to perfection while he was living in England. He knew all too well the special nature of the British-American connection. "The Idea of England" inspired Americans with "a hallowed feeling of tenderness and veneration, as the land of their forefathers . . . the birthplace and mausoleum of the sages and heroes of our paternal history." The family ties were strong, but how were Americans to respond to the constant abuse heaped on their country by English writers? The United States would gladly take England as a model. "We are a young people, necessarily an imitative one, and must take our examples and models . . . from the existing nations of Europe. There is no country more worthy of our study than England." But the defamation of our institutions was putting a strain upon our enthusiasm for our mother country. "Is all this to be at an end? Is this golden band of kindred sympathies, so rare between nations, to be broken forever? Perhaps it is for the best; it may dispel an illusion which might have kept us in mental vassalage, which might have interfered occasionally with our true interests, and prevented the growth of proper national pride." Irving had no doubt about the future. England was an old country, born of a "rude and ignorant" age; the United States was a new country, born of "an enlightened and philosophic age" and "in all our relationships with England, we are the rising and the gaining party." He had clearly spelled out the interplay of ideas and sentiments between the two nations: England's continuing role as a model for the United States, the ambivalence of young America's feeling for England, and the increasing competition of models between them in the early decades of the nineteenth century.[17] With no less perspicacity than Irving, Emerson understood the peculiar relationship between England and the United States. The English national genius, he said, had been the most successful "in the universe for the last millennium. The American is only the continuation of the English genius into new conditions, more or less propitious." With remarkable clarity, he recognized the compelling impact on America of the English model. "Those who resist it do not feel it or obey it less."[18]

WITH THE COMING OF PEACE to Europe after the defeat of Napoleon, the antithesis of ideals between the United States and Britain became intense. For the quarter century of European wars, from 1792 to 1815, Britain found in Jacobinism and Bonapartism a greater ideological and military foe; and the United States was as much concerned with protecting her existence (indeed at times against the French revolutionaries) as with proclaiming her ideology. One has only to remember the XYZ affair and the undeclared naval war with France during the administration of John Adams (1797–1801) to see that preserving and protecting the new nation's independence were every bit as important as proclaiming republican ideology. In the circumstance, there was a relative muting of the conflict of ideas between the two communities. But with peace, the conflict flared up again. Europe knew, and none better than Britain, that it had defeated Napoleon's armies, but not his principles. The America that had successfully survived the massive European confrontation between aristocracy and democracy now loomed greater than before—an enlarged and prospering society, an engine of power without standing armies, a relatively tranquil democracy without Jacobinism.[19]

The question in Britain was not whether there should be change, but how far it should go. Metternich's formula for holding fast in times of duress against all demands for reform did not find a wide acceptance among British leaders, though some, like the Duke of Wellington and his aristocratic cohorts, clung to the belief that the prevailing institutions could be changed only at great risk to the nation. And in the face of a rising, expanding, ever more powerful insistence that British society be reformed, what more relevant example could there be than that of the kindred republic across the sea?

In the new age, republicanism became a cult of enthusiasm. It was not only that, vis-à-vis the world outside, the United States wished to parade its special form of civism. It was also that, in the world outside, civism had come to replace the religious sectarianism of the earlier centuries. Moreover, the modes of deference that had characterized colonial America, and that had not been radically altered by the Revolution, now began to give away to an ethos of egalitarianism.[20] Then too, the newer immigrants, wishing to show that they were more American than the Americans, readily espoused republicanism. This was true of the

Germans and Scandinavians, and especially true of a Scottish family such as the Carnegies, who came here in 1848, and of the masses of Irish, particularly distressed refugees from the United Kingdom: praising American republicanism was the other side of the coin of damning the harsh rule of British aristocracy.

Tocqueville noted that he rarely found deviation from the articles of American faith for the reason that every citizen, regarding himself as the source and maker of the faith, was its ardent keeper. It had a universal dominion. In the revolutionary era, "loyalists" and "patriots" shared as many premises as they differed on. The patriots' insistence on the rights of property and liberties of the subject was perhaps the most important article of their faith. In the early days of the republic, the Federalists joined the Jeffersonians in a common perception of the American polity and, as David Hackett Fischer has told us, they quickly adopted the democratic forms of party organization that the Jeffersonians were introducing.[21] In the 1830s and 1840s, even those who criticized American institutions, such as James Fenimore Cooper, Emerson, Hawthorne, and Philip Hone, did so from within, as it were, considering American institutions, for all their defects, as superior to those of Britain.

And the premises of the Whig Party, the rival of the Democratic Party, were a variant statement of the American ideology, as Louis Hartz has shown, not a contradiction of it.[22] Insofar as the contrast between America and Britain was concerned, no one, in these decades, perceived it better than Ralph Waldo Emerson. Some of his observations in *English Traits* (1856) bear repeating.

> The feudal system survives in the steep inequality of property and privilege, in the limited franchise, in the social barriers which continue patronage and promotion to a caste, and still more in the submissive ideas pervading these people. . . . An Englishman shows no mercy to those below him in the social scale, as he looks for none from those above him. . . . The American system is more democratic, more humane. . . . The feudal character of the English state, now that it is getting obsolete, glares a little, in contrast with the democratic tendencies. The inequality of power and property shocks republican nerves.[23]

Here, then, were some of the conditions framing the contest of ideals between the two kindred societies in the decades after 1815. Those speaking for Britain defended the ordered, established, deferential, historical, conservative society; those speaking for America proclaimed the rational, democratic, disestablished, reformed society. The question before British leadership was not whether there should be reform, but what kind and to what degree. Even Wellington and Castlereagh disdained the modes and premises of continental politics. However they inclined, British leaders almost invariably appealed to native traditions. They could not ignore the American republic sprung from their own stock. In the two decades after the Congress of Vienna, one found in Britain a wide spectrum of opinion on the issue of reform that ranged from the far right to the far left. But even Wellington, staunchest of Conservatives, sponsored Catholic Emancipation and the repeal of the Test Act. Somewhat to his left stood the younger Tories—men such as Canning, Huskisson, and Peel—and from there one moved into the respective camps of Grey and Russell, of the more radical Whigs such as Durham, of the philosophical radicals, whose leaders were Jeremy Bentham and the Mills, father and son; and, at the extreme left, of the lower-class radicals, including the Chartists.

Where one stood on domestic reform determined to a great degree how one viewed the United States. Between the ultraconservative's view that America was a rowdy, uncivilized republic and the radical's view that it was paradise regained, there spread out a wide variety of perceptions that blended almost without demarcation, one into the other. For strife-ridden Britain, America was an object lesson in possibilities. The republic offered the monarchy alternative routes to reform. Here is why the number of Britons who came to study American institutions rose to a flood in the period after 1815. Here, too, is why their attitudes to the United States were at bottom an expression of their attitudes to British reform, as John Stuart Mill noted in his reviews of Tocqueville's *Democracy in America.*

For two decades, the war of ideals raged between the reformed and the reforming societies. It was nowhere more bitterly expressed than in the so-called battle of the quarterlies, in which reviewers on one side of the Atlantic attacked, almost without restraint, the men and institutions of the other side.[24] If the war summed up the doubts of the two societies in periods of great change as they were taking stock of themselves by taking stock of their kindred community, it also reflected more tangible, specific factors. They were continuing, in verbal hostilities, the War of 1812, which was itself a war of ideas. Territorial controversies—over the 49th parallel, over the Oregon territory, to name but two—kept alive the ideological conflict. The British were increasingly conscious that the United

States was fast becoming a powerful rival nation, and particularly in a hemisphere where they were seeking influence and wealth. As Mordecai M. Noah, an American traveling in the United Kingdom, put it, Britain viewed with increasing discomfort a nation "once their subjects, now their equals . . . with a population nearly equal to theirs, and territory and resources far superior."[25] The rising tide of emigrants from the United Kingdom to the United States bespoke more than the relative shift in population and power between the two—the emigrants were also bearers of animus toward the society they were leaving, and none were more outspoken than the Irish Catholics.[26] English travelers to the United States, noting the important role the Irish were playing in American urban politics, attributed to their erstwhile countrymen a considerable part of the republic's hostility toward the monarchy.[27] But, as Washington Irving saw it, the English travelers themselves were largely responsible for creating a spirit of malevolence between the two polities. They were a crude and motley assortment, including such types as "the broken-down tradesman, the scheming adventurer, the wandering mechanic, the Manchester and Birmingham agent."[28] Regrettably, said Irving, the British were accepting as true their travelers' virulent, grossly distorted account of life in the United States of America.

In his extensive, probing reviews of Tocqueville's *Democracy in America*, John Stuart Mill cautioned against the partisanship of the scores of books about America that were currently appearing. "America is usually cited by the two great parties which divide Europe (and Britain, of course) as an argument for or against democracy. Democrats have sought to prove by it that we ought to be democrats; aristocrats, that we should cleave to aristocracy, and withstand the democratic spirit."[29] It was clear enough, from Mill's review of Tocqueville, that Americas stood as an example of the democratic ideas and that for aristocratic Britain, the kindred community was a vital, challenging, and threatening antithesis.

Indeed, for the very reason that Mill underscored, English aristocrats, democrats, reformers, supporters of the establishment, and adventurers were writing up their grand tours of the kindred society. Many caught the attention of the reading public, but none as much as Frances Trollope's *Domestic Manners of the Americans*. Appearing in 1831, it could not have come at a more critical time in the inflammatory debated raging in England over parliamentary reform. Having lived in the United States for some four years (1827–1831), she could speak with some authority about life among the democrats and particularly about their attitude toward their English cousins. Her words bear citing at some length.

> The national feeling [is] of unconquerable dislike . . . at the bottom of every truly American heart against the English. [They] see themselves as more modern, more advanced than England. Our class literature, our princely dignities, our noble institutions, are all gone-by relics of the dark ages. Not a single word can be said hinted at a different opinion, which will not bring down a transatlantic anathema on my head. [There is] one single feeling of enthusiasm of which they appear capable, namely, the triumph of their successful struggle for national independence. They rest satisfied with the praise and admiration they receive from each other; and turning a deaf ear to the criticism of the old world, consent to be their "own prodigious great reward."[30]

Speaking with an experienced authenticity, her book argued a thunderous no against the "democratic" reform of the House of Common that the British leaders were then considering. But, as we know, despite intense aristocratic opposition, the reform bill was finally enacted on June 4, 1832. The democratic "revolution," as Tocqueville's great book would very soon declare, could apparently not be resisted. More than ever, America stood as a minatory model.

A GROWING AMERICAN CIVISM broadcast the antithesis of ideals after the Treaty of Ghent and particularly in the Jacksonian age. Increasingly diverse, scattered, and multifarious, the Americans were increasingly bound by a formal patriotism in which England figured large as the enemy. The code and rituals of patriotism were ever more necessary as the America union grew in its territory and in the number and diversity of its population. It was axiomatic to those who superintended American public life that an ever-increasing number of immigrants, both of English and non-English origins, needed a course in republican virtues. There were many agents of American civic instruction, among which the fairly universal growth of elementary education and the proliferating number of newspapers were the most important. Expanding political parties outbid themselves in extolling their adherence to the national faith. Patriotism, loudly proclaimed and ceremonially paraded, bound Americans into a ritualistic anti-English union. In their civic celebrations—in which the American eagle screamed, and recent immigrants often screamed more loudly than those with deep-rooted American genealogies—it would not have occurred to them that the "loyalists" of the revolutionary years had in essential ways been the "patriots" of their day.

History is indeed written by the victors. The history that was taught in the free public schools in a multitude of "national readers"[31] and the common school histories (Charles A. Goodrich and Samuel Goodrich were the most popular) celebrated the victory of the American Revolution.[32] When visiting foreign travelers came to American shores, they were regularly greeted by American celebrators of republican institutions, who almost tirelessly repeated the antithesis of American and European ideals.[33] In the victorious historiography, England was the arch antagonist—yes, even the arch enemy. The antithesis was never a simple antimony; American intellectuals recognized their connection and indeed their debt to England. But in the new democratic age, a patriotism had surged that submerged discrimination. A visceral antagonism did not stop at fine distinctions.

Faith is a dual ceremony. It is as much rejecting one set of principles as it is espousing another. In a democratic polity, what defines its citizens is not merely what they affirm but also what they deny. What defines them no less is their dual perception of the political community to which they belong; the ritual of belonging testifies both to an approval of their own nation and a disapproval of other nations. There are ranges, of course, of popular sentiment, depending on the circumstances that govern the relations between the citizen's community and the communities of the world outside. The special task of public education is to inculcate civism as an affirmative creed. But as historians have been reminding us, civism rests on disavowal no less than on preservation. From the writings of later twentieth-century historians (Hofstadter, Benson, Higham, Wiebe, to name some of the more obvious ones), we have been arriving at the sense that the politics of American faith, the creed of American political culture, is often expressed as the other side of optimism and affirmation, a mass psychology of anxiety, xenophobia, paranoia, and hostility.[34]

Robert Kelley has offered us the very helpful insight that the cardinal element of a political persuasion is "the image of the enemy . . . a shared vision of the enemy does more to bind men together than anything else."[35] Basic to the antithesis of ideals that locked the United States and Great Britain into a strange symbiosis was the fact that Britain was, for most Americans, the great antagonist. Anglophobia was intense all through the nineteenth century, but particularly so, as we have seen, during the early decades of the century. However true it may have been, as H. C. Allen reminds us, that American travelers to Britain were largely sympathetic to the former mother country, the harsh reality was that "the mass of the American people at home tended to be hostile."[36]

Faith must have its sacraments, and iconoclasts merely supplant the worship of forms that are more overt with those that are less. In their quest for symbols, said Daniel Boorstin, Americans had, by the time of the semicentennial of the Declaration of Independence, made the celebration of the Fourth of July a festival of national purpose. The day's ceremonies were a "ritual of self-justification," performed with an excess that revealed less the depth than "uncertainties of national patriotism."[37] The celebrants condemned the empire from which the colonies had freed themselves; in lionizing the American "heroes," they reviled their British foes. When he had made his way up the Hudson River to Albany, Alexis de Tocqueville witnessed the celebration of the Fourth of July. After a long series of parades involving deputations from the many trades or associations of the city, he joined with other citizens in a patriotic service at the Methodist Church. What impressed him particularly was the reading of the Declaration of Independence, with its massive rehearsal of "the injustices and the tyranny of England."[38] The Albany of 1831 was the United States in microcosm. In Great Britain, most Americans beheld the vision of the enemy.

Francis J. Grund, an Austrian who said that he had long lived among the Americans, noted that "the customs and peculiarities of the English are generally not liked in the United States."[39] It was a matter of the pride of a young nation. "The Americans . . . are the readiest to take and resent an insult, but they are more particularly sensitive with regard to the offenses of the English."[40] Grund regarded the American attitude toward the English as part of a larger ambivalence. The Americans looked to English manners as a guide and they dressed in the English mode; indeed, American wealth and English style ascended the social stairs together. But the other side of modish imitation was the fear of being condescended to, which the Americans resented deeply.

Especially helpful in understanding the Anglo-American antithesis of ideals are the experiences of some distinguished French visitors. Very memorable of course was the grand tour in the United States, in 1826, half a century after the Declaration of Independence, of the venerable

Marquis de Lafayette, who had played an important role in the American Revolution and who had long since been celebrated as one of the republic's great heroes.

Shortly thereafter came the widely noticed, but nowhere as prominent two young French aristocrats, Alexis de Tocqueville and his close friend, Gustave de Beaumont, two scions of the nobility who visited the United States ostensibly to inspect the American penitentiary system but far more significantly to observe, at close hand, the workings of American democracy. At that famous Albany 1831 celebration of Independence Day, Tocqueville heard a striking part of the ritualized antithesis of models.

> [A] profound silence reigned in the meeting. When in its eloquent plea Congress reviewed the injustice and tyranny of England, we heard a murmur of indignation and anger run about us. . . . When it appealed to the justice of its cause and expressed its generous resolution to succumb or to free America, it seemed that an electric current made the hearts vibrate.

Behind the shuttered windows, particularly among the Boston Brahmins, the young French aristocrats had heard about the unruliness, indeed the mob spirit of the new American democrats. But in public ceremonies they heard the voice and beheld the civic rituals of an ever-vital Anglo-American antithesis.

It particularly rankled the Americans that English reviewers disparaged their literature—this in the age of Washington Irving, James Fenimore Cooper, Ralph Waldo Emerson, Henry Wadsworth Longfellow, George Bancroft, and Nathaniel Hawthorne. Sydney Smith's query in the *Edinburgh Review*—"Who now reads an American book?"—contemptuously arrogant as it was, dug deeply into American sensitivities and inflamed their resentments.[41]

Half a century later, James Bryce recorded the anti-English sentiments Tocqueville had found on his 1831–1832 visit. At that time, said Bryce, "the hatred felt by the United States toward England" was intense, "rekindled by the unhappy war of 1812, kept alive by the sensitiveness of the one people [the Americans] and the arrogance of the other [the English], imprinted afresh on new generations in America by silly school-books and Fourth of July harangues."[42]

The animus between the republic and the monarchy had always flared up in times of war. Never was this more true than during the American

Civil War, when the Union was at last defining its cause as ending slavery while the official classes of the monarchy, for their own material interests, supported the slave-based Confederacy. "In countless hearts and minds [in the United States]," Henry T. Tuckerman wrote in 1864, "pleasant and fond illusions in regard to English character, government, and sentiment are forever dispelled."[43] He quoted a letter with the sentiments of "a scholar and a gentleman, who, on the score of his lineage as well as culture and character, claims respect for his deliberate views . . . which indicate without exaggeration the change which has come over the noblest in the land."

"Let John Bull beware," said the letter. "War or no war, he has made an enduring enemy of us. I am startled to hear myself say this, but England is henceforth to me only historical—the home of *our* Shakespeare, and Milton, and Wordsworth; for all her best writers are ours by necessity and privilege of language; but farewell the especial sympathy I have felt in her political, social, and total well-being. With her present exhibition and promulgation of jealousy and selfishness and heartlessness and ungentlemanly meanness, she has cut me loose from the sweet and cordial and reverent ties that have kept me so long to a second fatherland." There were moments of trial, of greater and lesser affinity between the monarchy and the republic. However close the affinity, it could snap. Underneath ran a deep-seated antithesis of ideals.

In probing the antithesis of ideals one must of course be careful. For some American groups, England was not the perennial enemy, and in their private schools and academies they were not taught the homogenizing lessons of national civism. For them, the enemy was not distant and foreign, but rather internal and nearby. The Jeffersonian age witnessed the passage of republican politics from deference to democracy. The insistence on the former and the acceptance of the latter, says David Hackett Fischer, marked the distinction between the Old Federalists and the New.[44] The "status revolution" of the early decades of the nineteenth century was no less a political displacement of entrenched elites than an economic one. In its wake it left embittered men, who turned their animus on the foe within. In their perspective, Britain seemed increasingly to be benign, if not friendly. "It is certain that the well-educated and well-informed class of our citizens," said Washington Irving, "entertain a deep-rooted good will, and a rational esteem, for Great Britain."[45] When the patriots took to the streets on the Fourth of July and pulpits and platforms rang with denunciation of British tyranny, families of the "better sort" closed their shutters and, in a sullen nostalgia that bordered on Jacobism, celebrated the monarchy across the water. Boston, the center of patriotism in 1776, became the domicile of a new loyalism half a century later. Said Henry Adams: "The tone of Boston society was colonial. The true Bostonian always knelt in self-abasement before the majesty of English standards; far from concealing it as a weakness, he was proud of it as his strength."[46] The line between the Boston Brahmins of the 1830s and the genteel reformers of the 1880s ran straight. For both, the newer ways of the republic marked a decline from civic probity and culture, and for both Britain was the paradigmatic polity.

For the foremost American writers in the years after the Treaty of Ghent, the approach to British-American relations was also of a special nature. In their individual search for recognition no less than in their collective venture at creating a new nation's literature, the writers came up hard against the terms of American identity. To examine the national myth, they stood outside it. They could not accept a portrait of American and British values drawn to the scheme of a simple antithesis. They resisted easy formulas of morality by which America was praised and Britain damned. In a larger way, their problem was to add to innocence the dimension of experience, to give up ideology for actuality. As R. W. B. Lewis has put it, they wished to leave an eternal present and return into time. They undertook to transfer Adam, the archetypal American, from the insulated purity of Eden to the trying corrupting realities of the world outside.[47]

Cushing Strout has detailed how several of these writers construed America's intellectual relationship with England. Washington Irving and Emerson saw England as the native land of the American imagination, joining Longfellow in the belief that "the torch of national culture was 'lighted at the old domestic fireside of England.'"[48] Hawthorne was fully conscious of the impoverishment of Britain's lower classes, but he could not resist the conclusion that aristocracy had given British society a sense of community and that "palaces, pictures, and parks" ultimately "do enrich life."[49] However hostile his view of English values and institutions, even Cooper ventured the hope that America and Britain "might benefit a good deal by a critical examination of each other."[50] But, as we have suggested, this sentiment had a very limited appeal. In the popular vision, the ideals of America and Britain represented a clear difference between right and wrong. Outside the room of Hawthorne's self-probing imagination, there were thirty million Americans who did not try to understand the national myth. Instead, they lived it.

R. R. PALMER HAS SAID that the American Revolution "dethroned England, and set up America, as a model for those seeking a better world."[51] The model was nowhere more diligently appealed to than in post-1815 Britain. Having quashed Napoleon's revolutionary challenge, the British withdrew to the long overdue rearrangement of their own affairs. Britain's ancien regime was under attack by virtually all the major classes, including members of the establishment itself. In Britain, as elsewhere, aristocrats joined the assault on the aristocracy. From right to left, the attacks on the old regime ran to increasingly more radical demands for the reconstruction of society. The years immediately after the Napoleonic wars saw a fearful confrontation between the establishment and the massive bloc of forces clamoring for change. As reform proceeded, the ranks of the reformers thinned out, with those who had attained their goals moving to the side of the establishment. By 1851, the challenge to the British order had passed. The reason why, of course, was that a new order had emerged.

Tocqueville said of the United States that it achieved democracy without having had a democratic revolution. In a comparable way, Britain passed through revolutionary crises and achieved the consequences of a revolution without actually experiencing one. The reason it was able to do so has long posed a challenge for historians. Probably the most widely accepted explanation has been that of Elie Halevy, who said that the extensive impact of Methodism, with its doctrine of submission, was to keep England's lower classes in check.[52] Tocqueville, in his visit to England in 1833, at the very height of the reformist upsurge, had found other reasons. The English aristocracy, far from being the exclusive caste that it was in France, was far more open.[53] Precisely for this reason, the English had fewer deep-seated reservations about the aristocratic principle.[54] Indeed, even the English Radicals, said Tocqueville, worked within the premises of the English polity. They accepted the law, respected property rights, were genuinely religious, and were individuals of "easy financial circumstances," "careful education," and "recognized as 'gentlemen.'"[55]

The sociology of British reform was very largely the sociology of the British perception of America. The United States served all reformers as the paradigm of a reformed society. But, for many reformers, America was a polity to learn from, not to imitate. For them, the question was how to filter American principles through British actualities, how to adapt the suggestions offered by American institutions to the conditions of British life. But as one moves leftward among the reformers, one finds that their programs went beyond merely revising British life in the light of American ideas. The more radical the reformers, the more they sought to replicate American society. Those at the extreme left attacked the most basic premises of the British polity: the aristocratic principles, the monarchical establishment, the idea and forms of status and deference—indeed the whole panoply of institutions political, religious, military, and educational that were fundamental to the privileged, ordered society. They wished not merely to republicanize Britain, but to make her a republic. In eastern Scotland's Chartist districts of the 1830s and 1840s, in Dunfermline, suffering from a starkly depressed weaving industry, the Carnegie family made a daily litany of the radical program for a better life. Little wonder that the principles of the republic across the seas became the essential doctrine of *Triumphant Democracy*.

The British-American relationship during those years is seen too simply if one concludes that America served Britain as "a beacon of freedom"[56] or that the relationship connected groups of "outsiders" in both societies.[57] The problem here is what one means by "outsiders." Insofar as their connection with America went, the constituency of the British "outsiders" was hardly fixed or readily defined; it changed according to the nature and degree of their connection with the British establishment. As for the Americans, it is most improbable to suggest that they were "outsiders" to the premises of their own society; the remarkable thing that men such as Tocqueville, Chevalier, and Grund noted was how "inside" virtually all Americans were in an embracing, almost immuring structure of values.

In the British perspective on America in the years 1815–1850, there were many Britains and many perspectives. The antithesis of ideals between the two nations was variously perceived, depending largely upon the degree to which America was to serve in the British reformer's program as *the alternate society*. Between Basil Hall's fierce assault on American institutions and Alexander Mackay's celebration of them, opinion ranged widely. For those defending the British establishment in the grim days of parliamentary reform, accounts pointing up the flaws of American democratic life offered welcome sustenance, and the defenders embraced, with an almost indiscriminate enthusiasm, both the condemnation of American principles, such as Frederick Marryat's, and the censure of American manners, such as Frances Trollope's. Among those who sought to change British institutions, many groups can be discerned, and it would be hazardous to fit them to a simple pattern. Nonetheless, with an awareness that they shaded off one into the other, both as to their reform program and the perception of America as a society that was antithetical and corrective to Britain, one can, following the suggestions of Frank Thistlethwaite and David Paul Crook, make out four larger groups of reformers whose vision of America played an important role in the British-American relationship in those decades. These were the moderate Whigs, the Manchester Liberals, the Utilitarian (or Benthamites), and the lower-class radicals.[58]

Far less ideological than other reformers, the moderate Whigs looked to America for suggestions about redistributing power in Britain rather than for more fundamental ways of reconstructing the social order. Interested in the general tenor of life in the United States, they did not, however, wish to adopt the premises that defined that life. Indeed, there was much about American culture that they found questionable. In their own metaphor, they saw America as a new house and theirs as an older one, and they wished not to tear theirs down but rather, in light of the American mode of living, to refurbish it and live more commodiously. They "commended the stability of America's political system, the lightness of her financial burdens, the freedom of her press, her religious toleration, and her unparalleled system of education. They were divided upon the subject of democratic institutions, but as good Whigs, sympathized with the broad characteristics of American liberalism."[59] The moderate Whigs differed among themselves as to how far the American model could be applied to British institutions, and their opinions changed from one decade of the great period of British reform to the next. They were firm in their belief that change should be gradual, pragmatic, and undoctrinaire. Men of 1688, they hailed the American leaders of 1776 as men of responsibility and property and the republic itself as an enshrinement of stable and conservative values.

Related to the Whigs in outlook, yet far more doctrinaire and ideological, were the Manchester Liberals, who belonged largely to the manufacturing class. "It was this class, with its Non-conformist business ethic, rather than Chartist *sans-culottes* or Bloomsbury intellectuals, who felt the closest affinities to the United States. These particular British people, intent on republicanizing British institutions, responded most sensitively to the American image."[60] The details of their program for Britain rehearsed the tenets of classical liberalism. They wanted free trade, full religious liberty, more frequently accountable parliaments, and retrenchment in government expenditures. Looking across the Atlantic, they saw all they wanted for themselves: a society without hereditary privilege, a polity without an establishment, a Dissenters' manufacturing community where religion was nobody's business and business was everybody's religion. Their efforts to change Britain were, perhaps more than any other group of reformers, acts of zeal, commitment, energy, and power. They achieved their greatest triumph with the repeal of the Corn Laws in 1846.

Cobden and Bright were by far the most prominent of the Manchester Liberals; so regularly and passionately did they appeal to the example of the overseas republic in their speeches in Parliament that they were dubbed "the two members for the United States." For them, the most important fact of the nineteenth century was the almost incomparable economic progress the United States was making.[61] The secret of the republic's productivity, Cobden was convinced, lay in her institutions. Britain would be wise to adopt them and soon, because already she was being fast outstripped by America.[62] "We believe the government of the United States," said Cobden, "to be at this moment the best in the world, but then the Americans are the best people."[63] His colleague, Bright, warmly agreed. The Americans, he reiterated almost endlessly throughout his long public career, offered "a spectacle to the world to which history has no parallel, and which it would be a happy thing for the population of this country if we were only at some rapid and sensible pace approaching."[64]

The Benthamites constituted a third British group of reformers who used the American example as a guide to domestic change. Wielding the yardstick of utilitarianism, they challenged the philosophies, traditions, and controls of the landed interests. The United States, as they saw it, offered much of what they wished to achieve in their native land: decentralization in politics and administration, an open economic society, a formal separation of church and state, simplicity and clarity in law, the conduct of public affairs by men of talent and distinction, an economy run on the principles of laissez-faire, a democratic and egalitarian society, and a public policy that was liberal and directed to achieving the greatest good for the greatest number. In strictly utilitarian terms, *The Westminster Review*, the principal Benthamite journal, averred that "the Americans possess a greater amount of happiness than the same numbers have enjoyed before."[65] And Jeremy Bentham, the founding father of the Utilitarian school, wrote with assurance to President Jackson that he was "more of a United States man than an Englishman."[66] The product of domestic needs, the Benthamite image of America changed along with the needs. Vital in the 1820s, when reform was a program, the image waned in the 1840s, when reform was an achievement.[67]

The working-class radicals, and above all the Chartists, warmly embraced America's ideas, considering them the complete antithesis of Britain's. In October 1839, William Carpenter, the editor of *The Charter*, a leading Chartist journal, appealed to the example of the United States, whose "inhabitants . . . are governed on the principles of Chartism, the consequence of which is that all legislation is bent toward the welfare of the many, and not of the few."[68] The United States was, for the Chartists, the truly modern society, rational, enlightened, innovative, individualist, an environment for achieving man's perfection. It was, in sum, the Chartist commonwealth.[69]

If America was the Chartists' ideal commonwealth, Britain was the exact opposite. It had been despoiled and misgoverned by self-interested aristocrats and men of wealth. It denied men the political equality that was their legitimate claim. Attacking the establishment, the Chartists insisted that removing privilege would set the British polity right. Monarchy was an expensive and corrupt institution; installing a republic would purify British politics and redeem British life. A republic, they were certain, could produce more goods and bring a far higher standard of material comfort to the majority of its citizens. Nor need the propertied classes fear it, for the example of America showed conclusively that republican institutions do not threaten property.[70]

AS A YOUNG MAN, a fairly recent immigrant to the United States, Carnegie summed up the sense Americans had of their role in reshaping European ideas: "Our republic . . . was and still is the hope of reformers throughout the world. Great and good men in every nation glory in its prosperity and would lament over its downfall. Our mission as the representative of a new era, as the pioneer of liberty, is to serve as an example to other nations, to incite them to come up to the true standard, to impel the people to ask and obtain new reforms."[71]

Vis-à-vis Britain, the kindred society, enmeshed as it was in the problem of recasting its institutions to meet the demands of newer classes and new conditions, America was a particularly compelling presence. This is hardly to say that the British-American relationship consisted entirely of the symbols each presented to the other. Behind the screen of national ideals was the calculated game of international politics—less dramatic, perhaps, but hardly less important. Outside the public arena of embattled ideologies were the diplomatic exchanges, the Rush–Bagot convention, the Canning–Adams agreements, the Webster–Ashburton Treaty, and the compromise over Oregon, which secured the boundaries of the arena sufficiently to permit the play of American ideas to continue.

It was in the context of the confrontation of ideals between the kindred polities that Carnegie's ideas took form. Joseph Wall has done very well to make us aware of the Chartist origins of Carnegie's ideas.[72] Young Andrew's sense that he had found the Chartist republic in America was expressed in a letter to his cousin back home: "We now possess what the working classes of your country look forward to as constituting their political millennium. We have the charter [for] which you have been fighting for years as the Panacea for all Britain's woes, the bulwark of the liberties of the people."[73]

Triumphant Democracy, which appeared more than three decades after Carnegie wrote these words, was more, certainly, than a neo-Chartist tract. Written by a man of fifty who had risen high in the scheme of American power and wealth, the book spoke an intelligence that had been leavened by the other sets of values. Some of its arguments read like Utilitarianism; others had the fervid conviction of Manchester Liberalism and, in particular, of Cobden and Bright, whom Carnegie warmly revered; and others still had the stolid guardedness of the moderate Whigs. Carnegie was not rooted in a single doctrine. A man of slogans, he was not, however, a simple ideologue. *Triumphant Democracy* expressed a composite of reform ideas that sprang from profound social change in Britain and America and from the intense, searching debate about their respective ways of life.

By 1848, the contention over ideals had lost its edge. The force of ideology that had powered American expansion began to diminish when, with the Mexican War, the borders of the continental United States were achieved. Indeed, the war itself turned public discussion more pointedly than before to the joint issues of slavery and the union. Rent by internal controversy, blemished as its spokesmen felt it to be by the institution of slavery, the republic could not readily be paraded as a model. It lost a certain credibility when, as the revolutions of 1848 erupted all over Europe in the name of liberalism and democracy, it stood idly by. Americans feted Louis Kossuth and gave him some money, but they did nothing else.[74]

If supporting reform was a *cause manqué* in the United States, having achieved it was a cause triumphant in Great Britain. Shock after shock of revolutionary crisis had swayed the British regime, but it had remained standing. As their demands were met, the reformers came over in successive groups to the side of the established order, buttressing it ever more firmly with their support. By 1848, the Chartists stood alone; they could gather petitions, and they could demonstrate, but little more. The Crystal Palace Exhibition of 1851 testified to the resolution of internal crisis, the reconstitution of the British political order, and the advent and success of the Victorian compromise. As G. M. Young has said, "The Great Exhibition was the pageant of domestic peace. Not for sixty years had the throne appeared so solidly based on the national goodwill as in that summer of hope and pride and reconciliation. After all the alarms and agitations of thirty years, the State had swung back to its natural centre."[75]

Britain and America no longer faced each other as symbols of aristocracy and democracy. Britain had been somewhat democratized, and America, in its peculiar institution as well as its in northern gradations of wealth, showed the blemish of aristocracy. The conflict of ideals was far from over, and democrats in Britain would yet appeal to the American example. But the kindred communities no longer stood for a simple, neat antithesis. The relationship between them, as nations speaking for their respective ideals, had been significantly transformed.

4

Reconciling Ideals

MORE THAN ANY other event, the American Civil War marked a change in the antithesis of ideals between the United States and Great Britain. The end of slavery enhanced America's appeal to the leaders of British political reform and to Britain's working classes. The victorious Union could now be hailed as an effective democratic polity, all the more so in the light of the gigantic military prowess it had shown during four years of war and that it showed even more in its great industrial strides in the postwar decades. This was precisely the theme of Carnegie's *Triumphant Democracy*.

The antithesis of ideals between the kindred polities abated during the later decades of the nineteenth century. What began to emerge in its place was an increasing reconciliation of models. Movements proceeded in each country that, turning their energies inward, encouraged them to work out their differences and seek concord rather than discord. Both states faced problems, domestic and diplomatic, that were broadly similar. The problems grew largely out of a newer, massive industrialization and a concomitant population growth. Each society had major internal conflicts between capital and labor. Each had to find markets for its vast increase of goods.

Politics in both societies was shaped by the conflicts within their respective economies. In the face of democratic reforms, and its lessening political power, the British aristocracy was responding ever more to the sway of the manufacturing and laboring classes: indeed, it was itself, as a class, being transmuted from a landed class into one of finance and industry.[1] Meanwhile, postwar America witnessed the emergence of that aristocracy of manufactures whose brutal regime Tocqueville had anticipated, one spurred by a driving individualism and unrestrained by the mores of aristocracy that might otherwise have kept it in check.

The mores and politics of any polity are enduring. That very continuity shaped Anglo-American attitudes in the later Victorian years. Inherent in American identity was a civism that sustained anti-English sentiments. However much they were changing, anti-American attitudes continued in the upper ranges of a British aristocracy, and indeed a British polity, whose very essence was defined by strata of gradations and a civism of deference. That may help explain why the egalitarian doctrines of that vociferous Scottish-American, Andrew Carnegie, found such a negative reception in some segments of the British press.

But critical components of the British political classes were coming to regard the American model with increasing favor. The intelligentsia did not share Carnegie's assault on aristocracy per se. But they saw the virtues of American constitutionalism, with its checks on the exercise of central power. With a rising threat from the new, powerful continental nations, they joined British diplomats in seeking a new relation with the transformed nation across the Atlantic. It was into this changing context of transatlantic forces and events that *Triiumphant Democracy* appeared. Much as Carnegie might have resounded an older antithesis of ideals, the actual facts and forces of both economy and diplomacy were encouraging the emergence of a newer transatlantic relationship, indeed an age of rapprochement between the kindred polities.

IF THE PERCEPTION of England was changing among some significant groups of Americans, the official American creed was not. Hating England continued as an article of faith. Anglophobia was still a shared sentiment with American patriotism, flaring up anew during the Civil War, when the British ministry took actions that decidedly favored the South. The New England intelligentsia, whose feelings for the older country had wavered between affection and alienation, bitterly concluded then that England and America represented two hostile ideas, that there could be nothing but "irrepressible conflict between the Old World and the New."[2] In the decades that followed, the bitterness subsided at best into a lack of cordiality. If American travelers in Britain found much to approve of in the old country's ways and monuments, "the mass of the American people at home tended to be hostile."

The sources of American hostility were not merely ideological; they had some basis in the conditions of American life. Carnegie, while pleading for friendship between the republic and the monarchy, said that several factors were causing continuous "irritation in the United States against Britain." Prominent among them was the Canadian question. "Imagine Scotland republican," argued Carnegie, "owing allegiance to the United States, and constantly proclaiming its readiness to attack Britain at their bidding."[3] The truth was that Canada was more attacked than attacking, but, as John Bartlet Brebner has shown, the dominion served as a constant source of friction between the two larger powers.[4] America and Britain were also coming into conflict in their respective quests for empire. In the age of the new "manifest destiny," Ernest May has observed, American bellicosity produced sharp encounters with Britain. Diplomatic clashes over Samoa, Chile, and Venezuela signaled the running antagonism.[5] American public opinion was consistently, if not universally, negative in its view of British diplomacy. The only way to solve Britain's perennial problems was for her to be annexed by the United States. Indeed, Victorian Britain regularly afforded the American press examples "of how not to manage foreign affairs."[6] During the Boer War, strong sympathy for the Dutch evoked what John Hay described as a "mad-dog hatred of English . . . among newspapers and politicians."[7]

The prominence of Irish immigrants in the more populous cities of the northeast, particularly in Boston and New York, was another vital spur to Anglophobia. Affairs in Ireland, and certainly the movement for Irish Home Rule, were a constant issue in that politics of ethnicity that American parties so regularly practiced. Pursuing the "Irish vote," candidates for office regularly exploited Anglophobia in municipal campaigns.[8] The Irish factor entered national politics as well, and nowhere more prominently than in the bitter presidential campaign of 1884, when the Democrats were denounced as the party of "Rum, Romanism, and Rebellion."[9] H. C. Allen has suggested with a certain validity that there was a close relation between the American dislike of Britain, on the one hand, and the extent of Irish immigration into the United States and their role in American politics, on the other.[10]

Making Americans meant, in no small part, making Anglophobes. Instructing citizens to love their country was a universal practice in Western society, indeed an essential component of the nationalistic movements and rivalries of the nineteenth century. Civic education in the

United States, as elsewhere, depended heavily on a pious study of the nation's history, and each generation of American schoolchildren began its study with the account of patriots, heroic and selfless, rising up against a monarch, oppressive and tyrannical, who was taxing them without representing them.

If it was true, said Carnegie, that Americans did not, on the whole, hate England, it was also true that some of their hostility could be ascribed to the history they had been taught.[11] James Muirhead, an Englishman who spent three years in the United States in the early 1890s and who wished to promote friendship between both countries, worried about the one-sided view of British-American relations that was taught in the primary schools.[12] What impressed him was that it was the very process of Americanization that made for Anglophobia. "It is the American in the making . . . that, as a rule, is guilty of blatant denunciation of Great Britain."[13]

One could not say, with certainty, how far the denunciation was deeply felt and how far it was merely an act in the ritual of patriotism. Inveighing publicly against Britain was part of a civic performance in demonology; as an Englishman who had lived in the United States for several years explained it, "The speakers that denounced Great Britain, as a general rule, like Englishmen greatly, and did not hesitate to admit to us in private that the whole business was electioneering clap-trap."[14] There was a difference, surely, between "electioneering clap-trap" and the passionate animosity that Tocqueville had heard and that brought him to write in the 1830s: "One cannot find a more acrimonious hatred than that which exists beween the Americans of the United States and the English." The old men he had checked this out with, reported Bryce in *The American Commonwealth* (1888), pretty much corroborated Tocqueville's observation.[15] There were even now, said Bryce, lingering elements of rivalry with England and a suspicion that the English were still patronizing in their attitudes toward America. But, he felt sure, the rivalry and suspicion were far outweighed by "the growing sympathy for 'the old country,' as it is still called. It is the only European country in which the American people can be said to feel any personal interest, or towards an alliance with which they are drawn by sentiment."[16]

Sir Charles Dilke had, in *Greater Britain* (1868), an account of his tour around the English-speaking world, reported earlier evidences of a widespread favorable American attitude to England: "It is impossible to spend much time in New England without becoming aware that the people of the six Northeastern states love us from the heart."[17] And indeed, the underlying theme of Carnegie's *Triumphant Democracy* was that the Americans of 1886 had great affection for Britain, and that it wanted only the introduction of republican government into Britain to restore entirely the harmony that had a century before prevailed between the kindred peoples. In 1897, Carnegie returned a resounding "No!" to the question whether Americans hated England.[18] What he said echoed an ever widening sense among his contemporaries that American attitudes toward Britain were changing.

Why the change? Bryce saw it as part of a larger cordiality between the United States and Great Britain and this in turn he attributed to the settlement of the *Alabama* claims, the democratization of British politics, the growth of American science and literature, and the greater respect in which the United States was now held by Europeans.[19] Improved relations with Britain, he said, were also due to the Americans' awareness of their country's increasing stengrth.[20] James Muirhead pretty much concurred. "The American," he found, "has become vastly more pleasant to deal with since his country has won an undeniable place among the foremost nations of the globe. The epidermis of Brother Jonathan has toughened as he has grown in stature."[21] Howard Mumford Jones has suggested that American attitudes became cosmopolitan in the post–Civil War decades. In the earlier period, said Jones, the accounts Americans wrote about their European travels had three principal characteristics: they had an antimonarchical bias, ascribing a country's faults to its monarchical institutions; they were militantly Protestant; and they were "naively pedagogical or didactic." After the war, American travel literature "no longer tended to be addressed solely to political, or religious, or democratic man." Their outlook was cosmopolitan. Europe was now a place for extending one's education. Particularly noteworthy was the new American attitude toward England. "The monarchy now becomes a wise institution; Great Britain is the home of poetry and history. English political institutions, English literature and the 'Anglo-Saxon' inheritance are assumed to be joint possessions of the two countries."[22]

In the politics of ethnicity, which was a key feature of the American democratic system, it was almost inevitable that immigrant groups should array themselves in partisan lines on the basis of their national and religious origins. The Anglophilic cult that burgeoned in the late nineteenth century contained two sets of adherents, both impelled by their animosity toward American Irish Catholics and therefore by their desire to redeem what the Irish were vilifying. In the instance of the first group, British immigrants in the United States other than Irish Catholics, loving the homeland would seem to have been a natural enough sentiment. But it should be recalled that there were active home rule movements in the nineteenth century in Scotland and Wales and that American immigrants from both these principalities had, at times, nurtured strong resentments against England. But in the 1870s and 1880s, as Irish Home Rule became a powerful cause in the United Kingdom and found passionate support among Irish Americans, the Welsh and the Scots in the United States warmly joined their English fellow immigrants in defending British policy. As Rowland Berthoff has shown, they rallied to Her Majesty's Government whenever an Irish crisis arose at home. To cite a notable instance, English, Scottish, Protestant Irish, and even Canadian immigrants in the United States proudly celebrated Victoria's Golden Jubilee in the summer of 1887, sharply attacking Irish slurs on the Queen and on the Empire. Indeed, says Berthoff, "apart from that ostentatious republican Andrew Carnegie, a few radicals, and a handful of eccentric Boston Jacobites, Englishmen and Scotsmen of every class revered the Queen and her family."[23]

Finding Carnegie's republicanism in the same company as Boston's Jacobitism is almost too much to contemplate. To combat the anti-British activity of the Irish Americans, their fellow immigrants from the United Kingdom formed many British-American newspapers and associations. Thus it was that a British-American community of opinion emerged, strongly supporting the British cause.

The second significant pro-British group was the American Pan-Anglians, whom we shall discuss more extensively in Chapter 7. They were an elite, an intellectual and political aristocracy, an Eastern establishment. In Irish-Catholic politics, they saw the awesome realization of the worst of the American democratic system. It impressed them that Britain alone offered the example of probity and competence in the conduct of democratic government that could well serve the United States as a model. Descendants of British forebears, they found their appeal to the example of the mother country a warming renewal of kinship. That they had been the ardent American patriots of a century before made of their present devotion to Britain an ironic latter-day Loyalism. Yet as Pan-Anglians, they felt that they had transcended the superficial partisan labels of time and place. Indeed, in their vision, they were joined in a quest for the very best principles of government that the English-speaking peoples, in their long historic evolution, were destined to achieve.

The American perception of Britain thus ranged widely between those, like the Irish, who sharply attacked British ideals and those, like the Pan-Anglians, who espoused them. But invoking Britain as the national enemy had, by the later decades of the nineteenth century, taken on the ring of an empty ritual. A clue as to where things stood in America's view of the kindred society could be gotten from the oration delivered on July 4, 1876 by William Maxwell Evarts, one of the most famous lawyers of his time and a prominent member of the Republican Party. The oration was part of the festivities in Independence Square, Philadelphia that marked the high point of the centennial celebrations of American independence from Britain. Evarts wished to show, above all, that the nation's key institutions had been proven valid over the course of the preceding century. Inevitably, he compared American ways with European ones. In the process, he not only found the comparison favorable to the United States, but also revealed why and how the American perception of Britain, along with its perception of other nations, was changing. True enough, he agreed, Americans owed something to the European example in the fields of philosophy, science, industry, and wealth.

> But in the institutions and methods of government; in civil prudence, courage, or policy; in statesmanship; in the art of "making a small town a great city"; in the adjustment of authority to liberty; in the concurrence of reason and strength in peace, of force and obedience in war, we have found nothing to recall us from the course of our fathers, nothing to add to our safety or to aid our progress in it. So far from this, all modifications of European politics accept the popular principles of our system, and tend to our model. The movements toward equality of representation, enlargement of the suffrage, and public education in England . . . the constant gain to the people's share in government throughout Europe, all tend one way, the way pointed out in the Declaration of our Independence.[24]

Americans were, from what Evarts was saying, seeing their relationship with Britain in a changing perspective. The age of antithetical models was passing. It seemed, to many Americans, that Britain was inclining ever more toward American forms. If it was true that older British institutions were being transformed, it was also true that older American ideals were no longer being realized. British and American institutions and ideals were moving toward a rough approximation, if hardly a close similarity: this seemed to be the transcendent fact of their newer relationship.

ON APRIL 9, 1865 General Robert E. Lee, commander of the Confederate forces, surrendered to General Ulysses S. Grant, commander of the Union forces, at Appomatox Courthouse in western Virginia. The Civil War was effectively over. The Civil War armies were the largest organization ever created in America. In the course of the war some 2.3 million Union fighters faced over 800,000 Confederate fighters. Around 360,000 Union soldiers were killed; over 250,000 Confederates lost their lives. The total of casualties on both sides was over a million. The population of the United States in 1860 had stood at 31.5 million. The cost of the war exceeded $20 billion, five times the total expenditure of the federal government from its creation until 1865. Ratifying the true meaning of the war, the Thirteenth Amendment to the American constitution, abolishing slavery, was formally proclaimed in effect in December 1865. In all of its aspects and dimensions, the American conflict was the first modern war—in its massive provisioning and clothing of so many men, its new technology and weaponry, the ways the war was financed, the radical strategems of its land and naval campaigns, the scope of its major battles, and in the impact of the war on the daily lives of all Americans.[25]

All through its long bloody course, the Civil War had figured prominently in Britain's mind. As many British leaders saw it, the war had begun as a quest for independence by the South's cotton kings against striving "Yankee" industrialists. Many British conservatives favored the South, which seemed to offer a quasi-aristocratic society they could sympathize with.[26] Southern cotton could abundantly supply the midlands' textile mills. In October 1862, a month after Lincoln's preliminary Emancipation Proclamation, Gladstone himself, chancellor of the exchequer in Viscount Palmerston's cabinet, one heavily laden with aristocrats, made a famous speech at Newcastle voicing what must have been a widespread official sentiment: "Jefferson Davis and other leaders of the South have made an army; they are making, it appears, a navy; and they have made what is more than either, they have made a nation."[27] Palmerston's foreign secretary, Lord John Russell, however, tried to keep British diplomacy to a policy of strict neutrality, so that despite such imbroglios as the *Trent* and *Alabama* affairs, Britain withheld from recognizing the Confederacy.

British pro-Union sentiment equivocated at first. In the pre-Civil War decades, affection for the United States had always been widespread among the middle and lower classes. The abolitionist cause in particular evoked great appeal: indeed, *Uncle Tom's Cabin* had sold more widely in Britain than in the United States.[28] During the American election of 1860 and at the outset of the conflict there were indeed many uncertainties about the North's position on slavery. But successive declarations and actions by the Congress, by the Union's military leaders, and by Lincoln himself eliminated the uncertainties. The war, in rapid stages, became a crusade against slavery. And as it did, so too did Liberal and radical opinion in Britain turn favorably toward the North.[29] In the United States, declaimed John Bright, "you find a people passing through a great war and a great revolution with a conduct and a success, with a generosity and a magnanimity which have attracted and aroused the admiration of the world."[30] It was Abraham Lincoln who, to the British, came to personify the magnetism of American democracy. In Lincoln, "the United States had found a leader without parallel in modern history, proof that a democracy could produce a head of state, from the most meagre of backgrounds, superior to any aristocrat."[31] The American Civil War—its epic proportions, its deprivations and sufferings, its humanity and heroism—vastly impressed all classes of awestruck Britons. But what particularly impressed Gladstone, the keeper of Her Majesty's books and of the nation's conscience, was the stoicism with which the Lancashire textile workers, supporters of the war to abolish slavery, bore the Union blockade that deprived their mills of cotton and them of their jobs. Without complaints, without envy, without murmuring against God's dispensations, they had borne their lot: they were clearly fit to enter the pale of the British constitution, he said, as indeed they did with the great Reform Bill of 1867.[32]

From 1865 to 1886, Britain was a country in continuous change and often in turbulence. 1832 had shown irrevocably that the old order could be shaken and remade. Two major franchise reform bills (1867 and 1884) bookended British politics during the years of Gladstone's two great ministries, when he and the Liberals superintended affairs at Whitehall. A remarkable amalgam of progress and piety, Gladstone personified mid-Victorian Liberalism.[33] Whenever franchise reform threw into question the premises of the British polity, as it did in 1865–1867 and 1884–1885, America's virtues and vices filled parliamentary rhetoric, no less of course than the pages of the British press. The 1870s were hardly a period of placidity: depression hit the British economy, workers spent their energies on getting rather than spending, British parties set up networks of local associations that would contest political control in parliamentary eminence, and new nations on the continent changed the agendas of liberalism as well as conservatism.[34]

The reform bill of 1884 extended the franchise to the counties and enlarged the electorate by around seventy percent.[35] If the monarchy had not quite arrived at universal manhood suffrage, it stood close enough to invite comparison with the transatlantic republic. The State of England question had perennially challenged British minds inside and outside of parliament. In the tumultuous days of the reform bill of 1884 (and the Redistribution Act of 1885), the question was two-sided and it called for probing democracy in both England and the United States.

Even as the sources of wealth among the aristocracy and its adherents were changing in the post–Civil War years, the attitudes of the British upper classes toward the republic remained largely negative, all the more so as the American model was regularly invoked to assault aristocratic prominence in British government. Throughout the mid-Victorian decades, "the old pattern of attitudes remained, with the hostility to America appearing most strongly at the top of the social scale." The "friends of America" were precisely those British groups who felt aggrieved (dare one use Carnegie's somewhat excessive word, "insulted") in Britain's aristocratic polity. The list was long and various. It consisted of groups that at times converged on different causes or no less frequently espoused one cause and not another. The Whigs led the list. Rooted in Britain's great landowning and mercantile families, they claimed an authority within the polity that was at least equal to the monarch's and which indeed they had at times contested. They found instruction in America, but not a duplicable model. Friendship with the United States: yes; greater affinity or connection, no.[36]

Closer to the republic were the parliamentary Radicals: a large group, with varying factions and programs, and surely different strong-minded leaders, but always sympathetic to the American model.[37] Their numbers included Joseph Chamberlain, of course, as well as Charles Dilke, Henry Labouchere, John Morley, and that inveterate Liberal, John Bright. A far more numerous group, clearly, were the working-class Radicals, who had no M.P.s, but who commanded a very vocal press, superb speakers, and "an enthusiasm for America not excelled by that of Bright."[38] Published weekly by a former Chartist, *Reynolds's Newspaper*, expressing working-class opinion, commanded a powerful role: its 1861 circulation of

350,000, compared to the 70,000 circulation of the daily *Times*, well served the American cause, to which it was passionately devoted.[39] Carnegie's newspaper chain, which he set up in 1884, was designed to serve the working-class program long espoused by *Reynolds's Newspaper*, and, of course, to promote Carnegie's always aspiring and ever-growing role in the British Liberal Party.

Among the monarchy's disaffected groups, there were reasons enough to find a better Britain in America. The parliamentary Radicals saw a less aristocratic, less class-ridden, less deferential society. They would not accept the absence of deference, that equality of status that Tocqueville had defined as the essence of democracy; they might agree with Adam Badeau, the American consul, that "in England, every body looks up"[40] and yet even Bright did not want the abolition of the aristocracy. British nonconformists applauded the disestablished society across the waters; they surely were aggrieved by the official government-supported role of the Anglo-Catholic church; it mattered to them that the Anglican regime had its special role in Cromwell's and Wesley's fair land; and yet, among so many of them, the American model was not entirely acceptable because it accommodated Catholicism, about which nonconformists were largely uncomfortable.

After the death of Prince Albert in 1861, many in England wondered about the role of Queen Victoria, the widow of Windsor Castle who so mourned her husband that she raised questions about her capacity to govern, from which doubts flourished an even stronger republican sentiment in England than before. America loomed ever larger as a far more economical, unostentatious polity. The American president did not have a civil list and roll, and national expenses were relatively minor. America's federal system, with its thirty-odd states, allowed a free play for the possibilities of home rule: not only for the Irish, whose unified party tactics in Parliament were constantly disrupting the conduct of parliamentary affairs, but also for the Scots and the Welsh; federal and sectional America was a land of Celtic fringes, which embraced Germans, Scotch-Irish, Scandinavians, Poles, Jews, and Italians—indeed, a federal government allowed a workable mutuality among a wide variety of ethnic and religious communities.

The working classes formed the largest pro-American constituency in Britain. They read the gospel about the republic in *Reynolds's Newspaper*. Their Trades Union Congress listened to speeches about America as an "El

Dorado of high wages" and a land where "you get pies and puddings."[41] They got letters from their relatives and friends in the United States gushing about the United States as the Britain they had petitioned and paraded for; as Carnegie put it to his Cousin Dod in Dunfermline: "We have the Charter . . . the Panacea for all Britain's woes, the bulwark of the liberties of the people."[42] Emigration statistics told a good part of the story. In the 1850s, 1860s, and 1870s, the number of British emigrants to the United States totaled one and a half million each decade; in the 1880s, the figure rose to two and a half million, drawing back to slightly under two million in the 1890s, and rising to 2,715,000 during the 1900s.[43] In Britain's referendum on America, the workers spoke most decisively: they emigrated to the United States; they voted with their feet.

Most of *Triumphant Democracy* read like a neo-Chartist tract. The statistics of the American economy proved that political equality was an almost magical stimulant. But, in the later chapters of his book, Carnegie clearly changed the nature of his argument. In his grand chapters on "The Federal Constellation" and "General Reflections," the Chartist republic became a fastness of fixity. The appeal to radicalism became an appeal to conservatism. Why did he move into another venue?

The reason is evident enough. Carnegie had written a program for Britain and Britain was changing very basically even as he was writing. The change that most commanded the attention of the British public leaders he was directly addressing was the way the franchise and redistribution bills of 1884 and 1885 were fundamentally remaking their constitution. What was happening was revolutionary, and Britain's leaders—in virtually every field of endeavor—saw it that way.[44] Signs of disorder were everywhere: in violent London demonstrations, in unrest in Ireland, in Fenian bombings in London, all arousing "nerves which had lost their mid-century calm."[45] The intellectual classes felt that their ideas were under attack. Consisting of England's educated classes, they included key members of England's literary establishment and some of the most luminous stars of her professoriat: James Anthony Froude, W. E. H. Lecky, John Richard Seeley, Alfred Lord Tennyson, Henry Sidgwick, Herbert Spencer, Goldwin Smith, Algernon Swinburne, Matthew Arnold, James Fitzjames Stephen, and his no less illustrious cousin, Albert Venn Dicey. In *Locksley Hall Sixty Years After*, which appeared in 1886, Alfred Lord Tennyson, the nation's aged poet laureate, expressed a widespread anger and confusion about both democracy and Irish Home Rule.

France has shown a light to all men, preached a Gospel, all
   men's good;
Celtic Demons rose a Demon, shrieked and slaked the light
   with blood
Envy wears the mask of Love, and, laughing sober fact to scorn
Cries the Weakest to the Strongest, "Ye are equals, equal-born.
You that woo the Voices—tell them "old experience is a fool,"
Teach your flattered kings that only those who cannot read can
   rule.

Lord Salisbury, the Conservative leader, feared the advent of democracy, intent as he was "on preserving the privileges of property, education, and established religion."[46] Hartington, Gladstone's Liberal Party colleague, was equally concerned about reforms being made "by the shock of revolutionary agitation."[47] Indeed, democracy was flooding the British landscape. Macaulay had earlier taunted the Americans that their Constitution was all sail and no anchor. The taunt was far more true of the monarchy in the mid-1880s, as Britain's contemporaries well realized.

How could one stabilize a liberal democratic polity? How could one keep it from the turbulence of a democratic franchise? Tocqueville had said that the question was the most important one a modern polity had to face and that there was no easy answer. In the mid-1880s, Britain's speaking and writing classes, aghast at the impermanence of British governance, and now looking for instructive models, turned to America. The republic had survived a great civil war, a gigantic constitutional conflict. They were quite clear that America should not—as a political society—be duplicated. But the republic had much to teach.

Indeed, before Britain's democratic crisis of the mid-1880s, prominent Britons had expressed admiration of the American constitution. As visitors to the United States in the 1860s, Goldwin Smith and Leslie Stephen voiced approval of the U.S. system of governance; and in 1871, J. R. Seeley, a professor of modern history at Cambridge, urged that the U.S. Constitution serve as a model for the "Greater Britain" that he envisioned.[48]

Seth Low, who had been a reform mayor of the independent city of Brooklyn, helped identify the cause of the crisis in the monarchy. "England's omnipotent Parliament . . . may before long become an instrument full of danger to the state, unless in some way, checks producing the same effect of those which have been found necessary in the United States are placed upon its omnipotence."[49] Low's point was widely reiterated by eminent Victorians. In his widely acclaimed *Popular Government,* Sir Henry Maine, a distinguished legal historian and professor of jurisprudence at Oxford, summed up the newer meaning of America for the British intelligentsia. "American Federal Government has provided against the infirmities of popular government . . . in a most remarkable way."[50] With the growth of democratic government in Europe, no paradigm commanded as much attention as the United States. The American Constitution was the basis of American liberty. What had hitherto not been understood, said Maine, was how essentially conservative the American Constitution and the American polity were: they curbed democracy rather than allowing it free rein. America was successful because it was conservative, because its founders had removed from the people control over property, private enterprise, and the obligations of contract.[51] Maine's argument was supported by W. E. H. Lecky, whose eight-volume masterpiece, *A History of England in the Eighteenth Century* (1878–1890), rested on a close knowledge of the kindred societies. In *Democracy and Liberty*, Lecky urged that the ills of democracy in Britain might be contained by a strong second chamber, like the American Senate, but unlike the enfeebled British House of Lords: the American model, he believed, could serve Britain very well.[52]

In his famous *Lectures Introductory to the Study of the Law of the Constitution*,[53] Albert Venn Dicey, Vinerian professor of the Common Law at Oxford, celebrated America for its surpassing respect for law and justice. "The main reason why the United States has carried out the federal system with unequalled success is that the people of the Union are more thoroughly imbued with legal ideas than any other existing nation."[54] The great virtue of the American Constitution, which defined the federal arrangement, was that it was beyond immediate alteration. It had come to command a special reverence. Its most important provision, said Dicey, in effect agreeing with Maine, was that legislation could not impair the obligation of contracts. He recognized, as had his fellow intellectuals in Britain, that the rules of the game were fairly permanent and universally accepted, that the demand for changing the laws by which the polity was run was therefore nowhere compelling, and that with an independent judiciary as arbiters, litigation supplanted legislation. All this had in a somewhat different way been argued by Carnegie.

It was James Bryce, of course, who transformed, for the British governing classes, the nature and meaning of the American paradigm. The

United States, he said, was conservative. Merely to call it a democracy was, in effect, to reduce a complex amalgam of phenomena to an empty typology. Bryce broke the paradigmatic mold into which Europe had so long cast American institutions. He freed America from Tocqueville and political science from Plato. He supplanted Tocqueville's philosophic realism with his own more careful nominalism. His account of American institutions read, therefore, more like a botanist's report than a philosopher's speculation, more like Darwin's *Voyage of the Beagle* than Pascal's *Pensées*. It was not true that the tyranny of the majority held sway in the republic: "The charges brought against democracy from the supposed example of America are groundless."[55] America was a conservative polity. "Property is safe, because those who hold it are far more numerous than those who do not: the usual motives for revolution vanish."[56] Prosperity contributed to their conservatism. They clung to older institutions and ways, in virtue both of the deep instincts of their race and of that practical shrewdness that recognizes the value of permanence and solidity in institutions. They are conservative in their fundamental beliefs, in the structure of their governments, in their social and domestic usages. "In serious matters, such as the fundamental institutions of government and in religious belief, no progressive and civilized people is more conservative."[57] In writing *The American Commonwealth* as a *vade mecum* to U.S. life, Bryce wished to caution his British peers against simply duplicating American institutions. But he also said that he was writing a book of edification. What he taught the British in those revolutionary times was that America was a model well worth contemplating, indeed one they might ignore to their own great peril.

In the larger Anglo-American dialogue, Carnegie was no Bryce. But saying that begs the question. True, Carnegie began with his conclusion; Bryce conducted an open-minded, remarkably complex inquiry. More significantly, both Scotsmen were members of a growing Pan-Anglian fraternity, as indeed were many of the British intellectuals whom we have been discussing. But yet another group belonged to this fraternity: the Anglo-American diplomats who well understood that nationalism and imperialism were reconstructing Europe's arrangement of power. Because of this, Britain and the United States were moving toward a grand diplomatic reconciliation, of which the settlement of the *Alabama* claims in 1871 was merely the first step.[58] The special relationship between the kindred polities was taking yet another and far more enduring turn. Itself a document of Europe's new age, *Triumphant Democracy* appeared in the context of deep-running, transforming developments.

IN THE YEARS after Appomattox, Britain's political leaders had to answer to the outcome of America's Civil War. That outcome defined the terms of the Anglo-American competition of models. Nothing could now be clearer, as Gladstone well understood, than that military power and political democracy were two sides of the same coin. The sweeping triumph of the Northern democracy seemed to have undercut the viability of an aristocratic polity. In the new world of European diplomacy, with recently unified nations challenging Britain's power with their massive conscripted armies, America stood formidably in Britain's vision.

What did the major British political constituencies see? The Radicals, the advanced bloc of the Liberal Party, had long applauded America and, equivocating only slightly during the Civil War, warmly celebrated American institutions. The Liberal Party, hardly a unified organization, largely approved of American ways. During the 1880s, years of great constitutional reconstruction in Britain, the Conservatives began to see redeeming virtues in certain U.S. institutions, while disclaiming the spirit of the constitution as a whole. Tory journals continued to praise those who damned the United States[59] and, as we shall see (chapter 5) in their reviews of *Triumphant Democracy*, to damn those who praised it. Frank Thistlethwaite notes that "from the 1890s, it was the Conservatives, taking their cue from people like Joseph Chamberlain, who made the most of the United States, both as a potential ally in a threatening international world, and as an example of stable, conservative institutions for an England threatened with further constitutional reform."[60] The newer Conservative Party attitudes were, of course, shaped by the accretion in 1886 of the Unionists, Liberals who had defected from the Gladstone's leadership over the Irish Home Rule issue: their more prominent leaders included Charles Dilke, John Bright, and Chamberlain, whose intensely pro-American outlook now found a voice in Conservative party councils.

Positive though they were, none of the foremost British political leaders favored embracing the American model. Indeed in the newer transatlantic relation, their principal spokesmen now felt they had to validate their own. This was the great importance of James Bryce's *The American Commonwealth*, which deftly lauded the republic while ascribing her greatness to her English origins and practices. This too was the importance of William Gladstone's essay, "Kin Across Sea," in which the leader of Britain's Liberal Party, while comparing the virtues of the kindred nations, paid his respects to America's Constitution while insisting on venerating

England's. Appearing in the fall 1878 issue of *The North American Review*, Gladstone's words would surely impress the educated, influential elite that constituted its readership. Apart from answering to the impinging presence of America, it is very likely that Gladstone was more immediately concerned with maintaining the leadership of his own party and with Joseph Chamberlain's attempt, through the National Liberal Federation, to organize the Liberal Party on the basis of the American "caucus."

The essential question about a nation's institutions, Gladstone began, was how far they would "contribute their maximum to the store of human happiness, and excellence." There could be no doubt that imperial Britain and her progeny constituted "a kind of universal church in politics" and that Britain and the United States were "the two great branches of a race born to command." They were, of course, alike in many respects—they prized self-government, rational politics, self-reliance, the ideal of liberty; they believed in the decentralization of power, in "publicity as the vital air of politics," in a government not only of force but of persuasion.

But however much one might stress the similarities between them, the fact was that "neither nation prefers [and it would be an ill sign if either did prefer] the institutions of the other." Indeed, their respective constitutions expressed the differences between the two polities rather than their resemblances. The British Constitution had grown over time; the American was made in a particular sitting, and by choice. Said Gladstone in a sentence that many quoted, and particularly Carnegie who emblazoned its concluding part on the cover of his *Triumphant Democracy*: "But, as the British Constitution is the most subtle organism which has proceeded from the womb and the long gestation of progressive history, so the American Constitution is, so far as I can see, the most wonderful work ever struck off at a given time by the brain and purpose of man." The burden of his essay Gladstone devoted to detailing the forms and spirit of British political institutions. In the process, he insisted on their essential difference from those of the Americans. At the root of American institutions was the belief in equality combined with liberty, "renewable at each descent from one generation to another, like a lease with stipulated breaks." Americans took it as a self-evident truth that all men were born equal. The English believed in inequality. "Their natural tendency, from the very base of British society, and through all its strongly built gradations, is to look upward. . . . The sovereign is the highest height of the system." All in all, the British Constitution was a unique creation, a machine so subtly balanced that it seems as though it were moved by something as delicate and slight as the main-spring of a watch. It has not been the offspring of the thought of man. . . . [It grew] not as the fruit of a philosophy, not in the effort to give effect to an abstract principle, but by the silent action of foces; invisible and insensible, the structure has come up into the view of all of the world. It is, perhaps, the most conspicuous object on the wide political horizon; it has risen, without noise, like the Temple of Jerusalem.

It was a remarkable statement on the competition of models, on the superiority of the English Constitution, and ultimately on the perennial yet ever-changing singularity of the great man whose ministries were truly ministerial and for whom there was no dividing line between politics and religion. What the pious man saw, indeed what transfixed him, was his own image. In Gladstone's ordered universe, one's eye moved from the outermost circles to the inner—from the civilized community of Christian nations to the British race that was "born to command," to the temple of the British Constitution, to the sacerdotal class within the temple, and ultimately to the high priest himself.[61] His essay on the spirit of England's laws and the contrivance of America's stood out large because he was the dominant figure in the Liberal Party from 1868 until his final withdrawal from politics (at the age of eighty-five) in early 1894, because he spoke for the preponderant group of Liberal M.P.s, and because the Liberals were at the time inclined to a pro-American attitude and much concerned with the interplay of power and sentiments between the kindred nations. What Gladstone said also testified to the wider sense among traditional Liberals that the road of liberal democracy that Britain had traveled during the second age of nineteenth-century reform had brought her as close as she could come to the American paradigm, and that the Americanization of British institutions—which many Liberals feared—was nowhere to be contemplated. This did not mean, of course, that Gladstone would not further attempt, for his party and in his pilgrimage, to disestablish what he considered to be privileged institutions. This is precisely what he proposed in the Newcastle Program of 1893, a fact that again revealed his refusal to address, as Joseph Chamberlain had urged him to do, the problem of social democracy in Britain.

5

The British Critique

Triumphant Democracy appeared on Saturday, April 17, 1886. The press on both sides of the Atlantic greeted it with scores of reviews. What they said constituted a transatlantic colloquy, all the more so as Andrew Carnegie was quite literally a transatlantic figure, an inhabitant if not quite a citizen of two worlds.

At least two questions about the British response immediately arise. First: Who were the responders, meaning what was the party affiliation of the respective newspapers that reviewed *Triumphant Democracy*? Surely, political orientation could enter into, if not necessarily determine, what the reviewer would say in a dialogue about the virtues of republicanism and aristocracy. Second: How far were current British affairs shaping their comments on Carnegie's assay of the kindred polities?

The dominant issue in British politics during the spring months of 1886 was Irish Home Rule. On April 8, nine days before *Triumphant Democracy* appeared, Gladstone introduced his bill for granting Ireland home rule. Nothing else mattered so much in British politics as that bill. Though he had certainly touched on the issue of home rule, it did not figure prominently in Carnegie's book. He subsumed it under the larger American principles of federalism and localism. What his British respondents said, accordingly, touched relatively little on the theme that almost totally dominated their politics.

And yet, somewhere alongside that theme ran another one, which was sounding most audibly and inescapably in British affairs, which Carnegie had surely made central to his argument, and which figured largely in the British reviews.

Irish Home Rule lay deeply embedded within the larger question of who should rule at home, not merely in Ireland but throughout the United Kingdom. That larger question had surely commanded the public mind throughout Gladstone's second ministry and surely Carnegie's mind as he was writing his masterpiece. The franchise act of 1884 extended the vote to the counties, virtually doubling the United Kingdom electorate. The redistribution act of 1885, with which the franchise measure had been coupled, divided the whole country into single-member constituencies, making numerical equality the guiding principle in the election of the House of Commons.

In effect, as Carnegie was laying down his pen in late 1885, his homeland was becoming, pretty much like the United States, a democratic polity. He had understood even when he started to write back in 1882 that the kingdom was democratizing; what troubled him was that it remained insistently aristocratic and deferential. From precisely a reverse perspective, this is what troubled many of his reviewers. The acts of 1884 and 1885 amounted to nothing less than a constitutional reconstruction—indeed, a revolution—in the governing rules of British political life. And because politics and political economy were one and the same, British ruling circles had reason to be fearful. Answering the question Carnegie had raised about the respective principles and stability of the kindred polities was therefore one in which the men who ran the British press and wrote the British reviews had a truly vested interest.

The terrain of Carnegie's reviewers was rumbling seismically. Their laws and therefore their wealth could be altered at the stroke of a mere majority in the Commons. What portents could one read in the fundamentally reconstituted Britain of the new laws of 1884 and 1885? Where else was the ever-unfolding Gladstonian Liberalism moving? That it would be evangelical was incontrovertible. But was the great political question of the day about Liberalism or really about Gladstone? When the Grand Old Man withdrew to his residence at Hawarden at the time of Lord Salisbury's first cabinet—during the latter half of 1885—what would the Liberal leader carry in his new emergence? The Hawarden kite—inadvertently sent up by Gladstone's son Herbert—carried the message that

Gladstone had been converted to Irish Home Rule. If we see the events of the mid-1880s as one unfolding British political drama, then Irish Home Rule surely belongs to the larger theme of that larger unfolding.

Carnegie's evangel about the redeeming principle of the American polity is then to be understood as part of that drama. A native Briton, he could claim a role in British politics. As member of the Celtic fringe, he carried some authenticity in a discussion over home rule. Indeed, the distinction afforded by his prominence as an industrialist seemed to imply that Johnson would now be writing a life of Boswell. But in that great British debate over aristocracy and democracy, he did not belong centrally because he did not carry the proper credentials, despite his contributions to the Liberal Party, despite the strident voice of the chain of newspapers his wealth had bought him, despite his efforts to work his way into the inner circles of Liberal councils. After all, he did not wish to purchase a lesser title and join the noblesse de la robe. He wished to uproot nobility and do away with titles. The very title of his book—*Triumphant Democracy*—carried its own message.

What his reviewers said about his book should be read in the context of the real conflict then going on in the United Kingdom. The issue was the reconfiguring of the British polity. In their confusion and apprehension about Britain's ever new directions, Carnegie offered them a subject for debate. That his position seemed so advanced to them, and that his argument was so stridently argued, made it easier for them to disclaim its validity. But his magnum opus should be placed in the context of British actualities in the mid-1880s. In the American democracy, his reviewers saw more than America. They saw the image of their own democratizing society.

If the reviews are to be seen as a vital, important part of the British-American dialogue, it is fair enough to ask for whom the reviewers spoke and what significance their reviews carried. In the Carnegie papers at the Library of Congress there are three noteworthy sets of British reviewers: those of the London press, those of the provinces, and those of Scotland. When *Triumphant Democracy* appeared, London was clearly the most important urban center in the Western world. The population of greater London in 1886 stood at well beyond 5 million and the population of the United Kingdom had reached over 35 million.[1] London had secured its position as the center of gravity of all that dominated British public life: its parliamentary affairs, its elegant and ostentatious high society, its financial and mercantile activities and institutions, its architecture, its theater, its literature.² Prominent in that literature, of course, were the London periodicals.

Among the journals that reviewed Carnegie's book were some of the most prominent in London—and therefore British—opinion. They included the *Economist*, the *Globe*, the *Saturday Review*, the *Spectator*, *St. James's Gazette*, the *Graphic*, and the *Academy*. Their book reviewers were anonymous, but the contributors to their pages included some of the most distinguished essayists and commentators of that later Victorian age. Just to cite some examples: the *Academy* writers included T. H. Green, Henry Sidgwick, George Saintsbury, and Edmund Goss; those of the *Graphic* included George Eliot, William Makepeace Thackeray, Anthony Trollope, Thomas Hardy, and Rider Haggard; the *Saturday Review* included Vernon Harcourt, Edward A. Freeman, James Fitzjames Stephen, Henry Maine, John Morley, and Matthew Arnold. One can readily see that British opinion was molded by a concentrated intellectual, literary elite—often enough, but hardly always, its university men, people who knew each other well, whether in their colleges, their clubs, their literary circles, or in the halls of Parliament.³

Most of the journals claimed to be "independent" in their political affiliation: insofar as the press was concerned, every little boy and girl born alive was not (as Arthur Sullivan had rhymed) either Liberal or Conservative. Still, their affiliation almost always put them to the right of Carnegie, who was self-proclaimedly a republican, a native Scotsman, a home ruler, with his bill of indictment against British institutions. Remarkably enough, his reviewers addressed the questions he was raising. Even more remarkably, they would see in America more than Carnegie and, while dismissing him, embrace those in America who shared their own ideals: the emerging Pan-Anglian community.

Carnegie had defined the terms for analyzing and appraising his book. In its simplest terms *Triumphant Democracy* could be regarded as the preachment of democracy to aristocracy. And indeed, flailing out at its formulas and the tone in which they had been preached is precisely what sparked the response of several of his reviewers. They knew that beyond the ostensible simplicity of the way he had shaped his argument lay deeper questions. What were to be the criteria for structuring a Western polity in the newer democratic age? How far were those criteria suitable to Great Britain, given her unique conditions and historical experience? How valid in fact was his portrait of the respective polities? Could it indeed by argued that political equality was the real reason for America's great industrial progress and achievement? If a portrait is only as true and useful as the portraitist, then what could one ask about Carnegie himself: Was he to be accepted, trusted? And, finally, to get to the purpose for which he had written his book: How far was *Triumphant Democracy* a useful book of instruction for Great Britain? Carnegie knew that his blaring message would evoke a strong response. Already part of that dialogue—money talks and so do the newspapers that money can buy — he would now inscribe his book in the pages of that ever vital binational competition of models.

RATHER FEW OF HIS reviewers directly addressed the thesis that Carnegie had argued: that democracy—as represented by the American model—was a far better type of polity than aristocracy—as represented by Great Britain. One who did was Henry Avray Tipping, the fairly distinguished author of several books on English gardening and architecture. His comments in the *Academy* constituted the only signed review of *Triumphant Democracy*. As Tipping saw it, the United States was a democracy in name only. Its activities and mores in effect contradicted the name. A truly democratic polity would become the settled and competent form of community when the members of the community could subject passion to reason, and self-love to the common weal. Until we reached something like that stage of ethical development, democracies would continue to be what they had always been—shams.

Until that time, the principle of monarchy and aristocracy, which signified that the few govern the many, would endure, either openly in recognized forms or covertly, in the minds and hearts of men. Inequality would govern political society as long as the leading minds of the age desired it. One could argue that the idea of equality was a nobler aim than aristocracy, but the argument for equality would take "the most wonderful dispassionate and intelligent philosophy." It would take, in effect, the very opposite of those qualities that characterized Carnegie's book.

How valid and accurate was Carnegie's portrait of the kindred polities? That surely was one of the most important questions to answer in considering his plea that the leaders of the monarchy should be guided by the republic. In sum, the most influential segments of the British press deemed his portrait to be of questionable validity. Yes, some newspapers granted, Carnegie offered very valuable—often startling—facts about the republic. But the larger picture was shaded, and therefore the conclusions he drew were seriously questionable.

Carnegie's claim throughout was that he was offering his British readers a book of facts about which they may have known virtually nothing. In that respect, some of his reviewers welcomed his disclosure. *Money* granted that he offered a "fair measure of practical information" that his careful readers would find "both useful and entertaining."[4] The *Spectator* agreed that Carnegie had very skillfully put together a volume of remarkable facts that show "in a single State . . . the [most] wonderful development of material and intellectual wealth that the world has ever seen."[5] And yet, even as a messenger of new tidings about the United States, the Scottish-American industrialist was challenged. One of the leading Tory organs, the *St. James's Gazette*, underscored the point that his facts had been "swept together from Scribner's Statistical Atlas, American Blue Books, and the works of such writers as Mr. Atkinson and Mr. Mulhall."[6] If Carnegie had promised Gladstone a book of revelation about the republic across the Atlantic, he came up with a not quite dry-as-dust set of figures in which, his critics said, there really was nothing new.

There was something far more important to question about his book, said his reviewers, than whether his facts were indeed all that new. He could be faulted for serious errors of omission and commission. That was surely true of his account of British institutions. The thrust of Carnegie's argument had been that monarchy and aristocracy imposed on their subjects a strong sense of inferiority. But that argument, said the *Saturday Review*, was grossly inaccurate. "Each rank . . . is as jealous of its own privileges as it is punctilious in the observances of those of others."[7]

More than that, said Avray Tipping, British aristocrats did not merely claim privilege: "they at least know that they are under some obligation to the nation," whereas "the American aristocracy of wealth [of which Andrew Carnegie was one of the most prominent members] too often feels none."[8]

Sharpest and most caustic in its attack on *Triumphant Democracy* was *St. James's Gazette*.

> Mr. Carnegie shows his extraordinary ignorance of England and the English on every page. He left his country in early life because he could not stand the constant insult of breathing the same air with a monarch. He believes that all monarchs, all princes, all

peers, and all their supporters detest America and would rejoice in her misfortunes. . . . He thinks England is languishing under the corrupting influences of a selfish nobility and a degrading monarchy. In other words, he knows nothing about his subject. The English respect and admire America, but they are also quite satisfied with their own Constitution. . . . He had better get rid of the idea that he can Americanize England by his agents in the English press or by means of such books as *Triumphant Democracy*.[9]

If nowhere as acidulous as some of his London reviewers, several of the provincial press found much to question in Carnegie's portrait of the monarchy, all the more so, of course, when the newspaper was Conservative in its affiliation. The *Somerset County Herald*, for example, scoffed at Carnegie's premise that "the government of England is as base as can well be, simply because it is monarchical. This is the substance of much of his work, and very frequently he betrays the superficiality of his knowledge of English institutions." To cite an instance: in his description of English local government, Carnegie had said that all power was vested in the hands of the squire and the parson. "He has not a word to say," noted the reviewer, "about the functions of the Board of Guardians, the Rural Sanitary Authority, the Highway Board, the parochial committees, and the special rainage districts, in the whole of which every taxpayer has a voice, just as he has in the United States of America."[10]

What Carnegie had found seriously wrong about Great Britain was monarchy and the principle of inequality; what he found wonderfully right about the United States was democracy and the principle of equality. But, persisted his reviewers, if "the star-spangled Scotchman" had been guilty of errors of commission in his portrait of the monarchy, he was no less guilty of errors of omission in his portrait of the democracy. The American republic was far from being the paradise Carnegie had made it out to be; indeed, there were serious troubles in paradise.

Said Avray Tipping in the *Academy*: "There is a remarkable inequality in the distribution of wealth in the United States. In terms of individual and wasteful luxury, the rich men of the republic surpass the ruling classes of the monarchy. The American industrialist entrusts conducting his business to his managers, "thus copying on a large scale the worst evils of [British] absentee landlordism." The United States was hardly a society of equality. Reformers in America indeed were stating that "the barriers of caste, greed, hatred, and bitterness must be cast down."[11] If Carnegie was so insistent on the idea of equality, said the *Saturday Review*, did he not find it "an intolerable outrage . . . that you are rich and your workmen at Pittsburgh or wherenot poor? . . . Divide your money, Citizen . . . and we shall consider you a softheaded but respectable person. Keep it and talk about your manhood being outraged by the existence of a royal family, and we shall take the liberty of calling you a most undoubted and a most illogical snob."[12]

The writer for the *Globe* found reason enough to jeer at Carnegie's assertion that ending the British monarchy would introduce a regime of "freedom, peace, and felicity." The industrialist's words hardly corroborated the news from the United States that "something like civil war" had broken out in Chicago at the Haymarket "massacre," where a radical protest had involved an exploded bomb, the killing of several policemen, and the imprisonment of the leading protesters. Was it true, moreover, as Carnegie had claimed, that America was the land of universal education? Indeed, the reports from the United States were "that growing illiteracy of the American Democracy is filling the minds of the most thoughtful Americans with anxiety." And was it quite true that the United States never taken up the sword except in self-defense? Try telling that to the Indians and the Mexicans, suggested the *Saturday Review*. Their treatment by the republic would hardly confirm the view that it always resisted aggression and arms.[13]

In sum, said his reviewers, Carnegie's American republic was, despite his protestations to the contrary, seriously flawed. In the land of "equality," some men were more equal than others. Caste and class had their own republican format. Lions did not lie down with the lambs. And swords had, after all, not been beaten into ploughshares.

AMONG CARNEGIE'S ARGUMENTS, one loomed much larger than all the others: that democracy, the political equality of its citizens, was the single source of America's prodigious economic achievement. Here was the principal reason why he urged Britain to follow the American model. Many reviewers left their comments at the point of wonderment about all the facts he had amassed. But several of them, and particularly those who had clear party affiliations and whose journals stood prominent in the circles of London opinion, sought to face Carnegie's argument head on.

They challenged the validity of his premise: indeed, they stood it on its head. Several of the reviewers advanced a reverse argument against Carnegie, and none more acerbically or derisively than that bastion of

Tory sentiment, *St. James's Gazette*. Statistics will prove anything, said the reviewer, but "tortured into illustrations of fantastic and impossible hypotheses, they become bewildering to the last degree." The logic of the American industrialist was flawed by his self-proclamation. He is "so blinded to everything but the 'Triumph of Democracy' that he fails, in the headlong jubilation of his career, to notice the inconsistency of his various arguments." And here the reviewer raised the counter-hypothesis: "In a country so wondrously endowed, we are tempted to ask whether any extraordinary excellence of government is required to ensure prosperity. Since America has every conceivable natural advantage, does the fact of her industrial pre-eminence prove that she had adopted the best form of government?"

Perhaps Carnegie should have "inverted his argument." If he could have said that "*in spite of natural disadvantages*, America was yet the greatest, or at all events the biggest, nation in the world, he might have fairly drawn the inference that she is one of the best-governed. *Of course he cannot do this.*"[14]

Equally tart was the *Saturday Review*, another major Conservative journal, which reduced what Carnegie had said to a self-evidently specious syllogism. "It was perhaps unnecessary for Mr. Carnegie to vary this very simple syllogism through five hundred pages, and it will be still more unnecessary to spend even five hundred words in criticizing it. *The major [of it] is false and there's an end on't.*"[15]

With far less asperity, the *London State* questioned Carnegie's thesis that political equality meant high productivity. "Starting from the incontestable hypothesis that the United States form a Republic, he proceeds to show that the country which they occupy is the biggest in existence." Much of what the American industrialist says "puts in rather clear a light the *non-sequitur* which vitiates the whole of Mr. Carnegie's contention." Let us, said the reviewer, propose an alternate argument. If the republic did not have all of its remarkable natural resources,

> and if it was the rival in commerce, manufactures, and general prosperity of nations not less liberally endowed by nature and fortified by situation and extent than itself, then we might admit that its success in material and numerical achievements was the result of its political institutions. But since . . . it has the advantage with which its Republican institutions have nothing to do, all that can really be said is, that a union of civilised States

occupying an isolated continent is not prevented by the existence of a federal Republic from making good use of altogether exceptional advantages—which is a very different proposition from Mr. Carnegie's.[16]

One has to look beyond the reviews to see that an embattled conservatism was facing the challenge of the times. The comments of his Conservative reviewers constituted not so much a discourse as a diatribe.

Some journals saw in *Triumphant Democracy* an idea that warranted exploring. The review of the *Spectator*, a Liberal journal, granted that Carnegie had "provided a most readable summary of the present condition of the United States, and some striking instances and reflections on the superiority of democratic institutions." But democratic institutions per se were not the cause of economic growth. Seeking a more universal source of dynamic expansion than "the mere form of government," the reviewer suggested that "the cause of growth is not so much 'triumphant democracy' and equality, which rather produce contentment, but the discontent caused by the democratic spirit working under worn-out aristocratic forms in social and political affairs, and particularly in regard to land. . . . The relics of feudalism which are a bar to the progress of the English at home" are a major cause of British expansion and growth overseas. Thus, the expansion that Carnegie found in the United States "has [also] been going on in poor, monarchical England, and a greater expansion in poor, old, slow Canada and colonial Australia."[17]

For the larger part, the provincial English press questioned Carnegie's argument. This was surely true of the Conservative papers. The *Salisbury Journal*, while granting that much in *Triumphant Democracy* held considerable interest, noted that the book as a whole contained "assertions and statements that a much less phenomenal personage than Macaulay's school boy would have little difficulty in refuting."[18]

The *Somerset County Herald* urged the careful reader to "ask for a large discount from the deductions which the author offers as infallible truths" and to be aware that "only one side of a great question has been put before him." It was only Carnegie's distorted view that material growth "is due wholly to the Republican form of government, for some of our [British] colonies have some very remarkable records in this direction."[19]

However much there were shades of difference between those newspapers that were regularly affiliated with either the Conservative or Liberal parties, they were broadly agreed that Carnegie's essentially republican argument was questionable. But a significant bloc of the Radical press, particularly those papers that had belonged to the Storey-Carnegie chain, enthusiastically embraced, even if they did not entirely subscribe to, Carnegie's explanation of the American achievement. Most of the papers were situated in the northern counties, a few in the midlands, and one in London. Typical of their comments were those of the *North-Eastern Weekly Gazette*, which hailed Carnegie as "an ardent politician and a brilliant writer" who had written "a strong, masterly, independent review of the triumphant march of Democracy as seen in the Republic of America." The reviewer questioned neither Carnegie's statistics nor his conclusions. "There has been great research and a careful verifying of facts, so that it will be valuable as a study and as a reference. We can only point our readers to Mr. Carnegie's *Triumphant Democracy* as one of the most remarkable and original books of the time." Taking up Carnegie's insistent argument for republicanism, the reviewer asked: When shall "such a Home Record" as that of the American Republic be written in Britain? "When shall pride of place and power, interminable debates, willful blocking of remedial measures give place to a close, cohesive, harmonious action of the Legislature to lighten the burdens and redress the wrongs of the people?"[20]

Reynolds of London, long a voice of English radicalism and republicanism, hailed Carnegie for "showing how the masses of Englishmen are purposely misinformed as to the immense advantages enjoyed by the citizens of the American republic over the subjects of the English monarchy." It was Carnegie's most admirable achievement that he had discussed "in a fair and impartial manner the different results of the [American and British] systems" and proven "by facts and figures that oweing to the manifold advantages of the Republican form of government" in all material and intellectual respects "America already leads the civilised world. . . . This work should be found on the shelves of every working man's library, club, and institute, and we trust it will hereafter be published in a cheap form, so that it may obtain a large circulation amongst those who have been duped and deceived."[21]

Yet even radical papers entered some caveats. Granting, said the *London Echo*, that "pure democracy has for the field of its greatest experiment the best of races and the best of lands [in the United States], not a few onlookers will be inclined to doubt whether race and land are not more important factors [in America's great achievement] than the absence of a monarchy and a House of Lords." And to look at the other side of the argument: "What if pure Democracy were tested under unfavourable old-world conditions?" Indeed, had not Carnegie himself admitted the role of other forces—such as ethnicity, climate, and a vast territory—in propelling America's progress?[22]

ANDREW CARNEGIE WAS A well known person among those who were reviewing his book. What he said could not have surprised them. But the intensity of his theme, the stridency of his voice, and the immediacy of his message to the inflamed political world of spring 1886 compelled the reviewers to look closely at the author no less than his ideas. Indeed, by disclaiming the author, one could either reduce or largely reject the ideas. Where the press was part of the very structure of power that Carnegie was calling into question, the reviewers went beyond challenging his premises: they fiercely attacked Carnegie himself.

They berated him as a self-important, self-proclaiming man. No one put this better than the reviewer in the *London State*. The author's "soaring soul never could abide the supposition that the world contained any one better or greater than Mr. Carnegie. In Scotland he could not conceal from himself that such was manifestly the fact. . . . As long as [he] can satisfy himself with the reflection that he has not his superior upon the earth, he ought be allowed to do so undisturbed." The real superiority of a society is to be found in its illustrious men and women. But Carnegie has not much to say about distinguished Americans. "On the contrary, he contends . . . that the Republic has not produced any one better than Mr. Carnegie."[23] Indeed, said Avray Tipping in the *Academy*, Carnegie stamped his own name in gold on the flamboyant red buckram cover of his book, over the inverted British crown. The message and tone of his book everywhere proclaimed his importance. "To him alone has been revealed the absolute perfection of the American Constitution. . . . He alone has fully realized the depth of degradation to which [Britain] has been brought by its baneful institutions. Upon him alone expectant populations depend for information as to the lives they lead and the occupations they follow."[24]

The fact of it was that, as his bridling at the British order of ranks testified, Citizen Carnegie was a snob: "irreparable and hopeless." So said the *Saturday Review*. Insisting on ostentatiously displaying his wealth on a highly advertised coaching trip all through Great Britain, Carnegie, said the reviewer, was "a most undoubted and a most illogical snob. Your sense of degradation makes the degradation, and if you were not degraded you would not feel so."25

His Scottish ancestry and his passionate Americanism raised serious wonderments for some of his reviewers. He had, so it seemed, abandoned one set of national ideals and warmly embraced another. No one put this wonderment better than the reviewer of the *Economist* (London). However much he had written a book of very carefully verified facts, "they lose much of their weight from the spirit of excited partisanship in which they are set forth." He had written "an unqualified and fulsome panegyric on everything pertaining to the United States." How was this to be explained? "Just as some people are said to be more Catholic than the Pope, Mr. Carnegie is more American than the Americans and far more Republican than any Republican 'to the manner born.' He is a convert. . . . And he has all the red-hot zeal of a convert."26

In a similar vein, the *Civil Service Gazette* saw Carnegie's volume as a profound change of faith. "Like all converts . . . his zeal for his newly adopted creed is burning, and his affection for that which he relinquished cold; he is 'a little more than kin and less than kind.'" He was indeed "more American than the Americans themselves in his appreciation of all their greatness and superiorities, and more depreciative [than they] of British littleness and inferiorities."27

Other reviewers in the London press faulted him for having filtered his facts through his faith. This theme was echoed in the provinces. Challenging Carnegie's arguments from statistics, the reviewer for the *Salisbury Journal* noted warily: "Republicanism is Mr. Carnegie's pet hobby. To [him], America is the apotheosis of all that is great, good, and beautiful. So intense is his enthusiasm—or rather so acutely does he suffer from American mania—that he is betrayed into writing passages that would be offensive to all Englishmen" if they were not so clearly absurd and easily refutable.

"THE PURPORT OF THE BOOK," said the reviewer of the *Globe*, "is to teach that the United States are an earthly paradise and that they owe their happiness . . . to the fact that they have never set a king over them." The *Globe* cited Carnegie's graphic image, one that was often quoted by reviewers with derision and anger: "Monarchy is the upas tree which blights all that is good in England, and when once it is cut down—as it will be . . . at the next demise of the Crown, England will flourish like America. . . . Get rid of monarchy, and then freedom, peace, and plenty will bless the world."28

In the long-standing dialogue between the kindred polities, the issue had always been about the paradigmatic role of each nation. For his reviewers, the besetting problem was how to separate the indoctrinator from the doctrine. Apart from Carnegie, indeed despite Carnegie, there still remained the hard-fisted question: How useful was the United States as a model for Britain? For most of the reviewers, the question was readily answered. They rejected Carnegie's facile equation of political democracy with material achievement. To the degree that great economic progress could be ascribed to other causes than those found in the republic, American republicanism lost its persuasion as an institution to emulate. Except for the advanced Liberal journals, and particularly those that until very recently had been part of the Storey-Carnegie chain, the press bought neither Carnegie's argument nor his proposal of the American model.

A few newspapers addressed his suggestion directly. The reviewer for the *London Sunday Chronicle* was impressed by Carnegie's figures on America's great number of newspapers, schools, theaters, and museums: in this respect, "we feel we are listening to a capable instructor, who is telling us of things not dreamt of in our philosophy, and describing a nation from which he has possibly a great deal to learn."[29] For all that, Carnegie's "British readers will be more inclined to smile at his republican fervour and his disparagement of monarchical institutions than to be converted to his pleading."[30]

London's conservative press was, of course, less disposed to be benign. *Triumphant Democracy*, said the *Globe*, contained "about as much pernicious nonsense as could well be compressed into 500 octavo pages." Most Englishmen would give no serious consideration to Carnegie's doctrine.[31] How far had the American industrialist persuaded Britons to follow the United States, asked *Court and Society*, a journal of a self-evidently Tory orientation. It indicted Carnegie's sharp attack on the ways of the monarchy: "Democracy will not gain by such advocacy as this. In fact, a book like *Triumphant Democracy* is a valuable refresher to the monarchical sentiment which has flourished for one thousand years in England . . . and is likely to endure for another."[32] Of course, no organ of English opinion rejected Carnegie's lesson on models as sharply as the *St. James's Gazette*: "Englishmen respect and admire America, but they are quite satisfied with their own Constitution. . . . They have nothing to say in censure of his ignorance . . . until he tries to set himself up as a political teacher. . . . But he had better get rid of the idea that he can Americanise England either by his agents in the English press or by means of such books as *Triumphant Democracy*."[33]

Several other English journals, particularly in the provinces, sounded the same theme. The United States, they said, could not, as Carnegie was suggesting, serve Britain as a model, except in one very basic respect: clearly, the British constitution needed far greater stability. The *Somerset County Herald*, a Conservative paper, quoted with approval Carnegie's ominous words to the kingdom's ruling classes: "I warn the people of Britain that the masses are prone to be carried away temporarily by passion" and that Britain needed "some more secure method of Government such as the Executive of the United States possesses."[34] The *Salisbury Journal*, another Conservative journal, having questioned most of the premises of Carnegie's instruction, subscribed to his description of Britain's current constitutional crisis. "The Ministers and members of Parliament," he had said, "are like so many agile performers on the tight-rope, no one knows the moment they may fall, nor, worst of all, the cause which may throw them." The reviewer agreed with Carnegie: "this is undoubtedly a serious evil of our present form of Government."[35]

It need hardly be said that the advanced Liberal press as well as the erstwhile Storey-Carnegie chain agreed with Carnegie that American republican institutions offered Britain a most worthy model. They did not address his warning that Britain's governors would be well advised to set up blocks to the direct expression, in Parliament, of popular sentiment. Carnegie himself understood that the warning might seem to be a contradiction of his key principle of democracy. "Some of my Radical friends," he had said in the closing pages of *Triumphant Democracy*, "may esteem this strange doctrine for a republican to preach, but such are yet to learn that the equality of the citizen in a State is the surest antidote for violent revolutionary measures."

THE SCOTTISH RESPONSE to *Triumphant Democracy* went through a complex filtration. Carnegie had, in his reductive presentation, written a tale of two nations—the American and the British—during the past half-century. But the Scots, as Carnegie well knew, were their own nation. Scottish nationalism had long been an active element in the history of the British Isles. The Act of 1707 had formally constituted a Great Britain that joined Scotland to the kingdom of England and Wales. If, by 1886, the governing classes of both kingdoms had long since worked out a functioning unity, there yet remained between the two the sentiments and the mores, if not quite the barrier, of two societies. Was Carnegie, as a native-born Scotsman, speaking to Britain as a yet vitally connected Scotsman? Was his America a surrogate for his Scotland? Was he wearing Esau's garment but talking Jacob's voice? The filtered complexity of *Triumphant Democracy* posed not only the national division and that three nations involved—America, England, and Scotland—but also the class divisions within their respective societies. Perhaps that is why Carnegie, speaking for the class-ridden Scotland that he had left but to which he was always affiliated, proposed an apparently classless America as a model for a thoroughly class-divided England. Did the zeal of his argument—which he took no trouble at all to conceal—speak to the legacy of his family origins in a nation-conscious and class-conscious Scotland?

His Scottish reviewers were fully aware of all this. That they did not often voice it meant that, in judging Carnegie's proposal, they took the knowledge of Scotland's complex relations with England as their point of departure. No one knew better than the Scots their own peculiar relationship with the British government and society centered at Westminster and Whitehall. Throughout the eighteenth century, the Scottish aristocracy had entered the pale of British power: collaborating in certain respects of power and jurisdiction; Scottish intellectuals took a special position, looking at Britain from the outside, as it were. It was no accident, certainly, that some of the greatest minds of the eighteenth century—the stars of the Scottish Enlightenment, including Adam Smith, David Hume, William Robertson, Joseph Black, and John Millar—constituted a stellar segment of the age of Enlightenment. But many of those less favorably advantaged had, seeking their own freer venue, emigrated to the colonies and led in the fight for American independence. Carnegie's *Triumphant Democracy* was a latter-day statement of that intellectual emigration from, and indeed antagonism toward, the hegemony of British aristocratic institutions and frame of mind.

Like the English, the Scots were also great traders. The Act of Union further enhanced the commercial interdependence of England and Scotland, and the Scots became the ever more active traders of Britain's great mercantile empire. Carnegie well understood that empire and worked in it virtually all of his life. He intimately knew the workings of the London and Wall Street capital markets; and, for his own great advantage, vaunted the ready access of his manufactures to Britain's open market while also arguing for the validity of American protectionism in closing out many of Britain's goods to the United States. These factors shaped the Scottish response to Carnegie. The Scots knew who they were, where they had come from, where they stood vis-à-vis British power, and they surely knew all about the "star-spangled Scotchman" and the doctrine he was proclaiming.

History and geography thus defined the Scottish press's view of Britain and of course its view of *Triumphant Democracy*. As the largest and in many ways the most advanced and achieved of the British provinces, Scotland inclined toward Liberalism, which was accordingly ingrained in the Scottish perspective. Their critique of Carnegie's message was filtered through this ingrained Liberalism. But Scotland was far from being merely antiestablishment; after all, by now it had long been very much part of the establishment. The major Scottish journals, such as the *Glasgow Herald* and the *Edinburgh Scotsman*, reflected this, in taking a distanced, measured view of what Carnegie said. The Scottish reviewers addressed pretty much the same questions as had the London press. But they largely centered on three of those questions. One: How far was Carnegie's basic premise valid? Two: How far could American institutions serve as a model for Britain? Three, and relatedly: In what way did their Scottish identity enter into their critique of an essentially anti-English book? And where did this all fit into the larger picture of the transatlantic Anglo-American dialogue and the ongoing competition of models?

Insofar as Carnegie's basic premise was concerned—that political equality had been the cause of America's prodigious achievement—nearly all of the Scottish press was doubtful. The reviewers expressed varying degrees of doubt about the premise, but none accepted the validity of a simple equation of political equality with high productivity. The *Edinburgh Scotsman* stated the case against Carnegie simply: "The impartial student of sociology and political science will not fail to perceive that [his] demonstration of the efficacy of the Democratic principles, as embodied and exemplified in the institution of the United States, is throughout weakened, if not absolutely vitiated, by sundry unwarranted assumptions."[36] To which the *Glasgow Herald* subscribed: "As a Republican, he is of course entitled to claim credit for the influence of Republican institutions, but then we are not bound to follow him in blind belief that the phenomenal development would not also have occurred under monarchical institutions."[37] Even the reviewer for Dunfermline—Carnegie's homeplace—questioned its native son, ascribing America's growth to what the new nation had borrowed from the mother country no less than from "material resources [that] were unrivalled."[38]

The Scottish reviewers turned with great concern, indeed more so than their English compeers, to the lesson that lay at the heart of Carnegie's book: that the United States offered its kindred polity an instructive model. The matter of instruction readily opened up to an immediately related one: Who is to learn what from whom? And that matter touched directly on the discourse the kindred polities had been having for nearly a century and the competition of models between them. This was precisely the point made by the reviewer of the *Edinburgh Scottish Reformer*. Many American institutions were "pregnant with lessons for British legislators and reflect the highest credit on the political genius of the people." Still, the reviewer wondered, is it "the republic as such that has produced all the good that is to be found in America?" Relatedly, several of the reviewers agreed that democracy per se might have a great appeal, but immediately added that the United States was hardly a reassuring model of democracy. "We confess to considerable sympathy . . . with [Carnegie's] faith in the soundness of the democratic principle, said the *Edinburgh Scotsman*, but "the American embodiment of the republican idea" is a questionable model. "Only a person who shuts his eyes to facts can deny that it has great imperfections, and admits of the existence of terrible evils." So far as Britain was concerned: "especially after the reforms which our Constitution has undergone since 1832, the government class evolved by our political machinery is at least as capable and as faithful in the performance of any of its duties as that of the republic." The *Glasgow Herald* agreed that "we have as much to learn from America, and have learned much—by her mistakes as well as her success—but let not America be arrogant enough to suppose that she has nothing to learn from her elders." Again, the relation between the two polities was mutual, and so, too, the instruction.

At bottom, the issue that Carnegie raised was the nature and depth of Scotland's affiliation with England. That this issue was raised at all, more than a century after it had been ostensibly resolved, was distressing to the Scottish establishment. That it was raised in so blatant a style was offensive. Even Carnegie's home city regretted both the substance and style of his central message. Noting the bold dedication with which he opened his book, the *Dunfermline Saturday Press* said that it embodied "a direct thrust at the aristocratic institutions of the mother country which might well have been omitted."[39] Much more irate about Carnegie's indictment of the monarchy was the *Glasgow Herald*, one of Scotland's major newspapers. The reviewer opened with an attack on Carnegie as "too successful, too self-contented and self-opinionated a man, and too enthusiastically a republican to be qualified to discuss calmly and seriously" the comparative virtues of republicanism and monarchy. Unlike Carnegie, "Englishmen are not wont to measure everything by the dollar, and they have a higher standard to regulate them than a mere comparison of costs. If Mr. Carnegie is not able to rise to that standard he not need insult it: yet we are bound to say that his reflections upon our Queen and institutions are gross in character and insulting to the nation. [His writing] is accompanied by a pervading and decidedly offensive egotism."

The longest and probably the most valuable of the Scottish reviews appeared in the *Elgin Courant*. What gives the review its great value, surely to the latter-day reader, is that it analyzed *Triumphant Democracy* from virtually every perspective. The reviewer touched on all of the major criteria that had entered the appraisals of the other reviews. For us, two points are notable about the review: first, it agreed with Carnegie's favorable view of the republic, though differing with him about the reasons for its achievement; and second, it very much regretted his attack on the monarchy. About America, the *Courant* did not doubt that it was all that the great industrialist had described: "the land of freedom, the land of wealth, the land of unlimited potentialities." As a description of America's progress, Carnegie's book deserved the highest praise. One could go so far as to agree with his holding up the republic as a polity to emulate: "in many things our country would benefit by following its example. We confess to a strong liking and profound admiration for our brethren across the Atlantic."[40]

But to Hibernians, however, Carnegie's book was a cause for great regret. "It is sad to see one whom we should be glad to acknowledge as a good Scotsman so persistently vilifying the institutions of the land of his nativity and glorifying those of that 'beloved republic' which has become the land of his adoption."

It was most distressing that Carnegie should flaunt the republic in their faces and "that it should be thrust down our throats as the pattern and mirror of everything that is noble, good and faultless, socially and politically . . . is scarcely what we should have expected from a man of Mr. Carnegie's antecedents."

How then, asked the reviewer, did Scots feel about his book's message? "We protest against [his] insulting allusions to our institutions and our social distinctions. Few even of our most advanced Radicals will agree with Mr. Carnegie in holding that a royal family is an insult to every other family in the land." Carnegie spoke with "the zeal of a convert": intelligent, yes, and prosperous, also true. That made the matter of Scottish affiliation, indeed identity, all the more important. "We in this country—in Scotland particularly—to whatever political party we belong, pride ourselves in our loyalty. . . . Scotland wishes no disloyal, no unpatriotic sons in her midst. Those who cannot love their old nursing mother—as she is—are right to desert the maternal nest. But to return denationalised, blinded, and purse-proud, to jeer at all her prejudices, and to laugh at all her defects . . . is, to say the least of it unfilial conduct at which she has a right to be justly indignant."

The words of the reviewer were of course not unexpected. They disclosed at once the deeper sentiments that coalesced the principal elements of the British establishment. There had been and indeed there still was a Celtic fringe, but the upper classes in the fringe had long since been absorbed into a larger English amalgam. It is noteworthy that the reviews never once said Britain. They upbraided Carnegie for his attack on the mother country, on England, but by 1886 the name England had become synonymous with Britain. And yet, not quite. Britain, after the Act of Union, remained an amalgam in which the component Celtic parts were, if hardly separate, then not quite equal with England. This is why home rule movements always had a certain vitality in the outer nations, though nowhere of the intensity of Catholic Ireland, which under England's rule was a suppressed and harshly ruled colony. Carnegie's impassioned evangelism aroused the profound feelings that bound the ruling classes of Great Britain into a shared sense of identity. The words of indictment that the *Elgin Courant* reviewer leveled against the native Scotsman bear repeating: that he was disloyal, that he was unpatriotic, that he had lost his sense of pride, that he had deserted his maternal nest, that he was denationalized, and that he was a convert who had in effect sold his birthright for a mess of potage.

His London reviewers could condescend to Carnegie, regarding him as a vulgar, conceited, spread-eaglish American, but they implied a name they would not use: that he was a Scotsman of a certain class and political orientation. His Scottish reviewers could hardly ignore his Scottish origins. The sentiments they expressed were a mixture of sadness, regret, distress, embarrassment, and anger. They resented deeply that Carnegie had returned home to jeer at his motherland and, using the enormous wealth he had amassed in America, was trying to convert her to an American doctrine.

THE BRITISH CRITIQUE of *Triumphant Democracy* was a major event in the transatlantic colloquy between the kindred polities. That Andrew Carnegie was a highly prominent member of both nations gave the book a unique importance and, accordingly, a distinctive role in the way it served in the Anglo-American dialogue. That importance was further enhanced by the immediacy of its theme: historically rooted though it was, it was a book for the times, an extended essay aiming to guide Britain through its current problems.

Yet remarkably enough, the reviewers, speaking in the voice of their diverse journals, almost intentionally failed to mention some of the great problems that were besieging Britain in that spring of 1886. Two sets of questions were impinging directly on the kingdom's affairs: How would it manage its external difficulties and how would manage its domestic strife? The reviews said nothing of Britain's foreign affairs, and particularly its growing difficulties with a Europe dramatically altered by the emergence of Germany, nor of the Franco-German antagonism, nor of the clear and present dangers with Russia in Afghanistan, nor of the growing difficulties with the British policy in India and the Near East, and nothing at all of the disaster of General "Chinese" Gordon's expedition in the Sudan and his annihilation at Khartoum.

Britain's domestic affairs were far more preoccupying, of course: Should they not have figured in discussing a book that centered almost exclusively on contrasting the two polities? Again, notably, the reviews said very little about the affairs that were then agitating Britain. Of the many issues that were then splitting British politics, none was more agitating than the social issue that had been variously raised by Joseph Chamberlain, representing advanced Liberalism, and by Lord Randolph Chamberlain, representing democratic Toryism. The reviewers said nothing about them. Nor in fact did they say much about the single issue that virtually swept all others aside: Irish Home Rule, although everyone, even then, knew that Britain would swirl almost beyond rescue in this great vortex. And indeed it did, for two long tortuous decades. It goes beyond our interest at this point to say that only a self-righteous, holier-than-everybody Gladstone would, in his singular formulation of Irish Home

Rule, have led the nation down this precarious course. What is directly germane here is that the Irish Home Rule issue was almost entirely passed over by the reviews.

The transatlantic dialogue over *Triumphant Democracy* thus had certain confines. The reason was that the book served each nation as a basis for validating its institutions. Using Carnegie's commentary, the American reviewers, however much they discounted his tendency to spread-eaglism, took heart that a son of a kindred nation had bountifully underwritten the republic. Because the essence of his book was to indict the monarchy, it was almost inevitable that his British reviewers would have to answer the terms of his bill of indictment. His reductive formula and his impassioned style shaped the substance of their response. Indeed, it robbed the response of something of the sophistication and even-handedness that it might otherwise have received. That Carnegie was literally the son of both affiliated nations and that he verged on a diatribe rather than a dialogue personalized the terms of the binational discourse. His British reviewers responded to what they took to be heated charges rather than a calm argument, to someone they saw as a perfidious anti-Albion rather than a sincerely affectionate native son.

Yet what they said was an important part of the transatlantic colloquy. Indeed so too was, for reasons basic to both polities, what they did not say, or did not feel concerned to say. More significant, in certain ways, was that the dialogue was being substantially transformed. Carnegie was a member of an emerging Pan-Anglian sodality, which we shall be discussing, and which was fundamentally redefining the Anglo-American competition of models.

6

Affirming America

IN THE TRANSATLANTIC dialogue between the kindred polities that Andrew Carnegie's book evoked, how would his American reviewers respond to what he had written about their society? Positively, one would imagine, and for the larger part so they did. But the conversation was more with themselves than with their British compeers. The British had to defend themselves against Carnegie's charges. The Americans were gratified that one of their greatest industrialists, a man who knew both worlds intimately, had written a paean to America. In Britain, *Triumphant Democracy* was part of an argument in comparative political science. In the United States, it was an internal debate over the validity of America as a polity.

The steelmaster's American correspondents were particularly positive. "You have done a great service to this country," said George B. Lathrop, a New York City author and editor. "In these days of carping criticism, *Triumphant Democracy* is much needed," wrote William T. Hornaday, a notable scientist at the Smithsonian. It gives "a great impulse to the American idea," said a New York friend, Jeanie Croly. The book will "teach our people lessons of loyalty and inspire more respect and love for our institutions," noted Stephen B. Elkins, a New York financier. "You teach both sides of the Atlantic that the U. S. A. is the only country based on the people's will, which is the only foundation for a state," wrote John Forrest Dillon, a prominent jurist. "You have rendered a great service to the English-speaking people," wrote William B. McKinley, then a congressman from Ohio; and, added Henry George, have contributed much to "knitting the English speaking race." Their comments touched every aspect of the importance of *Triumphant Democracy*. The book had been widely distributed and it might have been expected that his correspondents would sound their praises. True enough, not all were positive, and not all the newspaper reviewers refrained from entering their misgivings. But, in the main, they sounded a chorus of approval. To say that raises in turn a series of questions. Who were they? Just what did they say? And what did their evaluation of Carnegie's great book signify?

"You give us a tonic breeze," said T. J. Coffey, a Washington-based diplomat and lawyer, speaking for the editorial class that was reading Carnegie. In that spring of 1886, why were they so grateful for that tonic breeze? The answer is that everywhere they looked in that great American continental expanse they found little that was comforting. What their eyes could not avoid was the new type of conflict between the laboring classes and their employers. Strikes were a bitter struggle, indeed a war, between capital and labor. How could one pass over the violent events of 1877, when federal troops were called out to keep order in the Great Railway Strike? They shuddered at the great strikes of 1885 and 1886: those on the Union Pacific, at the McCormick Harvester Works, and the shocking riots and murders in Chicago's Haymarket Square in early May 1886, at the very time that *Triumphant Democracy* was being reviewed. But the strife between capital and labor was part of a larger unsettlement. Many of the strikers came with European ideas and accents. They often clustered within the cities, seeming to be alien groups with threatening cultures.

Though not clearly discernible at that time, these were the years of "the new immigration," when the ethnicity, the languages, the religion, indeed the character and civism of America seemed in peril. The gaps between the rich and the poor seemed wider than ever, and nothing made them more discernible than the rapid concentration of Americans in the growing urban centers. Many prominent writers of the day sounded the tolling of the bells, some of them fearful that the victory they had won to suppress rebellion and keep their union alive was now being overturned.[1]

In those early months of 1886, how did the American scene appear to the probing eyes of the editors and reviewers? The structure of American life seemed to reduce itself to a litany of problems.[2] The currents were real and tangible, their impact was often dire. Two decades after the bloodiest war in American history, what kind of a United States did men who were looking actually see? The two largest political parties were at war with each other. The South had in effect seceded again, setting up a solid bloc of

Democratic states, increasingly disenfranchizing the new freedmen, and vesting power in a somewhat transformed elite of planters. Elections were exercises in vilification, and the Republican Party—only so recently marching under the standard of morality and the American way—was now bitterly split. Could the house that was now divided against itself continue to stand? By redefining the Fourteenth Amendment and nullifying the Civil Rights Act of 1875, the Supreme Court was filling a void left open by ineffectual presidents and unacting congresses. Nothing seemed to be clearer than what James Bryce, among so many others, had been finding out: that the best men did not go into politics. Bryce was astonished at the thousands of public offices that were part of the panoply of American government. It was troubling, of course, that these holders of office gained by patronage, sold themselves out to the highest bidder, and as Lincoln Steffens would later say, not because they felt they were being corrupt but because they were doing the American thing. They were making money in an age when America, a land of vast multiplying resources and opportunities, was truly a land of bilk and money and in that way seemed to fulfill God's promise to make it the real promised land. The economy was in a recurrently perilous state: a depression lasted, with some ups and downs, from 1873 to 1896; most distressing was the continuous decline in the prices of agricultural commodities.

As the editorialists and newspaper owners of the United States saw it, how very far from wrong was the Reverend Samuel D. Burchard, a Republican clergyman, when he called the Democrats a party of "rum, Romanism, and rebellion"? A terrible slur, to be sure, and it certainly cost Blaine the election of 1884. Burchard was referring of course to the support Democrats had in Irish strongholds in different urban centers, particularly New York City; and of course to the fact that the New South was a thoroughly Democratic south. But as they looked around the United States in those middle years of the 1880s, it seemed that another America—and surely not a phoenix—was arising out of the pyre of the recent Civil War. The popular literature of the day sounded the knells—if not of the nation's death—then of its grave morbidity. In *Our Country* (1885), the Reverend Josiah Strong found that "the dangerous elements of our civilization are each multiplying and all concentrated in the city."[3] He feared the growing and pernicious influence of Catholicism. While the patterns of the "new immigration" (that is dated to 1881) were not yet clear, it was clear and troubling that the new immigrants were not Anglo-Saxon, that they spoke foreign tongues, that they resisted a ready acculturation, and that they lived in ghettoes that could threaten the civic culture that distinguished American life. Henry George had already warned, in *Progress and Poverty* (1879), that the United States was becoming a land of the very rich, the less rich, and the impoverished. The realistic novels of William Dean Howells, probably the most influential writer of his day, described a society that was deeply riven by so many social problems.

If further evidence were needed to underscore their worried sense of the condition of America, it came with the shocking Haymarket "massacre" of May 4, 1886. All the elements of their apprehension were suddenly realized: the class-oriented meeting had been called by a group of anarchist revolutionaries; circulars printed in German and English had been widely distributed; a column of 180 policemen had appeared to control the very small group that had assembled; a bomb went off; seven policemen were fatally injured. The disaster fit in with the ensuing, increasingly embittered conflict between capital and labor. Haymarket proved yet once again that America and American ideals were under siege. Here was the list: foreign-born leaders, foreign tongues, foreign doctrines, class warfare, alien views. The nation's newspapers were fairly universal in denouncing the meeting and its leaders.

And suddenly, it must have seemed, in that fearful season there appeared an evangel about the wonderful condition of America. A Scottish-American, a highly successful industrialist, a man who knew both America and Europe, presented them with a massive book of facts, solid documentation, one whose central argument that all was right with America—its premises were valid, its progress amazing, its prospect even more reassuring. In those uncertain, bleak times, the men who led American opinion needed uplifting. Carnegie gave them that tonic, and they seized his book zestfully and gratefully.

If the reviewers, following the practice of the time, were anonymous, the newspapers in which they appeared were obviously not. Those that had a declared party affiliation divided almost evenly between Republican and Democratic, but a larger segment than either of those designated itself as independent. By far the greater part of them were dailies; about a third were weeklies. A few of the journals had a circulation of over 50,000, but the largest number appeared in journals with a circulation of from five to fifty thousand.[4] In a nation of "island communities," they spoke for their respective cities and towns, virtually all of which had a political or commercial importance, though they varied much in population.[5] A few of the journals appeared in the nation's major cities, such as New York,

Philadelphia, Boston, and Chicago. But however major some of the cities were, they were not London. Commanding power did not lay in America's "island communities," nor the commensurate power of opinions and ideas. However much Americans subscribed to what may be called a larger consensus, they surely did not speak in a single tongue. The American idea was diffuse, variable, multiple, regional, and indeed local. London's response to Carnegie was what mattered in Britain, and it was largely negative. America's response, sounded in its multifarious communities, also mattered, and no less so in that it was largely positive.

Who were the newspapers' editors and publishers? Virtually all were northerners. Most of them were in their thirties when the Civil War broke out. Most were Republicans or independents. Several had been trained in the law and moved into journalism. A few combined professions: publishing, the law, and a commercial activity (indeed one was a housebuilder). Some had inherited their newspapers from their fathers. Many came from America's big cities (New York, Philadelphia, Boston, San Francisco) or those that were commercially well situated, such as Rochester, Troy, Utica, New Haven, Springfield. Some were truly prominent figures in American literary life, men such as Edwin L. Godkin, Murat Halstead, and George W. Childs. All were makers and shapers of opinion.[6] To an important degree, their role as publishers and editors modifies Bryce's conclusion that America's best men did not go into politics: many of the best men went into publishing and the shaping of politics. But there was of course a very palpable difference between the party politics of patronage and mediocrity, which Bryce was decrying, and the more individual, cognitive politics of editing and publishing, which many of the newspapers afforded.

What was the role of editors and reviewers in the American polity? In any liberal democratic society, the literary class will voice its malaise. It was particularly vocal in America. It formed a professional order of Jeremiahs. It saw life as a perennial moral conflict. And Americans, so it may have appeared in 1886, were still at war. It may help to list, in a somewhat different formulation, the seemingly endless conflicts of interests that were then roiling American politics: of agrarians and Wall Street financiers, of good government espousers and party patrons, of urban promoters and upholders of the yeoman tradition, of labor and capital, of monopolists and antitrusters, of greenbackers and gold standard bearers, of those who feared the new immigrants and those who welcomed them. In a nation of intensely partisan interests, editors and reviewers spoke the viewpoint of their particular group. Party lines were obviously organizing points of different economic interests, social divisions, ethnic orientations, geographical locations. Each of the two major parties had vocal and organized dissenters; but outside the Republicans and the Democrats other party groups were forming to shape state and national politics to help solve their problems and ameliorate their plight. *Triumphant Democracy* commanded their attention. It commanded no less the attention of his correspondents, whose names testify to the wide circle of friends and acquaintances Carnegie had formed and who constituted a fraternity of power that could shape American opinion.

In April 1886, the United States was more a question than an answer. Then, suddenly, it would have seemed, came a book of revelations, packed with solid, scientific, irrefutable facts about life in the United States. *Triumphant Democracy* was the answer to the questions that were then bedeviling America's editorial and political class.

Was the American idea of democratic equality still valid? Yes, the literary steelmaster proclaimed. Was not patriotism itself under serious challenge? Unreasonably so, responded the flag-waving immigrant. How far could the case be made for democracy against aristocracy? Very far, contended the transplanted Chartist. His formidable facts and figures—and who would know them better than a titan of industry—answered their doubts and shaped their reviews. And yet for all the facts, persisted some of the reviewers, were there not justifiable reservations about the way Carnegie had portrayed American democracy? This question also entered into the reviews and the correspondence. But the reservations, voiced by a few of the most important journals, were a smaller part of the whole.

For an important segment of American opinion, when it appeared, *Triumphant Democracy* stood as a testament of affirmation. Coming when it did, the book gained an immediate importance, but no less so because it belonged directly in the ever-continuing, ever-vital Anglo-American discourse. For, after all, the central question before the kindred polities was whether democracy was a valid, practicable, indeed superior idea.

Not all of America's editorial classes—and the varied interests they spoke for—embraced Carnegie's evangel. They had reservations not only about what he was saying but about Carnegie himself. Why did they doubt him? For two reasons that, in effect, were often one. The facts of American life, strewn all about them, contradicted his yea-saying. There was a second reason: they questioned the evangel because they very much doubted the evangelist. In early 1886 not only could the adversities of

American life not be denied, it could also not be denied that Carnegie was himself one of the causes of those adversities.

In 1886 several fissures ran through editorial opinion, and these fissures ran along lines that were regional, ethnic, religious, social, and economic. But one fissure sundered the editorial classes: their affiliation to the two dominant parties that were fighting for political control. Were they Republican or Democrat? Because they had no clearly defined programs, the differences between them did not, at least on the surface, seem to matter, said James Bryce. But he understood that the differences mattered very much. The fight between the parties was over patronage—the literally hundreds and thousands of jobs throughout the United States—that the victorious party and its leaders could disburse. The fight was also over legislative policy and where the policy was formulated: whether at the local, or state, or national level. The fight between the parties and their editorial spokesmen thus went to the heart of the American polity.

Carnegie and his book very much touched that heart and the blood—the money—that coursed through the heart. His massive book of facts seemed to put him into the realm of a higher-minded and disinterested intelligence. But was he really? It was well known that he had a strong connection with the Republican Party. It was surely well known that he had a strong link, indeed friendship, with James G. Blaine, who had gone down to ignominious defeat in the very tight election of 1884. It was also known that Carnegie had ties with Pennsylvania's political boss, Matthew Quay, and with James M. Swank, the very hard-working congressional lobbyist of the American Iron and Steel Association. With his fellow industrialists, he contributed to the support of the Republican Party. However much his strongest political sentiments lay in Britain, Carnegie was hardly a hushed, still voice in American affairs. He wrote letters to many editors; he delivered speeches; he wrote articles for important journals; he wrote books. The reviewers who questioned Carnegie's role in American politics had many reasons to question his book. It concerned them particularly that he stood for protection on one side of the Atlantic and against it on the other: that a man who staunchly defended the high tariff on goods—particularly steel—coming into the United States was staunchly opposed to imperial preference, a system of tariffs, for the British. Was this self-proclaimed latter-day Chartist, they wondered, devoted to the greatest good for the smallest number?

It would be too simple and categorical to say that the reviewers who approved of his politics also approved of his book. Yet certain points about the reviews of *Triumphant Democracy* may be ventured. Those who embraced his portrait were regular Republicans; the newspapers they wrote for were most often not from major American cities; they spoke for middletown America; their editors were not men of national prominence; where the party affiliation was cited as independent, they were not "Mugwump." The questioners came from the newspapers that bolted the Republican Party in the searing election of 1884: they saw Blaine as corruption personified, and therefore supported Cleveland. The newspapers were usually located in major American cities. Their editors were often writers of national prominence, including such men as E. L. Godkin, Murat Halstead, Samuel Bowles IV, Melville E. Stone, and a notable Democratic leader, William M. Singerly. Some of the "Mugwumps" of 1884 had been the Liberal Republicans of 1872, strong in the cause of reforming the national government, outlawing the spoils system, cleansing democracy not merely of its corruption but of the idea that corruption was democratic. Many had been the moralists of the Civil War: for them that had been "the good war," of whose great victory the nation was now being despoiled. Carnegie's waving of his unbloody flag of democracy triumphant was, for them, a patent fabrication of the truth.

But it's also true that Carnegie's questioners had no high standing in public opinion. For the larger part, Americans wanted to hear good things about the condition of the republic and who, it would have seemed, was better qualified, more informed than Andrew Carnegie to have the American eagle scream loudly against the doubters?

How *VALID* WERE America's idea and institutions: that is, how well founded, just, good? That's the question Carnegie's book had raised. That's the question his reviewers addressed. The question was, in fact, rather complex and could be answered in several ways and perceived at several levels.

The American reviews had this importance, that they constituted an extensive, national commentary on "the state of America" question, a question and discussion that were roughly analogous to a similar discourse that was perennially ongoing in British journals and Parliament. What was noteworthy about the American newspapers was that, in the great diversity of the American press, there was widespread praise for Carnegie and his book, while there was, for all that, a certain degree of doubt about both his American portrait and the lines in which he had drawn it.

That the book appeared in such troubling times gave his reviewers an immediate basis for appraising it. For the jangled nerves of America's editorial class *Triumphant Democracy* could not have come at a better time. "This is a book for the pessimist," said the *Albany [NY] Times*. "The man who has the blues, that says the country is going to the dogs, that business is overdone and manufactures badly done, politics are too corrupt for consideration, cannot do better than to read this book from cover to cover."[7] Said the *New Haven News*: "This book is like a refreshing breeze, it is so full of honest admiration for American institutions and the American people."[8] The *New York Critic* agreed: Carnegie had offered "a good antidote to those works on the defects of American institutions, and of which we have had so many during the past few years."[9] Whatever misgivings the *New York Independent* reviewer may have had, he concluded with: "On the whole, we are glad that there is an angle from which the present realities and tendencies of American life can be surveyed with so much enthusiasm."[10] The *Rome [NY] Sentinel* added its praise: "We need plenty of optimism in these days and we have it in Mr. Carnegie's book. . . . It is a kind of glorified census, and we are sure as we read it that the millennium has come!"[11]

In that contentious country of warring groups, Carnegie had done something truly salutary: he had restored patriotism. Elevating the states united, he had diminished the conflicts that disunited them. The editors seized at once Carnegie's celebratory volume. His book, said the *San Francisco Argonaut*, "is one long paean of jubilant patriotism."[12] "When so many born to the purpose of American citizenship affect despondency, it is cheering to come across a bit of worship so unrestrained from a native of another country. . . . [He] indulges in one prolonged ecstasy of admiration for the American republic."[13] How could a patriotic citizen turn back Carnegie's invitation to celebrate America, asked the *Rochester Post-Express*.[14] The reader "realizes that the American eagle is about to flap its wings, soar high in the air, and scream for all that it is worth. And who is there but likes to hear that scream?"

Faith in the country had been flagging. Carnegie restored it. No one had chronicled the country more enthusiastically, said the *New York Star*.[15] His "magnificent panorama" glows with "life and color that must make every American feel a new pride in his country and its institutions." Had America come to seem a source of shame in all the scandalous events of "the Gilded Age"? Carnegie's "splendid work" would end the sense of shame. American citizens would embrace his book with "pardonable pride," depicting as he had "this blessed land of ours so desirable that no one can read [the book] without being made the better and more patriotic."[16] Carnegie's chapters on American politics were "among the most admirable essays ever written on the subject. Their clear ringing sentences come like a fresh whole gust of the sea breeze." But even more notable was the book as a whole: its account of America's rise to industrial primacy was "wonderful not only for the vigor and power of condensation that characterize it but for the enthusiastic patriotism that glows on every page."[17]

Patriotism had always been a lively issue in the history of the United States. It was particularly alive in the decades following the Civil War. Separating from the mother country in the 1770s and 1780s put a heavy burden and an intense meaning on the word "patriot," evidences of which one could find in the new nation's literature of the late eighteenth and early nineteenth centuries. Evoking a new call to arms, each of the postrevolutionary wars had evoked a new call to patriotism. If the issue was ever more lively in the 1880s, it was because the bloody flag of southern rebellion was still stirringly waving and present, not merely in politics but in men's minds. And the perennial disuniting of the American polity by a variety of conflicting interests was further aggravated by the inpouring of aliens whose familiarity with America's free, republican institutions was as distant as the lands they had come from.

Here is why so many newspapers—and the civic groups they spoke for—welcomed *Triumphant Democracy* with great enthusiasm. It should serve as a manual in patriotism. "It would be a good thing could every American read it . . . well calculated to increase every American's admiration for his country and government."[18] As to those who were doubting U.S. institutions, it would surely be "a tonic to those anemics who have suffered so much alarm over our corrupt politics and foreign immigration."[19] *Triumphant Democracy* was a book for citizens born in the United States and for those who had freshly arrived. "It would be a good thing for America," said the *Chicago Evening Herald*, "if every citizen of this great free land would carefully study this book: it would make their patriotism deeper and wider and more intelligent."[20]

No newspaper presented the civic virtues and appeal of Carnegie's book as well as *The Davenport [IA] Democrat*, whose comments merit a lengthy citation: "It is a good book . . . for the study of Americans to the manor born. It cannot but increase their pride and love and veneration for the land and institutions of the land which today stands out foremost among the nations of the earth. *There is no danger of training Americans to a too deep love of country.* Every teacher and every preacher in all the broad acres, from the Atlantic to the Pacific, should constantly impress upon the minds of the young the grandeur and the priceless value of their inheritance they have received. *Looking at our American institutions in their reality and possibilities in the future, through the eyes of an adopted son who glories in them, can not do less than to arouse anew patriotism in its broadest and best sense.*"[21]

A close friend of Andrew Carnegie's, a member of his New York circle of literati, had made the same point: The book, said S. B. Elkin, would "exert a wide influence for good on both sides of the Atlantic." Carnegie's statistics were attractive, interesting, "instructive. Apart from these and many other merits, the book will teach our people lessons of loyalty to the Great Republic and inspire more respect and love for our institutions."[22] Both the newspapers and his correspondents underscored the great "debt of gratitude" that America owed Carnegie.[23]

If the newspapers acknowledged the "debt of gratitude" that the country owed Carnegie, his correspondents were, as one might have expected, even more grateful. It mattered of course that many of his correspondents were men who shaped American politics and writing. They hailed him both for his patriotism and his conversion to Americanism. L. S. Metcalf, the editor of the *Forum*, a prominent journal of opinion and literature, congratulated him on "the strength of your book. *You have done a great service to the country of your adoption.*"[24] William Temple Hornaday, a scientist at the Smithsonian, thanked Carnegie for exciting his sense of patriotism. Before reading *Triumphant Democracy* he had had "no conception of the fullness of the blessings that came to me with my American citizenship.... Henceforth my loyalty to my country will be much more pronounced.... One rises from the book with the question, 'Who would not be an American citizen?' ... The country owes you a testimonial for your dedication, which is a confession of faith, an exhortation to loyalty."[25]

Similar comments came from men in official positions, including a few members of Congress. W. W. Phelps, a congressman and a jurist, said he admired Carnegie for many of his accomplishments: "but what I like you most of all is for the intelligent, persistent and ardent love you bear our Democracy. If our country has done much for you, you are repaying it with interest."[26] John Forrest Dillon, a prominent jurist, was grateful that Carnegie had enlarged his understanding of "the destiny of my own country, and for increasing the measure of my love for it."[27]

The theme in all these letters was the same: that in the trialsome days of April and May 1886, Carnegie had affirmed the institutions of the United States, that he was a remarkable patriot, all the more so as he had been raised in a monarchy and been converted to republicanism.

Carnegie's exemplary patriotism elated many of his reviewers. In those cheerless times, it mattered especially that an immigrant was sounding cheers for America. Native-born Americans, said the *Newark Advertiser*, were "diffident about their country, so it is a good thing that the book was written by a non-native. . . . [It] will open the eyes of all who read, be they of foreign birth or to the manor born."[28] The testimony of a naturalized citizen made *Triumphant Democracy* "a book which all Americans must read with pride." His fervor proved his sincerity, and his foreign birth made his spread-eagle cry all the more reassuring. "No native born citizen ever pulled feathers from the tail of the bird of freedom more enthusiastically or to better purpose."[29]

In the same vein, other reviewers found it refreshing that every page glowed with a patriotism that, they hoped, all Americans should possess, and deemed it "refreshing to find that one of our foreign-born citizens . . . [has] a deeper love for the Republic than her native-born sons can know."[30] The editor of the *Boston Pilot* summed it up best for those hailing the patriotism of the remarkable immigrant: "Mr. Carnegie is a Scotchman by birth, but a self-made American citizen, who began at the bottom of the ladder, and is too great a man to be influenced by the sycophancy of his native country, or the silly pride common to so many rich men in his adopted home. America is rich in possessing such citizens, native or adopted."[31]

It was of course important to America's editorial class that Carnegie had calmed their nerves in nerve-racking times. But there was a deeper question they had to address, one that Carnegie had made the central theme of his book: the superiority of American republican institutions over those of Europe, and of the British monarchy in particular. Was the United States still a valid, a soundly based polity, again in comparison with its British kin? Were his premises about the American achievement valid? These are the questions that the scores of foreign travelers to the United States had been raising since the republic's founding. But Carnegie's book had this significance: if it was yet another in the long line of travelers' accounts about the United States, it was the only one written by an inhabitant of the two societies he was comparing. It was therefore the most documented and personally experienced analysis of all of them.

Utilitarian? Surely. Biased? Without a doubt. Central to the comparative analysis of the kindred polities? Therein lay its greatest value.

Were the republic's institutions yet valid? Greatly reassured by Carnegie's book of facts, Rossiter Johnson, in the *Chicago Dial*, concluded that America's Fourth-of-July orators had indeed been telling the truth. He commended the book to "those who are accustomed to fix their eyes upon the defects of American institutions and manners, while ignorantly extolling the supposed superiority of something across the sea."[32] If Americans were dismayed by disclosures of political corruption, said the *Boston Pilot*, they would do well "to examine the greater corruption of a monarchical government, in which corruption is the normal condition of public affairs."[33] The United States conducted its public affairs far better than European governments did.[34] When Carnegie first arrived at our shores, said the *Chicago Evening Herald*, Europe's ruling order awaited "the failure of the republic." But his book proved conclusively that "the genius of history has reserved this virgin continent . . . for her sublimest conquests." It announced to "those effete old European nations the glories of the grandest republic the world has ever seen."[35] What Carnegie had done, said the *Philadelphia Ledger*, was to contrast "the political constitutions of Great Britain and America" and to show "incontestably the superiority of the government of the United States."[36]

How correct were Carnegie's conclusions about the superiority of American institutions? Most of his reviewers were reassured by his repeated insistence that he had diligently checked all his facts and observations: indeed, he was doing nothing more, said his introduction, than offering his readers a palatable and digestible form of masses of statistics. A few reviewers paused to take note of the authenticity of what he said. "All his statements are true inductions from undeniable facts," said the *Springfield [MA] Union*: they will sustain examination. By objectively explaining the reasons for America's great progress and achievement, Carnegie "disposes of several current scares founded on nothing more substantial than false data."[37] Carnegie had "studied the subject very thoroughly," said the *New Haven News*, "and no one is so well informed that he will not find in these pages much that is startling, all the more startling because it is true!"[38] Noting the Pittsburgh industrialist's intent "to prove by solid facts the superiority of republican over monarchical institutions," the *Washington Post* agreed with Carnegie that his facts "will surprise even our best informed citizens concerning the progress and tremendous resources of these States."[39]

How would the English respond to Carnegie's book? "We can imagine the caustic smile with which some British reviewers will contemplate" Carnegie's observations, said the *Brooklyn Times*.[40] The Anglo-American debate had, said the *Chicago Herald*, regrettably consisted of "a score of books of travel prepared by cads, snobs, or blackguards who come here gangrened with prejudice, and on returning have catered to the ignorance and bigotry at home." But because Carnegie had written "freely and intelligently . . . his work will have greater weight in England."[41] However prejudiced the English ruling circles might be against their erstwhile progeny, said the *Chicago Journal*, there was no doubt that "to the great mass of British people, [Carnegie's] book will appeal as revelation."[42] The writer for the *Philadelphia Bulletin* fairly well summed up a widespread American sense of how and why his British reviewers would scorn *Triumphant Democracy*: "His facts cannot be resisted by any but the most obstinate and most dyspeptic of Britons, for whom the book seems to have been especially written. . . . The English critics, if they notice his book at all, will try to pick it to pieces because of a certain literary roughness or unphilosophic method in the construction. But they cannot controvert it, for it is wholly founded on fact."

But defenders of their faith in England were not to be found only across the sea. Regrettably, there were Anglophiles enough on our own soil, said the reviewer. Therefore, "we commend it to all Americans and especially to the class, limited in numbers and in intelligence, that affects to think England and the English superior to America and the Americans."[43] A century after the break from England, there were still deep resonances of the great tractarian debate of the 1770s about the two polities. There was yet reason enough to hail *Triumphant Democracy*, said the *Boston Commercial Bulletin*: the book's "clear, ringing sentences come like a fresh, wholesome gust of sea breeze after the dead atmosphere of a limited class of American periodical literature in which self-depreciation and laudation of England are the chief constituents."[44] Surely part of a continuing transatlantic debate, *Triumphant Democracy* was also, as we shall soon see, part of America's debate with itself, and surely an answer to the neo-Loyalism that declared itself in the journals and salons of the Boston Brahmins.

The importance of *Triumphant Democracy* for most of his American reviewers was that, in that time of fearful doubt, Carnegie had affirmed the republic. The positive reviews came largely from mid-America. More important, the newspapers they spoke for were Republican. It aided their cause that *Triumphant Democracy* affirmed not merely the republic but also the Republican Party that had long held the presidency. That Carnegie had indicted Britain's institutions was, for his favoring reviewers, less important than his validating America's. They agreed with his explanation of America's great industrial progress and particularly with his stressing the role of British-Americans in contributing to that progress. If what America's editorial classes said about *Triumphant Democracy* was part of a transatlantic exchange between the kindred polities, it was no less significantly an internal dialogue between the two major political parties and indeed between the two conflicting groups of Republicans, the regulars and the reformers. Those reviewers who paused to appraise the book as a treatise on politics granted that *Triumphant Democracy* did not stand in the company of the great books. They understood its immediacy, its lively portrait of current actualities, its roots in the statistics of the 1880 census. But that is precisely, for many of Carnegie's reviewers, what enhanced his book's great appeal at that time.

HOWEVER WIDELY America's newspapers acclaimed *Triumphant Democracy*, many reviewers withheld their acclamation. They voiced many doubts about Carnegie's portrait of the American republic. Their voices sounded large. The newspaper editors were men of distinction, including E. L. Godkin, William E. Singerly, Murat Halstead, and Melville E. Stone. However considerable their influence, the newspapers that questioned Carnegie had a relatively moderate circulation, many of them running at just over 15,000; some, however, such as the *New York Star*, the *Philadelphia Record*, and the *Chicago News*, ran, respectively, at 55,000, 107,000, and 162,000. Several of those who questioned Carnegie identified themselves politically as independent; some were Democrats, but the most audible and influential in shaping the course of national politics were the Independent Republicans, those who had grown up in the party of Lincoln and had now come to see it as shackled by corporate greed. These latter-day Republicans spoke a politics of dissent. They were not so much political partisans as suprapartisan: they tended to see both parties as vehicles of corruption. Their mantra could readily have been that the victors were spoiled; they saw politics as a conflict over patronage. They had been Liberal Republicans in 1872; they were Mugwumps in 1884. To them, Grant's had been a sorry presidency; Hayes inherited his piece of patronage from a notorious electoral commision; they could see no palpable difference between Roscoe Conkling and James G. Blaine; Harrison was to them a party hack and Chester Arthur the keeper of the customs house gate. Cleveland seemed a partial redemption, not because he could enact but because he could veto. With some exceptions, the newspapers were located in the northeast, in those pockets of urban sophistication where the genteel reformers dwelled. When informed Europeans came to probe into the workings of the American republic, they were invited into the shaded, shielded parlors and libraries of the older city intelligentsia, whether in Boston, New York, Philadelphia, or in some instances in the District of Columbia. Finding flaws in the United States, several reviewers saw virtues in Europe and, indeed, in Great Britain. One could not say of them that they were latter-day Loyalists, but they belonged to a genealogy that included Emerson and Irving and Parkman and Cooper and Longfellow. In the newer Anglo-American politics that were taking shape during the 1870s and 1880s, they were founding members of the Pan-Anglian sodality.

The initial challenge was on the ground that Carnegie's facts were wrong, a remarkable challenge considering that he had presented *Triumphant Democracy* as a compendium of tirelessly reviewed details, culled from a group of highly respectable authorities. Not so, said the *Boston Beacon*, which closely detailed a long list of errors that littered Carnegie's pages. Are we the nation with the smallest proportion of illiterates? Many nations presented far better scores of literacy than we did. Do we in fact have fixed, permanent fundamental laws? "Our constitution has been changed quite materially since its adoption, and *has occasioned the most destructive war of modern times.*"[45] Carnegie's assertion that the United States had universal suffrage clearly ran against the facts. Our national House of Representatives was very certainly not an "offshoot of the House of Commons," no matter how much Carnegie wished to draw close affinities between the kindred nations. And by the same token, it was seriously questionable that "the American of to-day is certainly more than four-fifths British in his ancestry. Our negroes are native Americans, and our population of Asiatic, Scandinavian, German, Latin, and other non-British antecedents is much larger than Mr. Carnegie allows. Moreover, the Irish are not British." More than that, Carnegie's presentation of the facts was grossly inadequate. His account of American art was rather limited, as was his presentation of the American literary achievement.

More important to his reviewers was that he almost totally passed over what was questionable in the great democracy. Henry George, to whom

Carnegie had sent his book and who was at that very time running for mayor in New York, made this point very succinctly: "You have given only one side of the picture, ignoring the shadows."[46] The same point was made by the *Boston Gazette*: "Mr. Carnegie has taken for consideration the sunny side of our life as a nation; the shadows he does not touch, except incidentally."[47] Talking about *Triumphant Democracy*, the "Senator," a commentator anonymously featured in the Independent Republican *Brooklyn Times*, acerbically noted that "we have made many blunders, many errors, many almost criminal mistakes, and . . . we are even now reaping the whirlwind in our strikes and labor troubles and all the entanglements of labor and capital."[48] The *Rome [NY] Sentinel*, a daily Democratic journal, more than agreed. "The vexed question of capital and labor is not touched upon and if, while reading the book we should hear any one say 'strikes,' we would say 'that must be something happening in Europe.'"[49] The strikes and troubles did not mar Carnegie's pages. Nothing was shaking the American terrain as much as the bitter strife between capital and labor and nothing was as conspicuously absent from his pages. Clinton Rossiter, in the *Chicago Dial*, a monthly literary journal, noted that in some instances Carnegie's rhetoric outran his facts: "he forgets the wholesale suppression of the votes of the freedmen in the South . . . and he forgets the Mexican War."[50] The Republican *Dallas News* rejected Carnegie's vaunting of American political institutions, warning that they "have not prevented the growth of social conditions full of danger and complexity. The chief features of unequal reward, by governmental license and encouragement to monopolies, are becoming as conspicuous in the United States as in Europe, and Democracy will have to do something about this or its long triumph will be rather problematical, to say the least."[51] Again, these "chief features" were nowhere mentioned in *Triumphant Democracy*.

The Nation, an independent journal under the editorship of English-born E. L. Godkin, rejected Carnegie as an unmitigated Philistine and an undisguised worshipper of material success. Godkin found unacceptable the celebration, in *Triumphant Democracy*, of electing judges. "The proposition," said the reviewer, is "beautifully illustrated by the existing labor troubles." He derided Carnegie's counsel that Britain follow the American example in her handling of "less powerful and advanced nations" such as, "for example, of the Indian tribes."[52] If the United States was so rich in agriculture, asked the *New York Graphic*, why did it not share its vast resources with Europe in some way rather than compel Europe to spend its monies coming here to buy American farm goods?

Carnegie misrepresented the principles of our government. Should Britain indeed have a body similar to the American Senate? What the writing industrialist had failed to mention, said the *Graphic*, is that "the Senate does not directly represent the people, but the sovereignty of the individual States which compose the Union." Carnegie was wrong, moreover, in comparing the expense of political campaigns in the United States and in England: he had made erroneous assumptions in describing the politics of both countries. Most telling, in the reviewer's deprecation of Carnegie's argument, was the industialists's plea for free trade for other nations and protection for America. "When it is remembered that [he] was enabled to make most of his money out of the protective tariff it is not difficult to appreciate his reason for advocating its continuance and endeavoring to show that it has been the cause of all the industrial prosperity which the country has seen." In sum? "The United States, for all that Carnegie had made it out to be, was no more "an earthly paradise . . . than England, France, or Germany."[53]

The Democratic *New York Star*, a daily whose circulation ran over 55,000, and which had supported Cleveland in 1884, voiced several of the same reservations. Carnegie's picture of our legislators and judges did not show the dark side of the picture. The fact is, as British readers would well know, referring to the Tweed scandals, that "the municipality of the greatest city in the Union is on trial for a criminal offence, and that this is no novelty in American life." In Carnegie's paradisical democracy, "there ought to be no poverty," but the fact was that there is great poverty in New York and in many other centers of American life. As to the great virtue of our presidential politics, the election of 1884 was hardly less scandalous: the national vote was so close that "an additional $50,000 would have given the win to Blaine rather than Cleveland!" Carnegie's American canvas was too bright. Impressive though they were, his facts were incomplete. His inferences were questionable. His omissions were glaring.[54] The *Philadelphia Record*, a daily independent paper with a circulation of over 100,000, added its strong misgivings about Carnegie's presentation of how the American government works. "His treatment . . . does not portray a very close study of the Constitution, of the real character of the United States Senate, or of the powers of the President and his Cabinet."[55]

The *Star* faulted Carnegie with more than a charge of omissions. He could be faulted even more seriously with a charge of commission. Here the question touched the very basis on which Carnegie had built his monument to America's achievement: her principle of political equality which he deemed the essence of her free institutions. Carnegie, said the reviewer, had shown only one side of the medal. "Every medal has its reverse. A democracy, no less than a monarchy, must work through a human organism, and is subject to the imperfections of everything human." True, the prospect of American citizenship, based on political equality, had attracted European immigrants and may have been the source of some part of the American achievement. But "we cannot accept [Carnegie's] statement without serious modification." Nor do we believe "that the possession of liberty is a panacea for all human woes." If it was true that "America is, on the whole, the most prosperous country on the earth," Carnegie had erred in "asserting that it is wholly due to republican institutions." And here the *Star* moved to a critique sounded widely in the British press: "It is questionable whether any form of government could have successfully hindered the progress of a country whose resources are practically inexhaustible and whose people have a habit of sweeping away obstacles without thinking of looking to government for aid or assistance. Our glorious climate and fertile soil . . . are *not* heirlooms bequeathed to us by the framers of the Constitution." Climate, soil, and yes the hard work of inflowing immigrants had contributed greatly to the American achievement. The newcomers "assist in driving the desert before them, converting unproductive regions into fertile territories, and with the benefit of their labor [and] personal fortune . . . help in the aggregate to swell the national wealth."[56]

Doubts about *Triumphant Democracy* went beyond the premises and argument of the book: they went to Carnegie himself. (In most American reviews, as we have seen, he had been hailed for his achievements, his conversion to the virtues of Americanism, his worldwide travels and experience, his literary prominence, his widecast philanthropies.) But several reviewers questioned not only the book but the man himself. Said E. L. Godkin in *The Nation*, "It is to be feared that Mr. Matthew Arnold would regard [Carnegie] as an unmitigated Philistine. He is an undisguised worshipper of material success, and delights in big figures."[57] The review in the *Chicago News* concurred: the fact of it was that "dear Mr. Arnold, as Mr. Carnegie calls him, would find him very much of a Philistine." *Triumphant Democracy* was "a book of brag." Carnegie's writing had no style. "He is entirely without the historical sense."[58] Far from promoting Anglo-American affinity, Carnegie, said the *Boston Courier*, perfectly represented "the ideal of Yankee vulgarity and obstreperousness as conceived by the average English mind. . . . No native born American could hope to rival him in his peculiarly blatant offensive patriotism."[59] It was fair to judge Carnegie by his book's cover: one could not hope to produce "a book cover so characteristically ugly" as the one adorning *Triumphant Democracy*, with its flamboyant flaming red and gold cartoons, all shouting a republican message. His book, said the reviewer, bespoke Carnegie's offensive mannerisms, his egotism, his lack of culture.

Why had Carnegie written his massive volume? Carnegie's close interest in British politics was well known. So too was his having sponsored a whole chain of radical newspapers in England.[60] *Triumphant Democracy*, the reviewer for the *Dallas News* concluded, fit into a larger Carnegie scheme. "In fact, it is tolerably evident that the work is essentially a campaign document for use by the British Liberals."[61] The charge against the industrialist author was not unfair: as Gladstone's advocate in British politics, Carnegie was indeed warmly supporting the Liberal prime minister's jousting with the Conservatives' Lord Salisbury. More than that, Carnegie's personal interest in proclaiming American institutions had more immediate, self-serving purposes, as several of his reviewers noted. Said the *New York Graphic*, "When it is remembered that Mr. Carnegie was enabled to make most of his money out of the protective tariff, it is not difficult to appreciate the reason for his advocating its continuance and endeavoring to show that it has been the cause of all the industrial prosperity which the country has seen."[62]

FOR THE LARGER PART, in sum, the American reviewers looked at Carnegie's book favorably and in considerable measure because he had looked so very favorably at America. Even those who had reservations about his portrait of the republic and about the premises of his argument found positive things to say about his book. The reason for their approval lay largely in the reassurance Carnegie's book gave them in those uncertain times. If we are not the best of polities, so ran the lesson offered by the rich industrialist, we are far better than the most advanced nations of the Western world. And far better than Great Britain, the world's foremost power and, most important to us, our kindred society. It was not only the troubled times that gave *Triumphant Democracy* its importance: it was also that these were important centennial years for the republic, years of taking stock and seeing things writ large. The years from 1876 to 1887 marked continuous anniversaries of the critical years from the founding of the republic to the adoption of the Constitution of 1787. Carnegie's book hailed half a century of the democracy's progress. A book of hard facts, it was a major contribution to the high-sounding odes with which America's public figures were celebrating the republic.

Carnegie's reviewers constituted an editorial class in the United States, a guiding force of the public opinion that so many commentators, James Bryce most prominently, had found to be the mainspring of American politics. Ordinarily they voiced the party affiliations of their newspapers, dividing largely into Republican, Democratic, or in some instances independent camps, and speaking to the larger issues that then faced the republic, including adjusting tariff schedules, distributing the spoils of office, managing the flow of immigration, containing the battle between capital and labor, or devising a financial and banking system that would serve a rapidly growing nation.

Carnegie's book appeared in turbulent and stocktaking times. Looking inward, the reviewers saw a landscape that seemed convulsed with troubles. But Carnegie summoned his reviewers and readers to look outward: to compare their nation with others. Looking both inward and outward, the United States could indeed be seen as having taken gigantic steps during the half-century that Carnegie had focused on. If most of his American reviewers judged Carnegie so favorably, it was largely because he had so favorably judged America. Even those who expressed reservations about it were reassured by Carnegie's very positive evangel. Very few reviews were uniformly negative.

How far had *Triumphant Democracy* succeeded in promoting that transatlantic interchange between the United States and the United Kingdom that he had declared as one of the major aims of his book? Not far at all. Some of his American reviewers hoped for a greater affinity with the motherland, but more took the occasion to fall into traditional views of Britain as a land of snobs and effetes. The centenary celebrations encouraged more hostility than affection.

It was simple enough to explain the larger difference between his British and American reviewers. Carnegie had vaunted America at the expense of Britain. The British establishment responded self-defensively, challenging both Carnegie's premises and his effrontery. American reviewers, beset with serious doubts about their country, found reassurance in *Triumphant Democracy*.

Where did *Triumphant Democracy* stand in the array of books about the United States? Was it ephemeral or a classic or something in between? Some reviewers, even those who thought well of it, said that as a commentary of the American polity, it did not rank with Tocqueville or the *Federalist Papers*; but one or two thought that it did. What only a very few of the reviewers could have known was that in fairly short order (indeed, just two years later) would be appearing the three-volume canvassing of *The American Commonwealth* by James Bryce, an Oxford don, an M.P., a member of the British establishment, and, as if to enhance his credentials further vis-à-vis Carnegie's, a Scotsman. His book was truly magisterial, the product of a long experience with America, and offered a more balanced judgment of the kindred polities than Carnegie's. The important item for us is that both books, each prominent in its own way, were part of a larger colloquy between the kindred polities and that both Carnegie and Bryce belonged to the same Pan-Anglian sodality that was reshaping the contours of British-American diplomacy and politics in the late nineteenth century.

7

The Pan-Anglian Persuasion

THE APPEARANCE OF Sir Charles Dilke's *Greater Britain* in 1868 marked a new turn in the British-American relationship. His preface sounded its principal theme: "Through America, England is speaking to the world."[1] That Dilke's book gained a wide popularity and influence in Britain signaled a changing British perspective on the connection between the two nations. He spoke in particular for the growing group of British Pan-Anglians. *Greater Britain* manifested the emergence of a set of convictions about the British-American relationship that might best be termed a persuasion. It was hardly a formal creed, and it contained no rigorous articles of belief. There were variations of orientation and emphasis in the way its many adherents perceived the interplay of the kindred nations. But there was a larger group of ideas to which the Pan-Anglians subscribed and which, indeed, identified them. And though they came from different walks of life, they were alike in being makers and leaders of opinion. Standing at the threshold of the democratic age, they were conscious of the importance of public opinion, of its malleability, of their own role in educating it. They were also conscious of standing outside the frame of attitudes and conventions of their respective national communities. Understanding, indeed fearing, the dangers of misguided public opinion, they wished to seize the opportunity of guiding it. Conditions were favorable, they felt, for reaffecting relations between the older country and the newer, for healing wounds, for bringing both nations together on the meeting ground of their common ideals. In the face of a new Europe, with powerful states and different (therefore threatening) ways of life, an entente between America and Britain seemed to them not only desirable but necessary.[2]

In the Pan-Anglian glossary, two terms recurred: "the Anglo-Saxon race" and "the English-speaking peoples."[3] The special virtues of Britain and America, many Pan-Anglians believed, derived from their Anglo-Saxon legacy and from their belonging to the Anglo-Saxon race. As used by Hitler and some of his ideological forebears, the word "race" has taken on particular notoriety. In the nineteenth century, it had a variety of connotations, some relatively neutral and benign, others less so. In the main, it was used to denote a group of individuals who shared common characteristics of ethnicity and traditions.[4] But the demarcation itself served inevitably to single out as worthy those who were members of a particular race and to designate as less worthy, by a contradistinction that could only be invidious, those who were not. The term "the English-speaking peoples" was certainly more benign and neutral. It signified a program no less than a conviction, more a prospect than a retrospect, for it said, in effect, that what had not been gained by history could be gained by language. Through that medium, of course, the great institutions of Britain and America could be transmitted and spread. It is difficult to draw a categorical distinction between the ways the Pan-Anglians used the terms "Anglo-Saxon race" and "English-speaking peoples." Some used one term, some another, and some both interchangeably. Indeed, said the Earl of Rosebery, a prominent Pan-Anglian, "whether you call it British or Anglo-Saxon, or whatever you call it, the fact is that the race is there and the sympathy of race is there."[5]

In whatever terms, Pan-Anglians on both sides of the Atlantic, including among them the most eminent Victorians of their generation, announced the details of their vision of the British-American relationship. Joseph Chamberlain urged closer connections between Britain and America, for both were, as he saw it, dedicated to the defense of "the ideals of the Anglo Saxon race of humanity, justice, freedom, and the equality of opportunity."[6] Albion Tourgee also hoped for an increasing affinity between both nations, confident that it would help guarantee world peace as well as "the maintenance of those ideals which the Anglo-Saxon holds above any consideration of material or political advantage."[7] Addressing the Committee for the Celebration of the Centennial of the American Constitution, John Bright expressed a common Pan-Anglian hope: "As you advance in the second century of your national life, may we not ask that our two nations may become one people?"[8] In the later days of the Civil War, Bright wrote an eminent American historian: "I have been a friend of your country . . . and I live in the expectation that from you much will be learned that will advance the cause of freedom: not only in Europe, but throughout the world."[9]

Conan Doyle dedicated *The White Company* (1890) "To the Hope of the Future, the Reunion of English-speaking Races." Doyle expressed the consciousness of British Pan-Anglians that Britain could no longer claim to be the principal power in the English-speaking world. Writing from the United States in 1894, he said: "The center of gravity of race is over here, and we have got to readjust ourselves."[10] In the shifting balance between the kindred nations, in the revived community of their values, what then would be the British-American, this new (or renewed) individual? Some prominent Britons had clear answers: "We are all Americans now." "I feel as proud of the Stars and Stripes as I do of the Union Jack."[11] The most searching answer perhaps was that of Henry James, Pan-Anglian par excellence, who made the fusion of both societies his commitment and his art: "I can't look at the English-American world, or feel about them, anymore, save as a big Anglo-Saxon total, destined to such an amount of melting together that an insistence on their difference becomes more and more idle and pedantic. . . . I have not the least hesitation in saying that I aspire to write in such a way that it would be impossible to an outsider to say whether I am . . . an American writing about England or an Englishman writing about America."[12]

WHAT WERE THE TENETS OF Pan-Anglian belief? Because the Pan Anglians were above all writers and publicists, the literature one could cite in answering the question is vast.[13] For our purposes, it will suffice to center on two men, a Briton and an American, Sir Charles Dilke and John R. Dos Passos, and the principal book in which each advanced his ideas. Born in 1843 into the English aristocracy, Dilke achieved his fame as a committed democrat. A member of Parliament, he espoused many of the progressive causes of the day, including the move to disestablish the monarchy and set up a British republic. It appeared, in the early 1880s, that he would succeed Gladstone to the Liberal premiership, but his career was virtually ended, early in 1886, by his involvement in a divorce scandal in which he was named as co-respondent. Up to that point, together with his closest supporter Joseph Chamberlain he had led the energetic parliamentary band of radical reformers. Both he and Chamberlain were ardent progressives and ardent Pan-Anglians, a fact that discloses how the example of America, however slackening the appeal to it in British politics, continued yet to serve British radicals as a guide to the remaking of their nation's institutions. Dilke established very early his intellectual leadership of the Pan-Anglian movement. His *Greater Britain*, almost surely the most influential statement of the Pan-Anglian persuasion, appeared when he was twenty-five years old.

The book was an account of Dilke's travels in English-speaking countries in the years 1866 and 1867. He had, he said, followed England round the world, visiting lands that were English-speaking or English-governed, the principal ones being the United States, Canada, Australia, and India. The guiding idea in his long journey was "a conception, however imperfect, of the grandeur of our race, already girdling the earth, which it is destined, perhaps, eventually to overspread."[14]

Everywhere he went he saw a conflict of ideals between the English and the natives, between what he called the "dearer" races and the "cheaper" ones, between those who, to his mind, carried the progressive beliefs of civilization and those who clung to beliefs that were retrogressive. Wherever they had colonized and established their dominion, the English had extirpated the "cheaper" races. The issue of the conflict was clear to him. He was persuaded that the races would not blend, "that the dearer are, on the whole, likely to destroy the cheaper peoples, and that Saxondom will rise triumphant from the doubtful struggle." The English would triumph by numbers no less than by culture, and over their European rivals no less than over the dark-skinned races they were ruling. "No possible series of events can prevent the English race itself in 1970 numbering 300 millions of beings of one national character and one tongue. Italy, Spain, France, Russia become pigmies by the side of such a people."[15]

That the English were spreading their dominion over the face of the globe was surely desirable. The "mission" of the English race was to make "it impossible that the peace of Mankind on earth should depend on the will of a single man." Where the English went, they brought liberty. In this respect, the other European nations had failed singularly. "The map of the world will show that freedom exists only in the homes of the English race ... America, Australia, Britain, the homes of our race, are as yet the only dwelling-spots of freedom." In time, India would also "be fit for freedom."[16]

Regarded in this way, America, Australia, and India were of the utmost significance in shaping the course of world affairs. They represented a "Greater Britain," carrying English ideas to the distant parts of the globe. Which section of the race would triumph—the British, the American, or the Australian—was of little moment. What mattered was the victory of the race as a whole, for "the power of English laws and English principles of government is not merely an English question: its continuance is essential to the freedom of mankind."[17]

In Dilke's image of a Greater Britain, the United States stood large. It surged with English vitality, grew with English fecundity, triumphed over the cheaper races with English superiority, advanced the level of civilization with English freedom. For all its impressive spectacles, for all its diversity of ethnic and religious groups, "there is not in America a greater wonder than the Englishman himself, for it is to this continent that you must come to find him in full possession of his powers." If the English were everywhere increasing, the growth of American numbers was staggering. By 1930, Dilke ventured to predict, there would be 250 million English living in the United States alone. The apparently infinite variety of American types should not deceive one, for the land was a vast crucible: "they are run into an English mould: Alfred's laws and Chaucer's tongue are theirs whether they would or not." "It is only when one has left the mind-staggering diversity of cities and men, land contours and institutions that there rises in the mind an image that soars above all local prejudice: that of the America of the law-abiding, mighty people who are imposing English institutions on the world."[18]

Because it was the key constituency of Greater Britain, because its power was equal to that of homeland of the race, America had to be understood and befriended. If Americans are offended by the way Britons have conducted themselves, it is because they so much respect British opinion. By recognizing the Confederate rebels as belligerents, by confronting the North in the *Trent* Affair, Great Britain had harshly disaffected American opinion. It was best that both states arbitrate their differences. "Let friends settle their disputes as friends." Having received her language and history from England, "America offers the English race the moral directorship of the globe, by ruling mankind through Saxon institutions and the English tongue. Through America, England is speaking to the world."[19]

John Randolph Dos Passos, an American lawyer, was far less prominent a figure than Dilke and, in this sense, a more typical Pan-Anglian. A specialist in corporate and banking law, he became the confidential adviser of many Wall Street firms. The author, moreover, of books on stock exchanges, commercial trusts, and the Interstate Commerce Act, he opposed the federal regulation of trusts, calling the Sherman Antitrust Law an unnecessary and dangerous piece of legislation. In *The Anglo-Saxon Century*, which appeared in 1903, he urged "the establishment of a common, interchangeable citizenship between all English-speaking Nations and Colonies by the abrogation of the naturalization laws of the United States and the British Empire, so that the citizens of each can, at will, upon landing in the other's territory, become citizens of any of the countries dominated by these governments."[20] He laid out with painstaking exactness the terms of alliance between Britain and America. His plan showed how far the Pan-Anglian movement had gone in the three-and-a-half decades since the publication of Dilke's *Greater Britain*. The fraternity of those proposing a closer collaboration between Britain and America had grown in numbers, power, and enthusiasm. The Pan-Anglian persuasion had advanced from a recognition of the power of shared ideas to the idea of shared power. In charting the course of the Pan-Anglian movement, it is fair to say that the first edition of Carnegie's *Triumphant Democracy* certainly bespoke, in 1886, the movement's growth, arguing as it did the increasing assimilation of British institutions and urging the introduction of American republican forms into Britain. Indeed, in a new chapter that he wrote for the second edition in 1893, Carnegie showed how rapidly the Pan-Anglian idea was advancing. He proposed a British-American union, suggesting simply, without a lawyer's finesse and under his own conviction as to where power and wealth stood between the two polities, that Britain be merged into an enlarged, federated United States of America.

To Dos Passos, the facts of history underwrote compellingly the need for a British-American alliance. The great European powers were heavily armed, and militarism threatened peace. An "Anglo-Saxon aggregation" could "arrest and destroy this dreadful modern tendency." America and Britain stood at a new juncture in their international relations, facing new responsibilities and contingencies, as a result of their respective wars with Spain and with the Boers, and the mutual understanding they had shown each other in their difficulties was surely a basis for an even closer entente. No other great powers than Britain and the United States were capable of assuming the guardianship of the future of mankind. Properly read, a millennium and a half of history showed the continuous progress of the Anglo-Saxon race "as it journeyed from its primitive, formative condition to its present enlightenment." To cap his argument, Dos Passos devoted his last chapter to quotations from notable Britons and Americans, showing that, for the larger part, they too supported the idea of a Pan Anglian alliance.[21]

Dos Passos returned repeatedly to the essence of the Pan-Anglian perception: that both polities shared common values and institutions. "We belong to the same national family." America's most prominent citizens—her presidents, statesmen, jurists, soldiers, financiers, writers, and scholars—were of British descent. "We speak the same language," he said. We read the same literature, have the same political institutions, and the same laws, legal customs, and modes of judicial procedure. We share "the same religious impulses, thoughts, freedom, education and growth."[22] As he saw it, the present circumstances of Britain and America, and the new condition of world affairs, made an alliance between them imperative. The Anglo-Saxon people had to assume power. With the conviction of a seer, Dos Passos kept reiterating his rhetorical questions: "Are we the chosen race of Israel? Are we the peoples of the earth elected to lead the van of civilisation and peace?"[23] His answer was a Pan-Anglian's sermon and vision.

> The course of this great race cannot be retarded. It must go on. It must move forward in the mission to spread Christianity and civilisation everywhere, and to open up the undeveloped part of the world to the expanding demands of commerce, and of all that commerce, liberally conducted, implies. Let us take up together the work so magnificently performed by the United States and by England down to the commencement of this century. Once for all let prejudices be cast aside. Let us unite in a great English-speaking family. Let us be content to learn from each other. And when the curtain of the twenty-first century is raised, may the successful anglicisation of the world be revealed; may the real spirit of our institutions and laws prevail everywhere, and the English language have become the universal dialect of mankind.[24]

Dos Passos shared with Dilke the essential tenets of Pan-Anglian belief. Whether in exercising their dominion over backward peoples on other continents or in seeking security vis-à-vis the unstable nations immediately around them, they had a mission to perform: to bring peace by means of their joined power and to advance civilization by means of their progressive ideals. During the later decades of the nineteenth century, Pan-Anglianism remained a persuasion about culture. It was part of a larger set of beliefs held by the North Atlantic nations that man's cultural history showed continuous progress and that Western culture was clearly superior to any other. By the turn of the century, Pan-Anglianism changed from having been a persuasion about culture to one about the need for using power to guarantee that culture. From having been a movement among intellectuals in Britain and the United States to effect a rapprochement between the hitherto estranged polities, it became, with a considerably enlarged membership, a movement for using British-American power to enlighten the world with British-American culture. Men of intelligence and sophistication, the Pan-Anglians were no simpleminded altruists and hardly unaware that advancing culture and advancing power were two aspects of the same act, that remaking the world in their own image was a political no less than a civilizing mission.

IN THE PAN-ANGLIAN PERSUASION, as in any other, the past was an indispensable component of the present. Proposals for reform, political and social, are almost necessarily theories of history. Edward Augustus Freeman, in some ways the pivotal figure in Pan-Anglian historiography, summed up this intelligence in his famous aphorism that "history is past politics, and politics present history." The Pan-Anglians shared with their age the sense that man's experience bespoke progress and that it was governed by universal laws. The past was, to them, a record of continuity, and beneath the superficial appearance of cataclysm and severance, one could find the unbroken course of social evolution. The Pan-Anglians rewrote the past in two principal ways. They saw British-American history as part of a continuous Anglo-Saxon experience. And, in their account of the relations between Great Britain and her North American colonies in the seventeenth and eighteenth centuries, they began to find fault with the policies of their own leaders and to rehabilitate their erstwhile foes.

The key tenets of the Anglo-Saxon hypothesis constituted something of an orthodoxy among many British historians during the third quarter of the nineteenth century and was borrowed from them by the new "scientific" school of American historians in the 1870s and 1880s. They believed, in essence, that the English ideas of liberty, constitutionalism, and local government originated among the Teutonic tribes of northern Germany, who implanted them in Britain when they invaded the island during the fifth and sixth centuries. Surviving the Norman Conquest, these ideas served as the rationale for Parliament's attack on the crown in the seventeenth century and as the basis of colonial government in English America. The Anglo-Saxon hypothesis had many proponents among British historians, including John Kemble, William Stubbs, John Richard Green, James Froude, and Edward Freeman.[25] It was Freeman who was particularly important in directing American historians to a study of the Anglo-Saxon past, serving as he did as an intellectual mentor to Herbert Baxter Adams and the newly founded school of history at the Johns Hopkins University. Declared Freeman: "To me the English-speaking commonwealth on the American mainland is simply one part of the great English folk, as the English-speaking kingdom in the European island is another part."[26] Adams, who had organized graduate historical studies at the Johns Hopkins when it opened its doors in 1876, and who was central to the growth of professional history in the United States, very largely echoed Freeman's postulates: "It is just as improbable that *free local institutions* should spring up without a germ along American shores as that English wheat should have grown here without planting. . . . The town and village life of New England is as truly the reproduction of Old English types as those again are reproductions of the village community system of the ancient Germans."[27]

John Fiske, perhaps the most popular historian of his age, widely disseminated his Pan-Anglian views. Among his most influential works was a series of lectures he had given to large audiences and that were published in 1885 under the title of *American Political Ideas, Viewed from the Standpoint of Universal History*. Humanity's story, he said, could be understood only in terms of evolution and continuity. What Stubbs and Freeman had taught us about the Germanic origins of England's admirable political institutions was true. It was no less true that England's colonies in America were a "highly-civilized community, representing the ripest political ideas of England." Only now, a century later, could we see the true magnificence of the American Revolution, which was "a struggle sustained by a part of the English people in behalf of principles that time has shown to be equally dear to all. And so the issue only made it apparent to an astonished world that instead of *one* there were now *two* Englands, alike prepared to work with might and main toward the political regeneration of mankind." Fiske shared with his fellow Pan-Anglians their sense of a transcendent England and of a British-American mission. The hegemony of English institutions will spread, Fiske was certain. The world's business will be conducted in English. Even the nations of Europe will learn America's lesson of federalism: they will form a United States of Europe and, as a result, wars will no longer be fought. The principles of the English-speaking peoples will then have triumphed. "Indeed, only when such a state of things has begun to be realized, can Civilization, as sharply demarcated from Barbarism, be said to have fairly begun. Only then can the world be said to have become truly Christian."[28]

The Anglo-Saxon hypothesis was a way of looking at human experience, particularly European. It was a device for proving the superiority of one national culture over another, a proof, in those decades when scientists had established evolution as history and historians sought to establish history as evolution, that had to reach into the primitive times of the nation to have any ring of authenticity. A reconstruction of the past that made the future inevitably British-American, it was a way of looking over all creation and pronouncing it remarkably good because it was remarkably English. But if the Pan-Anglians, American and British, had captured the past for their own political culture against the outsiders, there remained yet the task of reconciling the two branches of the race to each other. There remained, after all, the not easily glossed over revolution of the Americans against the British, and however much the British had in their own history books shunted aside the American story, their war for independence was implacably central to the Americans. If rapprochement was the Pan-Anglian program for British-American politics, it was no small part of that rapprochement to attempt a sympathetic understanding of what had led to the rupture between the kindred peoples a century before. Thus there appeared in Britain and in the United States interpretations of the War for American Independence that moved off from the standard national ones that had hitherto prevailed.

The task of the Pan-Anglian historian was, in effect, to abjure so much of the past policy of his nation as to underwrite and promote the friendliness in its present policy. In Britain, this was done most grandly by George Otto Trevelyan, who, together with his more famous uncle, Thomas Babington Macaulay, belonged to the "Whig" school of historiography. Whig historians ritually condemned kings and their ministers in whatever century, and "voted reform" at every point of constitutional crisis in the nineteenth century: 1832, 1867, and 1884. Trevelyan was for many years an M.P., a devoted Liberal, and a leader in franchise reform. He was also a member of Gladstone's second ministry. His histories were, in this way, a retrospective diary. His six-volume *American Revolution* castigated George III and his advisers, admired the rebellious Americans, and supported the conciliatory moves toward the colonials by Edmund Burke as well as their stalwart defense by Charles James Fox, on whose rise to fame

Trevelyan had earlier written.[29] In the United States, a benevolent view of British policy during the revolutionary era was advocated by the "imperial school" of American colonial history, whose principal members were Herbert Levi Osgood, George Louis Beer, and Charles McLean Andrews. Their larger conviction was that far too little was known by Americans about Britain's policies, needs, institutions, and attitudes during the troubled years before and during the revolutionary crisis. All three rejected mere patriotism as a basis for understanding the relationship between Britain and her mainland colonies, arguing for an imperial view of the relationship rather than one that was exclusively American.[30]

While not formally considered to have been one of the members of the "imperial school," Moses Coit Tyler was every bit as concerned as they were to promote the Pan-Anglian view of the British-American past. This he regarded as his particular responsibility in his *Literary History of the American Revolution, 1763–1783*, in which he undertook to present "the several stages of thought and emotion through which the American people passed during the two decades of the struggle which resulted in our national Independence." A "new breed of scholars," he said, was rewriting the history of those decades "in the light of larger evidence, and under the direction of a more disinterested and a more judicial spirit." He was especially concerned to show that there were two parties in contention at that time—loyalists as well as revolutionaries—and to give a fair hearing to those who argued against seceding from the British commonwealth. It was unjust, Tyler said, to continue branding the "Tories" as men who were profligate, unprincipled, or reckless. The truth was that they contained "a very considerable portion of the most refined, thoughtful, and conscientious people in the colonies."[31] We ought to dispel very grave errors that we have long been making in our approach to the Loyalists, errors that continue to be found in popular American writings on the movement for independence. The Loyalists were not "a part of mere negation and obstruction . . . they also had positive political ideas, as well as precise measures in creative statesmanship." They were not opposed to altering relations between the mother country and the colonies; they sought "to reform through reconciliation, rather than reform through separation." They too were patriots, "nowhere lacking in love for their native country, or in zeal for its liberty, or in willingness to labor, or fight, or even to die, for what they conceived to be its interest."[32] Tyler questioned the premises of those who pushed for separation from Britain. And he proceeded to entertain serious doubts about that great pronouncement of the American Revolution, the Declaration of Independence itself. The Declaration was an overly praised production, said Tyler, a "patchwork of sweeping propositions of somewhat doubtful validity." Full of "verbal glitter and sound," it was "at the best . . . an example of florid political declamation belonging to the sophomoric period of our national life, a period which, as we flatter ourselves, we have now outgrown."[33]

Tyler's preface announced the larger cause he believed his intellectual history of the American Revolution would serve. He considered the conflict between Britain and America a period of tragedy and pathos, "the birth time of a most bitter race feud . . . altogether needless . . . between the two great branches of a race which, at this moment, holds an historic opportunity, not only the most extensive and the most splendid, but the most benignant, that was ever attained by any similar group of human beings upon this planet."[34] The feud had gone on far too long. It was time "to bring together once more into sincere friendship, into a rational and sympathetic moral unity, these divided members of a family capable, if in substantial harmony, of leading the whole human race upward to all the higher planes of culture and happiness." To do this was, indeed, "an object which, in our time, draws into its service the impassioned desires, the hopes, the prayers, the labors, of many of the noblest men and women in Great Britain and in America." His history, he trusted, would serve that object. He hoped it would help "the promotion of a better understanding, of a deeper respect, of a kindlier mood on both sides of the ocean."[35] They were all there, the details of the Pan-Anglian's sense of politics, history, and society: the lofty mission of the English race; the tragic feud between its two branches; the need for their reconciliation; the work of the prominent men and women in both nations on behalf of this high cause; and the use of the past, judiciously rewritten, as an instrument for serving the present.

WHAT WERE THE principal features of Pan-Anglianism? It was a forward-looking persuasion. As a transatlantic fraternity, its adherents were, in some respects, comparable to the abolitionists in Great Britain and the United States who, in the 1830s and 1840s, had pooled their moral energies to redeem the white Anglo-Saxon Protestant world. They were comparable also to the radicals of the 1760s and 1770s who, in both polities, argued on the ground of natural rights and an ulterior justice against a government they deemed oligarchic and ethically bankrupt. The Pan-Anglians were above all reformers, spurred as well by a sense of moral purpose, working with the consciousness of a mission, seeing the English-speaking people as the vanguard of mankind. What impelled them most immediately was their wish to reform their own societies. That the United States and Great Britain were, by the 1870s, evolving broadly analogous institutions made it almost inevitable that reformers in one society should use the other as a yardstick for achieving the kind of change they considered desirable and that indeed the other society should suggest to them the reforms they should work for. For British Pan-Anglians, as indeed for all British reformers, the question was: should their institutions be Americanized, and to what degree? For those persuaded that Britain had to change, America could yet be appealed to as a model. In considering how to relieve the social strains and stresses of later Victorian Britain, British Pan-Anglians could yet ponder the transferability of such American formulas as the principle of federalism, the separation of powers, the disestablishment of religion, the prohibition of a hereditary aristocracy, indeed, the installation of a republic. American reformers, on the other hand, did not propose the anglicization of American life; the very suggestion was ideologically impermissible. The principles of British society continued to represent, in the official American political culture, the traditional antithesis. But in the republic of long-hallowed "purity," a sacerdotal class could say that there had been grievous lapses from purity, and this is precisely what the American Pan-Anglians did in their appeal to the example of the British civil service as a device for restoring American government to its pristine republican honesty.

The Pan-Anglians belonged to a single generation. They were, so many of them, born in the 1830s. In 1835 alone were born Albert Venn Dicey, Charles Francis Adams, Jr., and Andrew Carnegie. And 1838, another annus mirabilis in Pan-Anglian nativity, saw the birth of James Bryce, John Morley, George Otto Trevelyan, and Henry Adams. As younger men, they smarted, almost all of them, under the hostile neutrality of Lord Palmerston's government toward the United States during the Civil War. They rode in the wake of the new cordiality between the two nations that followed the arbitration of the *Alabama* claims. They came into their own in the 1870s, into important positions as writers of note, editors of major national journals, university professors, men of business, key members of political parties and of ministries. The suggestions that Stanley Elkins and Eric McKitrick have made about the founding fathers as young men of the revolution is apt here: for the Pan-Anglians were young men of their own significantly transformed world.[36] They were bursting with energy, initiative, and ambition, looking for a wide berth for their talents, disdaining their elders for not being able to rise above the limits, indeed the parochialism, of a straitly national view.

The Pan-Anglians were an intelligentsia. The nature and role of an intelligentsia vary, of course, from one polity and time to another. What made the American and British Pan-Anglians similar and, in some roles, broadly collegial, was that they were writers, editors, publicists, and university men seeking to play an active role in public affairs, to shape the course of political life, to reform their respective societies to the measure of their own basic premises. They functioned in essentially liberal democratic societies, as opposed to authoritarian ones, and therefore had legal sanction for their role as critics in such societies, the one disestablished, the other passing through the straits of disestablishment. They played the role of a priestly class, appealing not to Christian doctrine, but, as seemed more fitting in those metaphysics-eroding years of positivism and Darwinism, to the higher laws of what they deemed progressive civilization. (The religion and priesthood of Marxism were as yet a fist, no bigger than a man's becloudedness.) They sought to establish their position in society by means of the Pan-Anglian vision they projected, or to use that vision to compensate them for the position they felt they had lost. In appealing to the example of an external society, they sought to transcend their sense of the limitations their own society was imposing on them. Men of great intellect, they were also men of great ambition, but could not or would not quite see how far the one shaped the other. Men rich in ideas, they were also men beset with insecurity, and resisted concerning themselves with how two qualities were linked or how the linkage seriously impeached the scientific disinterestedness to which they pretended. But in this they were hardly different from any other group of questioners of the faith or, in fact, defenders. The Pan-Anglians were an articulate, earnest, influential transatlantic fraternity, vitally important in the changing nature of the British-American relationship.

In each society, the Pan-Anglians were, though for different reasons, an educated class without policy-making power. Inevitably, they appealed to education as the instrument for redeeming society and to the educated as its best leaders. Inevitably, they regarded aristocrats and plutocrats as men guided only by their own interests, and therefore seriously flawed directors of social policy. In contemplating how to achieve a better society, they professed a wish to rise above the dictates of private interests, and it did not often occur to them that their programs were a product of their own interests or that the powerlessness they felt in a world of affairs commanded by plutocrats or aristocrats was a principal factor in shaping their vision of the better world they were heralding. It was part of their rise to power that they directed the vital media of public opinion, particularly in the United States, where the world of genteel letters was theirs. Many of the principal American periodicals—the *Atlantic Monthly*, the *Independent, Forum, Scribner's, The Nation*, and the very prestigious *North American Review*—were under their editorship or an open forum for their ideas. They did not so much command the British periodical press, but with Morley and Stead as powerful editors, and with Bryce, Bright, Chamberlain, and Dicey, among so many others writing extensively, their presence and influence were imposing.

The Pan-Anglians were the new *philosophes*. They looked askance at traditional knowledge and the establishments in which it was purveyed. They were particularly wary of traditional religion. A highly learned coterie, they saw Christian belief as a shackled intelligence. Even Carnegie, who had little formal education, experienced a sense of liberation on discovering Herbert Spencer's teachings, which, he felt, came to him as a new revelation. The Pan-Anglians' disdain for established religion put them in direct confrontation with the men in power, who were generally traditional Protestants, and with the Irish-Catholic leadership which either shared power or was vigorously contending for it. The Pan-Anglians pretended to views that were rational, enlightened, universal. Essentially positivist, they were, in their way, confirmed ideologues, descendents of Calvin and Condorcet, architects of yet a newer heavenly city. Their opponents, the men in power and the Irish Catholics, they regarded as barbarians suffering from a want of culture or of an informed intelligence or both. They found their image of themselves and their opponents easier to sustain in the United States, where intellectualism and political leadership were almost antithetical terms; indeed, their Pan-Anglianism rested precisely on their appeal to the more sophisticated culture of the alternate society. Even in Britain, they could sustain their image by claiming for themselves a deeper discernment, a perception that the British aristocracy was one of manners but no culture, lineage but no merit, schooling but no education; and many of them felt toward Irish Catholics, whom they regarded as mired in a superstitious religion, an animus that ran close to what the American Pan-Anglians felt. Robert Kelley's suggestion that "the image of the enemy is the most serious and revealing element in a political persuasion" is surely appropriate here.[37] The Pan-Anglians had such an image. It was an essential quality of their social origins, education, and therefore ideology. However, they did not come as warring crusaders but rather as benign redeemers, men whose lofty and (they were certain) irrefutable ideals would improve the condition of their societies.

The Pan-Angles formed a new community of transatlantic voyagers. Sped by ever faster steamships, which accelerated not only their crossings but the strength and intimacy of their contacts, they traveled either to the new Atlantis or the historical metropolis with a changed intent and therefore a changed perception. In the new age, they came much more to probe than to describe; they wrote evaluations much more than Baedekers. Superb analyses of what they thought of the societies they visited have long been available in the excellent collections of Allan Nevins, *America through British Eyes*,[38] and Henry Steele Commager, *Britain through American Eyes*.[39] But particularly helpful is Richard L. Rapson's *Britons View America: Travel Commentary 1860–1935*.[40] His very extensive annotated bibliography, listing almost two hundred books that he had selectively drawn from a number about twice as long, offers a remarkable group of Pan-Anglians. Of course the long procession of British author-visitors was led by James Bryce. But his fellow travelers, as it were, constituted a very distinguished company, including William Archer, Matthew Arnold, Frederick C. De Sumichrast, Edward Augustus Freeman, Philip Gibbs, Rudyard Kipling, Alfred Maurice Low, James Fullarton Muirhead, A. F. Pollard, William T. Stead, and Anthony Trollope. A new generation, they now praised America. Giving up descriptive itineraries, they delved into significances and the reasons why. The numbers, wealth, and massiveness of the nation that had emerged from the Civil War evoked their admiration. They were Pan-Anglians in the sense that they knew that the British future must now be tied to America's power and energy. Americans visited Britain as well, of course. For the English-speaking world, London had long been and would long remain the cynosure of interest, a finishing academy of literature, art, learning, metropolitanism. The American Pan-Anglians went to London to contemplate a spectacular, affiliated culture; but, because they could not readily enter the higher ranges of British society, they saw England with affinity, not affection, with awe at the products of a long history compared to the prospects that their own short history held forth for themselves.[41]

A ministry of enlightenment, a band of covenanters, the Pan-Anglians had two principal congregations: one at Oxford University, the other in Boston and New York. The collection of so many men of a similar persuasion at Oxford puts one in mind of earlier religious movements, such as the one at Oxford inspired by John Henry Newman or, centuries before, of the zealots at Cambridge who dedicated themselves to propagating Calvin's true religion. The principal British Pan-Anglians, Bryce, Dicey, and Morley, were classmates at Oxford in the late 1850s and early 1860s; Trevelyan, who took his degree at Cambridge at the same time, was very early admitted into their "joyous and intimate circle." John Richard Green, another contemporary, studied at Jesus College. Among their intellectual guides were men, about a decade their senior, who were Oxford-educated or who taught at Oxford. Goldwin Smith, the archetypal Pan-Anglian, was Regius Professor of Modern History at Oxford from 1858 to 1866, a post in which he was succeeded by William Stubbs. Smith went on to teach at Cornell University for more than a quarter of a century. Freeman, who took his degree at Oxford, taught there from 1867 to 1879.

How shall we explain the growth of a particular, newer orientation toward the British-American relationship among this band of Oxonians? There is no facile explanation, to be sure. Yet it may help to note, at the outset, that their views of Britain and America had a large similarity, but were hardly coincidental at every point, or even in many significant details. Still, the similarity warrants analysis. It may be attributed, broadly, to their epoch, which was alive with ideas that were liberal, democratic, and universal. It may be attributed to their youth, for the educated young are attracted to formulas for change that question the established society they are called upon to succeed in. It may be attributed to their mentors, who could offer them such formulas, and who were themselves (Stubbs was an exception) of a liberal democratic orientation.

For some, it may surely be attributed to an awareness of being regarded as inferior in a society in which status and title seemed to count for more than ability or intelligence. One cannot generalize about the social origins of the British Pan-Anglians, but details about some of the more prominent ones may be helpful: Green was the son of an Oxford tradesman; Freeman came from a modest landowning family in Staffordshire; Morley was a poor youth who, at Oxford, lived a retired life at a small college.[42] Bryce came from a middle-class Ulster Scottish family, with strong Presbyterian convictions. (It will take us only slightly afield from the Oxonians we are discussing to remember that William Stead was the son of a Congregational minister and apprenticed to a Newcastle merchant, and that Andrew Carnegie was the son of a poor Dunfermline weaver.) In a settled age, one might accept with whatever reservations and hoping always for one's own improvement, the discriminatory symbols and rewards of an established society. And the university, if hardly an egalitarian agency for offering individual careers worthy of their talents, did offer possibilities of entry into areas of the established society: Parliament, the bar, the church. But in an age of reform, where the essential question was how far the governing order should be modified and who should be admitted inside the pale of the Constitution, the university, from having been merely a source of access to the establishment, became also an instrument for attacking it.

The 1850s and 1860s were a particularly unsettled time at Oxford as a result of the action of the Oxford Commission of 1850, which opened up university fellowships and scholarships to free competition, no longer restricting them, as before, to communicants of the Church of England. After 1854 one could receive a bachelor's degree without religious tests. There was, however, a requirement for holding office in the colleges and the university, as well as for membership on the university governing bodies. The tests were finally abolished in 1871. Bryce did not soon forget how in the spring of 1857, as a Scottish Presbyterian youth of nineteen, he went to Oxford to stand for a scholarship at Trinity and was asked, as a condition of receiving the scholarship, to sign the Thirty-Nine Articles. He resisted strongly, thinking of foregoing his university career, but in the end, the president and fellows of Trinity yielded and Bryce survived the ordeal without having to sacrifice his honor and principle. He felt he had scored a victory for conscience and dissent. Little wonder, then, why he found America so appealing, and why in 1870 on his first visit there in the company of his classmate, Albert Venn Dicey, he was so impressed by the United States. In particular, he appreciated the absence of rank and religious affiliation as criteria for success.[43] It was on this trip, incidentally, that he met many of the Americans who became the foremost proponents of rapprochement between the United States and Britain, the ardent adherents of the Pan-Anglian persuasion. The fraternity was already in formation.

The American Pan-Anglians constituted, as we have noted, an Eastern cultural establishment, whose leaders included editors of major journals, professors in prestigious universities, historians, and men of letters. The hub of their universe was Boston, and from it their influence radiated outward through the literary and educational media they commanded. Scions of families of the early republic, they turned inward and away from a present they found lamentable or insufferable to a past in which, as they saw it, right principle had governed public affairs. Francis Parkman, Henry Adams, James K. Hosmer, and John Fiske enshrined the past as though they owned it, holding it up as an object of moral instruction to the present. To them, the Civil War was a great awakening of morality and righteous indignation; God was stirring again in their everyday world. They saw the newer democracy as a defection from valid principle and purpose. Born to leadership, they had few followers. They had little in common with the newer values and the newer men: the newer political leaders in Congress and in the cities, the newer men of industry and commerce, the newer class of laborers, the newer immigrants. Savants and sages, they retreated into their books, incapable of perceiving that their scholarship was not so much an instrument for understanding as for defense.

Bereft of power, losing their audience, they wrote jeremiads about the changing society, testaments to their own anxiety about where they belonged in the new America and to their wondering if it was still listening. In their quest for a certain identity, they revitalized their ties to the English motherland, ties by which they could validate their claims as founders of the republic, keepers of ancient principles, possessors of a superior culture. The ambivalence about the motherland that had troubled men such as Hawthorne, Emerson, Irving, and Cooper a generation before, no longer troubled them. The choice was not really theirs to make. Neo-Loyalists in this way, they did not so much espouse the motherland as retreat to her for sanctuary. They were, in effect, exiles in their own country. When several of the principal journals and publishing houses moved their offices from Boston to New York, many of them sensed that their world was being dismantled. William Dean Howells, as *A Hazard of New Fortunes* (1890) indicated, made the move and understood what it signified; but then again, he was from Ohio and not a Brahmin. The Brahmin order of things could not have survived the relocation.

To help us identify the American Pan-Anglians of the later Victorian decades, immensely valuable is James Bryce's list of the distinguished individuals he met on the three trips he made to the United States while doing research on his study of American life. He said that the information they gave him formed the bedrock—eighty percent of it, in his own estimate—of *The American Commonwealth*, whose first edition appeared in three massive volumes in 1888. He came with searching questions and an insatiable interest; he was strongly interested in comparative legal institutions and history; a Scotsman among the English at home, he felt immediately at home in the U.S. transatlantic mentality. It was fortuitous that he sought out the men who figured large among the American intellectual class: editors of major reviews, writers, novelists, journalists, jurists, politicians, biographers, lawyers. But above all they were professors and indeed presidents at some of America's principal universities.

His prefatory list of acknowledgments almost takes one's breath away. To name a very few: Theodore Roosevelt, Thomas Wentworth Higginson, Oliver Wendell Holmes, Jr., Henry Villard, E. L. Godkin, John Hay, and Seth Low. Several taught law or comparative history at the major universities: James B. Thayer, Bernard Moses, Albert Shaw, and Frank Goodnow. A few were prominent university presidents: James B. Angell, and Andrew Dickson White. Many had written about both American and English law, and several had written about English history. It was not directly relevant to Bryce's inquiry or to their larger intellectual outlook to say how much they were committed to a close Anglo-Saxon diplomacy. Indeed, the issue itself was nowhere as pressing as it was soon to become. But there was no question that their perception embraced a knowledge of the relation of the kindred polities. Bryce's interlocutors constituted a formidable, indeed a leading body of American Pan-Anglians.[44]

The Americans who sought a renewed friendship with Britain were a significant segment of a larger patrician class that John Higham aptly designated as "anxious reformers." Their growing distress about the newer conditions of life and their proliferating programs for controlling or altering those conditions were twin aspects of their view of the world around them. Seeing threat everywhere, they responded with a consciousness that they must act now or be forever lost. What threatened them, Higham suggested, was the sense that society was being hopelessly polarized.[45] What threatened them, Robert Wiebe has said (looking at the patricians from a somewhat different but yet broadly similar angle), was the growing crisis they felt, as key members of America's principal "island communities," with the almost sudden advent, after the Civil War, of an impersonal, unknown, "distended society."[46] Each day seemed to bring "new evidence that a decent world where their word mattered, where their standards were honored and their families secure, was either rapidly passing or had already disappeared."[47] A helpful clue as to what was troubling the patricians was offered by Richard Hofstadter: they were victims of a "status revolution," in which their role as leaders in their respective communities was being seriously undermined.

In the struggle for the control of their communities, they were being outmaneuvered by men who did not have their scruples or their concern with social standing. "They were less important, and they knew it." They were frustrated aristocrats, beleaguered by "hostile forces and an alien mentality." They spoke of themselves as "the best people," desperately seeking, in the small toehold they held on public life, to build "barriers against the invasion of modern barbarism and vulgarity."[48]

The American Pan-Anglians belonged to the tradition of New England reform. Of a type with Emerson's man the reformer, they had a defined, articulated sense of the order of life they preferred and of the scale of values that should measure it. Unlike so many of the earlier generation and of their own, however, they did not wish to change the world they had known; they wished to preserve it. What needed changing, they felt, was the rash of newer institutions that signaled the growing dominion of selfishness, anarchy, irresponsibility, parochialism, and antagonism to community. They belonged to an interlocking directorate of past-oriented reformers. They sought to achieve their governing purpose by a variety of means: reforming the civil service, reconsidering the policy of unrestricted immigration, extending civic education, restricting the sale of spirituous liquors, changing the structure of urban government, reducing public expenditures, uprooting corruption in public life, promoting international peace, and keeping the United States from imperialistic and therefore race-mixing involvements.

They believed in nothing so much as the efficacy of a right education. It was precisely such an education, after all, that distinguished them from the new men of wealth and power. They wished to spread enlightened learning, as they understood it, by extending the schoolroom to all, indeed by making much of public life an extended schoolroom. However, the public school was not for them the only instrument of education: the lyceum, the Chatauqua movement, a responsible press, and high-minded journals were also devices, among others, for expanding among the citizens the domain of informed civism. Carnegie's gift of public libraries expressed their ideal; no less so did his 1868 memorandum to himself, when he was a very wealthy man of thirty-three, in which he expressed his most ardent desire: to get a university education at Oxford. Their educational program reflected, in variant form, the lively apprehension among all privileged groups in Western society, in the later decades of the nineteenth century, that the issues confronting a democracy could hardly be managed if its citizens did not first have the capacity to understand them, let alone the discrimination to judge the ways of resolving them. When, on the passage of the great English reform bill of 1867, Robert Lowe, a leader of the Liberal Party, advised his colleagues in Parliament to educate their masters, the newly enfranchised, he was expressing the distress of those who hoped to run the American polity no less than of those who had been running the British.

The American Pan-Anglians and their fellow reformers were not millenarians and their proposals were not simplistic. They did not imagine that a new life could be ushered in by means of a single tax. They were, in a very distinct sense, proto-progressives. They worried about the impact of forces that were eroding the older values. They attacked materialism and materialists. A man's lodestar, they felt, should be not his class interests but his ethics. For them, life was a labor of good works in behalf of good causes. They did not seriously doubt what represented the side of "good" in either works or causes, a subject about which their own upper middle-class education, in both genteel families and genteel colleges, had given them a firm, clear sense. To a society growing, as they saw it, more narrow and particular in outlook, they hoped to restore a cosmic, generous, and disinterested point of view. They were devotees of Spencer, Mill, Darwin, Comte. They believed in the rational world, and thus continued walking along the path Emerson had taken when he broke with Unitarianism and with what he considered to be the confines of formal theology. They were not sectarians. They replaced a benign deity with a benign evolution, trading one set of moral imperatives for another, persuaded that the replacement signified a forward step in the ever upward movement of humanity.[49]

Their projected version of the better America was a statement of what they felt was going wrong with it. Two problems troubled them above all. The first was that the nation was being badly governed. The evidence of mismanagement seemed so clear to them that it could hardly be a subject for debate. They saw it in the big cities, and most blatantly in Boston, where the rise of the newer urban politics with its bosses, ward heelers, patronage, vote-selling, and Irish-Catholic power offered a dire spectacle. Tales of corruption in Boston, New York, and Philadelphia, the new cities of the plain, filled endless columns in the journals of righteousness: *The Nation*, the *North American Review*, *Harper's Weekly*, the *New York Tribune*, the *New York Evening Post*. They regarded with horror the defense of "Boss" Tweed by some journalists, the proposal that he merited a statue rather than calumny, and the suggestion that he was, if anything, a modern Robin Hood. They saw disastrous mismanagement in the nation's legislature. The Grant regime was for them a study in bribery and blackmail. The money changers had taken over the temple of the republic. The Adamses synchronized the advent of the new perdition with their own loss of power in the nation's high councils. Henry Adams's novel, *Democracy* (1880), was a harsh portrait of the unmitigated immorality of the Senate, which, given the fact of a relatively weak presidency, had become the ultimate agency of law and power in the United States. From the pages of his *Education*, written decades later in the immurement of his home in the nation's capital, much like the cork-walled room in which Proust was almost simultaneously remembering his own things past, Adams looked out on a people besmirched in all aspects of its public life, "one dirty cesspool of vulgar corruption."[50]

What had to be done seemed clear enough to the reformers. To get rid of bad government, one had to get rid of bad governors. One had to ensure that the public service would be put into the hands of men of competence, men dedicated to disinterested service, men of education. As the reformers saw it, the three qualities were synonymous. In a popular democracy such as the United States, with so many elective offices, it would be too much to expect that all officials could offer the highest abilities. But it would be a major step in the right direction to staff the government bureaucracy with a well-trained, carefully selected, permanent civil service. Then the vagaries of each administration, its possible want of intelligence or probity, would not matter so much. The example that most readily commended itself to the reformers was the British, where, some two decades before, with the publication of the Northcote–Trevelyan Report, the civil service began being progressively converted from a preserve of the aristocracy to one of the university-educated. Lord Macaulay, Trevelyan's uncle, defined the ideal for the Americans no less than for the English: he wished to create "a public service confined in its upper reaches to gentlemen of breeding and culture selected by a literary competition."[51] The opponents of what they called "snivel service reform" attacked the proposed bureaucracy as an effete, hereditary class of college graduates, a charge the reformers sought without much success to answer.[52] The slogan of the civil service reformers, it seemed to the democrats, was that to the educated belonged the spoils.

The second matter that was causing the Pan-Anglians grave apprehension was their sense that Americans were losing their identity as an English-speaking, Protestant nation. If the nation were to change in either respect or both, its character as a progressive community would change. Inevitably lost would be the conscious civism that had distinguished America as a political culture, which so many notable visitors to our shores had identified. Americans were losing coherence as a group. The larger loyalty to the nation was being undermined by ethnic and religious particularisms. Great numbers of foreigners were pouring in who did not speak English and who might thus not have a ready communion with America's unique civic culture. Most threatening, it seemed, were the continuing inundations of Irish Catholics, who seemed to differ radically not only in religion but also in their political and social values. Protestant America responded to the change in America's ethnic and religious composition by proposing, variously, compulsory education, immigration control, and a strengthened Protestant church. The most dramatic statement of its sense of being completely at bay was the Reverend Josiah Strong's *Our Country* (1885), which broadcast dire warnings about the Catholic peril and which urged American Protestants to embark on a mission, indeed a crusade, for their own preservation.

To the Pan-Anglians in their Eastern cities, the Irish loomed as a forbidding, ominous presence, contending as they were for power and intent on using American diplomacy to assist Ireland in its bitter struggle with Britain for home rule. Nowhere was the social and political conflict that gave rise to the American Pan-Anglian outlook more sharply defined than in Boston. Barbara Miller Solomon's *Ancestors and Immigrants* still offers valuable insights about how the older leaders of the Boston community, the Brahmin elite and their cohorts, responded to the massive growth of Irish-Catholic numbers and power. From having been proponents of unrestricted immigration, which they had regarded as the vital blood of democracy, they now began to oppose it, fearing it would destroy democracy. From having been ardent Anglophobes, they now became ardent Anglophiles. "As upper-class citizens lost the balance of power in their divided society, English antecedents became the measure of all good things."[53] They embraced the Anglo-Saxon hypothesis about the essential nature and origins of American political life. Worried whether American institutions could survive the flood of "millions of newcomers alien to our traditions," James Russell Lowell was firm in the belief that the institutions had been made by "men of English blood with 'hereditary instincts' for democracy." Parkman celebrated the outcome of the French and Indian Wars, which he saw as a great struggle between the Catholic, priestly, authoritarian culture of the French race and the open, burgeoning, libertarian culture of the English. Fiske celebrated the outcome of the American Revolution, in his view a struggle between temporarily misguided imperial bureaucrats and colonists who stood valiantly for higher English principles of government. Hosmer regretted the dilution of the older stock, and by way of counterpoise called for "a closer interdependence among the great branches of the English-speaking race." Goldwin Smith warned against the "dynamite and blatherskite" of the Irish, pleading for the reconciliation of the two Anglo-Saxon nations.[54]

Thus, out of the welter of their discontents, their animus and their anxiety, Brahmins and Yankees turned increasingly to their English past and to a program for increasing amity with their ancient homeland. Losing status in a newly ordered society, they reclaimed their family connections with the kindred society across the seas, seeking their sustenance at "the original fount of national greatness." In a world of dissolving loyalties and new allegiances, in which their role as keepers of the keys to the American faith was challenged and undermined, they embraced doctrinal Anglo-Saxonism as "a kind of patrician nationalism." Wanting to establish their identity in a growing babel of ethnic stocks, they appealed to the standards of English ideas, English literature, English speech, English social priorities. Their Anglophilism was, in sum, the twin face of their fear; it was the only redemption they could find in the newer America, where the intellectual church they had commanded had come to count for nothing.

WHAT, IN SUM, was the significance of Pan-Anglianism for the British-American relationship? And what, in particular, did *Triumphant Democracy* signify for Pan-Anglianism?

In European times that were becoming more stridently nationalistic, the Pan-Anglians sought in the relationship between their kindred societies a vital meaning for their times and for themselves. Those who were conducting state policy—hereditary rulers, elected officials, and the principal bureaucrats—were everywhere concerned with ensuring national security. The democratization of politics in the late nineteenth century led to the growth of social imperialism, a drive for increasing national power that expressed the will of the mass electorate and their quest for identity through the persona of the state. Everywhere, too, in a direct ratio to expanding nationalist ideas and policies, but hardly with the same number of supporters or command of political strength, could be heard the countervailing voices of the internationalists. The latter were alike in seeing the threat of nationalistic policies and ideas and in seeking to transcend the confines of the nation and the impact of its programs. They differed among themselves in the way they read their times, each under a different dispensation—Marxist, Catholic, Positivist, or something else again. They differed too in the degree to which their readings were conscious expressions of their group or class interests and the way they perceived these interests.

As to the connection between the United States and the United Kingdom, there had always been—in the widest sense of the term—a "special relationship." The decades after World War II saw a vast growth of historical scholarship in Britain that centered on the Anglo-American relation and found that relation to have been of a "special" nature. Because the word was invested with connotations it could not carry—going far beyond the personal preferences of the respective nation's chief diplomats as well as the changing turns of their respective nation's diplomacy—the notion of a special Anglo-American relation was inevitably challenged. In a very fine essay on the subject, Max Beloff sought to demythologize "the special relationship." Yet however carefully demythologized, the relation emerges as particular and unique. In his close analysis, Beloff regularly returned to the theme, amply documented by the period's chief diplomats, that there was indeed a unique Anglo-American connection that took shape in the later Victorian decades and that it arose out of the respective international interests of the two powers.[55]

For the first century after American independence, the sense of that relationship had been negative: decidedly so on the part of Britain's ruling classes and many of its chief diplomats; intensely so in the United States where recurrent conflicts over British Canadian boundaries aroused a popular American antagonism. During the late nineteenth century, the relationship, as we have been noting, took a more positive turn, shaped in large part by international politics. Of course the British-American affinity grew in the soil of a common language. There had been an English-speaking union between the two nations that long antedated the diplomatic rapprochement that took shape in the late decades of the nineteenth century. There was an ever-growing literary bond. Post-Civil War

America, by the sheer dint of its exponentially increasing population, was a massive market for the major English writers of Victorian England: Dickens, Thackeray, Tennyson, Carlyle, George Eliot, Macaulay, and Trevelyan were read as widely and perhaps as voraciously as they were in Britain. At the same time, prominent American writers emerged whose books were warmly greeted in Britain. Half a century before, Sidney Smith had jeeringly asked: Who now reads an American book? In the later Victorian age, the question had lost its edge: Americans were writing their own notable, distinctive fiction, poetry, and history, and editing their own eminent journals read by a transatlantic audience. Travel between the two societies also increased, particularly on the part of socially conscious individuals and groups in both societies who were searching for models of improvement. To cite the most conspicuous example: Jane Addams founded Hull House in Chicago on the pattern of London's Toynbee Hall.

The flood of immigrants into America produced not only the need for a common public education but also, particularly for the new arrivals who had not been raised in Anglo-American institutions (especially those from Eastern Europe and Italy), for courses in civics that stressed the English origins of the American polity. Courses in English history now began to proliferate at American colleges and Bryce's *American Commonwealth* was required reading both at American colleges and, instructfully abridged, in American secondary schools.

Finding one's English roots now became a practiced art in the United States. Having a genealogy that went back to colonial times now served as a certificate of legitimacy: many of Carnegie's reviewers applauded his patriotism while, in the course of their reviews, cited their own deep-rooted American credentials. On both sides of the Atlantic, societies were established that sought to cement the transforming special relationship. Sir Walter Besant founded the Atlantic Union in 1901. A binational committee set up the Pilgrim Society in 1902, whose charter members were a *Who's Who* of the Pan-Anglian sodality, including Lord Frederick Sleigh Roberts, a hero of the Boer War, Charles Rolls, the American industrialist, Grover Cleveland, Thomas Nelson Page, and Mark Twain.[56] The growing Anglo-American affinity was most popularly celebrated by the marriages of English peers and American heiresses. Not quite the dynastic marriages of earlier centuries, but in the new age advertised by the popular presses in both countries, they cemented the English aristocracy of titles to the American aristocracy of manufactures.[57] If not quite of a transforming political consequence, it did enter the new diplomacy of Anglo-American relations that prominent men in British politics took American wives, including such notable English figures as Joseph Chamberlain, William Harcourt, Randolph Churchill, and George Curzon.[58]

Fashioned of the ties that bound the kindred polities came the most consequential Pan-Anglian achievement: the diplomatic revolution of the turn of the century. The individuals superintending foreign affairs in their respective countries designed the Anglo-American relation in a new way. Their impelling motive was practical, of course: they knew that a new diplomacy was needed for a new age. John Hay, the passionate American Anglophile who served at the Court of St. James, knew that, and so did the passionate British philo-American, Joseph Chamberlain, the monarchy's foreign secretary in Lord Salisbury's third ministry.[59] Each polity was looking after its own interests, and those interests drove them to search for nations with which they could act together. Bismarck had long since set the terms of the new diplomacy: alliances and ententes were drawn up as insurance against a world that could too easily be shattered by blood and iron. The Pan-Anglians who were directing Anglo-American affairs understood that an earlier affinity must now become a joint protective association. Once the *Alabama* claims had been settled, the road of Anglo-American diplomacy led, if not always in straight uncomplicated steps, to "the great rapprochement," as Dexter Perkins has so insightfully and persuasively called it, of the 1890s and 1900s.

Rapprochement was as much as the social politics of the respective nations would then allow: their leaders could not bring their polities to the point of alliance, as many of their prominent leaders proposed, and as the monarchical states of the European continent had in fact done. They could at best bring their polities to the point of a feasible mutuality. Their approach was situational, case by case; and among the men who conducted the diplomacy of the two states it was an entente of sentiment, of ethnicity, and of class. The high point of the entente came when each polity, faced by its own war—the United States by the Spanish-American War and the United Kingdom by the Boer War—extended to each other an understanding support while the other European powers stood aside both unsupportively and critically. Urging the need for cooperation between the kindred nations, famous men on both sides of the Atlantic formed an Anglo-American League in London in 1898. Among its members were the most notable Pan-Anglians of the age, including James Bryce as chairman, wealthy men like Andrew Carnegie and Albert Harmsworth, and peers, politicians, and celebrities whose names studded their impressive list: Herbert Asquith, Arthur James (Lord) Balfour, Richard Burdeon (Viscount) Haldane, Conan Doyle, H. Rider Haggard, and Alfred (Lord) Tennyson. Moribund though it became after 1903, the League testified to the newer vitality of the Anglo-American relation.[60]

Pan-Anglianism was a type of reform ideology. Reform ideals and programs were the stock in trade of politics in the new democratic age of Western society, and particularly in the kindred polities. Always looking for the improved society, each group of reformers appealed to the model of the other. America was, in its own perception and that of others, the paradigmatic reformed democracy, and Britain was, with no less self-consciousness, with gradualness and inevitability, attempting to infuse democratic ideals and forms into aristocracy. A distinct minority in a nation that clung to a ritual hostility to the former mother country, a hostility inflamed by the politically active Irish Catholics, the American Pan-Anglians found virtue in the modes of British government.

For those advocating change in Britain, two questions were virtually one and the same: How far shall we reform our society? How far shall we Americanize it? To many Britons, particularly the laboring classes, the nonconformists, and the educated, the American model held a continuing appeal. During the later Victorian decades, the laboring classes retained their earlier belief that borrowing the forms of American democracy would guarantee the plenty that America's common people enjoyed, and it was, in the main, this kind of thesis that Carnegie argued in *Triumphant Democracy*. To the nonconformists, the United States continued to offer compelling proof of the virtues of a disestablished society. The educated classes, from whom the British Pan-Anglians drew their principal support, also took a positive view of American life. What distinguished the British Pan-Anglians from other groups that had sought instruction in the American example was that, as the conditions of both societies and their perspective of each other changed, they did not give up their pro-American sympathies. By the 1880s, when recurrent strife between American labor and capital emblazoned newspaper headlines, some British working-class leaders, particularly those who had been educated in England's universities, began to revise their view of the American polity and supplant praise with disapproval. Gladstone's first ministry fairly well satisfied the nonconformists' program for the better society and, for them, lessened the great appeal of America's mode of disestablishment.

If the British Pan-Anglians retained their pro-American attitudes and their close American connections, it was because the terms of their understanding of the relationship between both nations were, from the outset, different. Insofar as their own interests as a group were concerned, they wished not to overturn the structure of British power but rather to enter it and help command it. They refrained, moreover, from too closely identifying the problems and institutions of one polity with those of the other. This they expressed clearly in several of the pieces they contributed to *Essays on Reform*, a collective plea for enacting the parliamentary bill of 1867 to extend the franchise to the British laboring classes. Maitland called the *Essays*, a collection by eleven writers, "a manifesto of Young Liberalism," and H. L. Beales has added that "it was the voice of the university mind of the day in anxious thought about the political needs of the day."[61]

Inevitably the American model figured in their argument, and nowhere more prominently than in Goldwin Smith's essay on "The Experience of the American Commonwealth." Smith, then a Regius Professor of Modern History at Oxford, subscribed to the virtues of U.S. democracy, but like the others, he was fully aware of its serious shortcomings. The immigrants, particularly the Germans and the Irish, lacked enterprise and a knowledge of American institutions. America had nothing that could be called an estimable culture. The American Constitution had notable deficiencies. "The elective presidency with its patronage has always been the grand incentive of faction, intrigue, and corruption." Indeed, the elective Presidency was very possibly a mistake. The American mode of paying politicians resulted in making politics "a trade in which low adventurers are drawn." Democracy breeds demagogues, and there was no question that demagogism was "a great curse of America."[62] Smith was reiterating the charges against American democracy that had been leveled by Tocqueville and many British commentators of the day, charges indeed that would be voiced two decades later, though with considerable modification, by Smith's fellow reformer and Oxonion, James Bryce. What should be noted here is that, in joining their American confreres, the English Pan-Anglians well understood the differences between the two polities. Pan-Anglianism was at best a conjunction, not a fusion.

Pan-Anglianism was in sum a special reading of the British-American relationship. The persuasion of an educated minority, it served the kindred polities as a vehicle for rapprochement. For each polity, Pan-Anglianism was a halfway house. Between them, it was the bridge of understanding that crossed from an age in which the two polities stood for polar ideals over to one in which their ideals grew very close. For the century beginning with its declaration of independence, America had been, for Britain's reformers and for her middle and lower classes, the model republic. It remained so in many respects after the Civil War; but the special conditions of both polities made America a particularly appealing polity for the British Pan-Anglians. Pan-Anglianism was, in this way, the philosophy of the educated Whig. It carried a century later the chastened political sense of Burke and the elder Pitt in the Commons, and of Dickinson and Galloway in the Continental Congress. Among its American proponents, it marked a removal from the patriotic myth that Britain was the land of a condescending, self-indulgent aristocracy. Among its British proponents, it marked no less a removal from the democratic myth that America was the land of a universally approving people and exemplary institutions.

There had been earlier fraternities of good causes in the kindred nations, self-righteous minorities who sought to lead their own community to the path of the other. In the 1770s and 1780s, for example, the passionate democrats of London, devout commonwealth men such as the Doctors Priestly and Price, held up the American model of democracy as the one for Britain to emulate; in the 1830s and 1840s, ardent abolitionists like William Lloyd Garrison and Theodore Dwight Weld called upon the United States to follow Britain's humanitarian lead and abolish slavery forthwith. No less self-righteous than the inter-Atlantic fraternities that had preceded them, the Pan-Anglians were not radicals. They did not wish to change the premises of their respective orders, but only to realize those premises, as they understood them, more effectively. Unlike their predecessors, moreover, they commanded major organs of opinion and influential readers. And in doing their virtuous, respectable work, they were as much concerned with achieving respectability as with achieving virtue.

Pan-Anglianism marked the ending of the antithesis of ideals. For a century, that antithesis had been the essential bond between America and Britain: America was the model of liberal democracy, Britain the model of liberal aristocracy; America was the paradigmatic reformed society, Britain the society undergoing reform. The year 1867 signaled the end of the politics of deference and the arrival of the idea of democratic reconstruction in Britain; 1877 signaled the end of political and racial reconstruction and the full installation of the principles of a business society in the United

States. The antithesis that had bound the two societies began to lose its sharpness and meaning. From having stood for polar ideas, America and Britain began to stand for ideas that were broadly similar.

The product of forces that had created the similarity, the Pan-Anglians were its enthusiastic evangels. Stressing the common political legacy of the kindred polities, they insisted on their need for mutual understanding, respect, and action. The bonds of mutuality with which they linked key classes in the kindred communities were strong and enduring. Out of them was fashioned, at the end of the century, the diplomatic entente between the United States and Great Britain that has since then governed their relations with the world outside. Pan-Anglianism was, thus, the intellectual entente that opened the door to diplomatic entente. But the Pan-Anglians were always fully aware that shared power was the correlate of shared culture, and fully persuaded that the power should be used to advance by peace the high ideals of the culture. Ambassadors of good will, they became, in time, ambassadors. They understood the mutuality of the two cultures, that each had its strengths and weaknesses, its modernity and its tradition. The journey of veneration and instruction that the young Bryce made in 1870 to Boston and Concord, where he met Emerson, Longfellow, Lowell, and the Holmeses, was rather similar to the early journey that the young Washington Irving had made to meet with Scott, Southey, Campbell, Milman, Hallam, and other prominent literary figures in post-Napoleonic Britain.

TRIUMPHANT DEMOCRACY was a major statement of Pan-Anglianism; the book rested on the key tenets of Pan-Anglian belief. Carnegie subscribed fully to the Anglo-Saxon "hypothesis." The language, literature, laws, and political institutions of the United States were English, he said. The British race had a special aptitude for colonization, enterprise, and government, an aptitude shown to the greatest advantage in America. He accepted Freeman's dictum that the American was but a Briton who had crossed the ocean. The Americans of his own day were, in his view, four-fifths British; they had remained "true to this noble strain." It was fortunate that they had: "I trust that they are ever more to remain truly grateful for this crowning mercy." The admirable traits of the race were everywhere evident. America's foremost leaders were British. In General Grant's "Scotch Blood," one could find the source of "that tenacious, self-contained, stubborn force, which kept pegging away, always certain of final victory." Equally clear was the achievement of "that English-American,

Lincoln . . . the greatest political genius of our era." Particularly noteworthy was the major role that first-generation British immigrants were playing in the growth of American manufactures, which Carnegie, the most illustrious among them, regarded as one of the principal achievements of the triumphant democracy. "So it can still be claimed that Britons do the manufacturing of the world, and we must credit to our race, not only the hitherto unequalled sum of products of our native land, but to a large extent the still greater sum of the Republic's."[63]

The security and achievement of the republic, for Carnegie, depended on its British identity. One of the great dangers besetting the republic, he said, was the massive immigration of foreigners from all lands, "many of them ignorant of the English language, and all unaccustomed to the exercise of political duties." Two factors happily removed this danger. Making the foreigner a citizen equal with all others instills in him a passionate fondness for his new homeland. No less important is the free common school, "the great single power in the unifying process which is producing the new American race." In Carnegie's steelmaking vision, a cavalcade of "various racial elements" was passing "through the crucible of a good common *English* education, furnished free by the State . . . all to be fused into one, in language, in thought, in feeling, and in patriotism." English-speaking America was the real America. It was a mistake to take "the semi-English, semi-foreign New York City for the country." It was also evident that relative to the more rapidly increasing numbers of whites, "the colored race" in America was shrinking. What then was Carnegie's American? "The American republican can never be other in his blood and nature than a true Briton, a real chip of the old block, a new edition of the original work." The American and the Briton were not two separate individuals, but rather "two members of the one grand family."[64]

Carnegie celebrated the growing entente between America and Britain and the men who were promoting it. In the United States, he said, they were clearly men of culture and status. The bearer of good will toward the mother country was surely "not the uncultivated man of the gulch." He was, on the contrary, a man who had learned "the past history of the race from which he had sprung." Indeed, said Carnegie, there was a direct proportion between the love an American had for Britain and the extent of his knowledge and power. Who were these men of knowledge and power who had been in the vanguard of pro-British sentiment in the United States? They were "the Washington Irvings, the Nathaniel Hawthornes, the Russell Lowells, the Adamses, the Dudley Warners, the Wentworth

Higginsons, the Edward Atkinsons, the men of whom we are proudest at home."[65] Among them were men who counted for little or nothing in American politics, a fact that, for Carnegie, in no way detracted from their importance or character. Indeed, it was axiomatic with him that men of great quality or talent did not go into politics because the basic issues of American government had long ago been decided and therefore evoked no major antagonisms or antagonists. The American admirers of Great Britain were "the best people in the land," and they were being sought out by their British confreres coming to the United States to seek a better understanding of the republic's institutions and promote a new understanding between the two branches of the English-speaking race. And so far as the British promoters of transatlantic amity were concerned, Carnegie was no less clear about their identity or the nature of the group they belonged to. They constituted a class of "really able Britons" and their names read like a *Who's Who* of British literature, historiography, and politics: Morley, Huxley, Froude, Freeman, Farrar, Irving, Rosebery, Bell, Seeley, Bryce, Arnold, "and others, who are all personages at home."[66] Carnegie had tabulated the Pan-Anglian sodality. His table was hardly complete, and in some respects, it was not entirely accurate. But that did not much matter. He was offering not so much a list of actual membership as much as his sense of the nature of the Pan-Anglian fraternity and of the good work they had undertaken to do.

That work, which Carnegie declared to be his "chief ambition," was to bring the two "grand divisions of the British race" into a closer union. He knew without a doubt "that in their genuine affection and indissoluble alliance lie the best hopes for the elevation of the human race." This was the central article of the faith he shared with other Pan-Anglians. To promote affection and alliance, it was imperative to educate both nations. He had been surprised, said Carnegie, to find such "lamentable ignorance" about America, "even in the highest political circles" of Great Britain. He was sure that the better the citizens of both countries got to know each other, "the stronger will grow the attachment between them." Currents of change in Britain were bringing her ever closer to the United States. "The assimilation of the political institutions of the two countries proceeds apace, by the action of the older in the direction of the newer land." In but a few years, "the political institutions of the two divisions will be practically the same."[67]

The year after he sold his steelworks, some eight years after the revised edition of his *Triumphant Democracy* appeared, Carnegie was interviewed by a young English reporter, Bernard Alderston, who wrote what appears to have been the first biography of the Scottish-American: *Andrew Carnegie: The Man and His Work*. Carnegie's greatest wish, wrote Alderson was to bind together the interests of Britain and America "and form them into one vast confederacy." He warmly espoused "the Federation of the English-speaking peoples." The world's "peace and progress depended on this reunion." It would become the arbiter of international disputes; its power would be invincible. Otherwise, he predicted, Britain would lose her primacy "as head of the Anglo-Saxon race and decline into a secondary place, and then comparative insignificance in the future annals of the English-speaking race." To realize the British-American confederacy, said Carnegie, he "would gladly sacrifice his fortune."[68]

Carnegie's was a special brand of Pan-Anglianism. *Triumphant Democracy* emphasized the thesis that the affinity of the kindred communities could be achieved only if Britain adopted the American model. He differed in this way with most Pan-Anglians, who were inclined to respect the distinctions between the two political cultures and who stressed the virtues of the alternate society. The portrait he drew of American perfection and British imperfection was too stark for Pan-Anglian sensibility, too improbable for the Pan-Anglian sense of history. Part of the reason for his special brand of Pan-Anglianism was that he had access to power in the United States, where he could not show it, and he stood obstreperously in the antechamber of power in Britain, where he could not get it. He was firmly rooted in neither society, amassing wealth in the one and conspicuously consuming it in the other. Lacking gentility and culture, he tried to buy them, in a surrogate way, by befriending men whose claims to both were impeccable. Lacking the power he wished for, he spoke loudly and carried a big, but hopelessly outmoded, thesis. His insistence on Americanizing Britain as the only way of achieving unity between them was out of touch with the Pan-Anglian orientation.

He could not, like most Pan-Anglians, find a balance between the two cultures; he could not, like them, attain that position of political strength that came from celebrating Britain and America for the institutions they shared and respecting them for those they did not. He fell back, inevitably, to the only intellectual ground he really knew, that of a remembered Chartism, seeing always the contrast between an aristocratic Britain, which badly needed reform, and a democratic America, which had gloriously achieved it. This explains the critical response to *Triumphant Democracy*: whether or not they were pleased with his representations of the republic and the monarchy, rather few of his scores of reviewers on both sides of the Atlantic considered the book a judicious, discerning analysis of the British-American relationship. It surely explains why the prominent Pan-Anglians regarded *Triumphant Democracy* the way they did. The Americans rejected it as fulsome, dishonest, patriotic effrontery; the British thought its premises specious and its understanding of their own institutions limited. In 1888, two years after the appearance of *Triumphant Democracy*, Bryce offered the consummate Pan-Anglian portrait of the political culture of the United States. His *American Commonwealth* was a balanced, sophisticated evaluation of one society by an admiring scholar of the other. And though he hardly intended his book to be that, it was also a refutation of what his Scottish kinsman and fellow Pan-Anglian had said about the British-American relationship.

But for all the eccentricities of his Pan-Anglianism, Carnegie was a confirmed believer. He belonged to that very small group within the fellowship, men such as James Russell Lowell, who had spent a number of years in both countries. He traveled in their world and knew many of them personally. He shared much of their social philosophy: he joined with them in many of their causes—international peace, universal compulsory education, anti-imperialism. He was one of the first among them to argue for an alliance between America and Britain and, somewhat later, for a political union.

And for all its obvious limitations, *Triumphant Democracy* was an important book. It caught the changing climate of American ideas about Britain. It marked the passage from an age of ideological antithesis between the kindred nations to one of mutuality. Standing in the passageway between both ages, Carnegie often blended their ideas and confused their arguments. He tied, in a patent contradiction, the popular myth, so rich a part of the American civic ritual, about the clear-cut differences between the two countries, to the growing sense among certain groups of Americans that the real nature of their polities had long since changed and that a new relationship between them had to be defined. He sounded the American citizens' old-time cry of antipathy toward the "feudal" monarchy, yet called on them to show it affection. He paraded America as a model democracy, but tried to sell her as a bastion of conservatism. He denounced British society for its lack of democracy, yet warned Britain's governing classes about the dangers of their new democracy. He spoke of the sharp antithesis between American and British ideals and institutions, while showing how similar they were and how they were growing more and more similar each year. Carnegie did not himself emphasize the contradictions, he lived them. His own life was a passage between two very different ages in the British-American world. In arguing the way he did in *Triumphant Democracy*, he could not accept all that the present meant because, already past fifty, he would have to turn his back on so much of his past. He could deny his premises only at the cost of denying himself. Seeing himself as a man who had made it beyond all belief in the land of American democracy, he presumed he had made it because of American democracy, because it was so unbelievably better than and different from British monarchy.

But if this was his intellectual shortcoming, it was also the reason why his ideas were important. He spoke in one voice for two worlds: the democratic world of the American patriots and the British democrats, and the elite world of the Pan-Anglian men of letters and public affairs. *Triumphant Democracy* was a compound of two ideologies. Janus-faced, it bound together two perceptions of the kindred nations, the one looking back on an age of ideological rivalry, the other looking forward to an age of ideological accommodation. The transformation of the British-American relationship was not the categorical replacement of one orientation with another. Particularly in popular understanding, where the perception of a changing world was filtered through the thick lens of national myth, old viewpoints blended into new ones. It was this blend that Carnegie articulated. It was this level of popular perception that he commanded. It was this transit of ideas that his *Triumphant Democracy* signaled.

8

Conclusion

TRIUMPHANT DEMOCRACY embodied Carnegie. From its publication to the years of his retirement from actively participating in public affairs, he resounded its basic themes. And yet, ironically it might have seemed in light of his impassioned commitment to his book's message to the British political world, events he could hardly have anticipated, in a sudden rush, pushed him and his book aside. The most important, probably, were the deaths of the immediate members of his family. His only sibling, his younger brother Thomas, a partner in Carnegie and Brothers, died of pneumonia in late October 1886 at the age of forty-three. His mother, who had been the dominant force of his family life, died shortly thereafter, at seventy-six. Carnegie himself, stricken with typhoid, hovered precariously at the fringe of death in those awful late fall months of 1886. As Burton Hendrick has so poignantly summed it up: "Carnegie knew that . . . he was the only survivor. At that moment he felt himself the loneliest man in the world."[1]

At that very time, the world of British politics that Carnegie had so intimately inhabited for so many years took a turn that largely disconnected him from his important associations. Gladstone's Irish Home Rule bill of April 1886 split the Liberal Party and effectively ushered in the Tory hegemony (with a minor Liberal interlude) of the next two decades. Carnegie's friends were out of office; his funds could therefore no longer purchase the access to power they formerly did; his message lost its currency and vitality. Gladstone did in fact return briefly for a third ministry, in 1892, but at a point when Carnegie's counsel in Liberal affairs would least have been listened to. July 1892 witnessed the explosive strike at the Carnegie Homestead Steel Mill. The embattled confrontation of steelworkers and strikebreakers, the use of Pinkerton guards, the killings of five workmen and the wounding of several more: whatever other meanings they had, the bloody drama surely made a mockery of Carnegie's pose as an advocate of working-class peace and good will and of his portrait of the United States as a *Triumphant Democracy*.[2] The British working classes to whom the Carnegie newspaper chain had disseminated his Radical republican program in 1885 could only wonder what had happened to the disciple of Cobden and Bright, to the self-proclaiming scion of the militant Scottish Chartists. Indeed, as if to underscore their distrust of U.K. party politics, British labor leaders began organizing a party of their own. Keir Hardie, a Scottish labor radical, helped organize the Independent Labour Party in 1893, and in the election of 1900, the Labour Representation Committee ran its own set of candidates, indicating that organized workers were giving up their traditional affiliation with the Liberals and were now striking out on their own. In the new world of British politics, Carnegie's voice and role were diminished, if not totally stilled.

Once he recovered from his own near-death illness and from the deaths of his brother and mother, he invested, one may almost dare say sublimated, all of his driven energies into his business. He was at last free to marry a young woman, Louise Whitfield, the daughter of a wealthy New York City merchant whom Carnegie had courted for some years in the face of his mother's disapproval. But he was also entirely free to continue his marriage to the great steel industry that he regularly revolutionized by adopting the latest inventions and by maximizing his steelworks' production and underselling all his competitors. Before 1901, steel was America's major industry and Carnegie was king of steel. Then, in 1901, at the age of sixty-five, Carnegie decided to sell his world-dominant steel partnership to the United States Steel Corporation formed by the great financier, J. P. Morgan. The purchase price was $450,000,000. Carnegie was the richest man in the world. He was at last free to give all his energies to the provisions of the memorandum he had written in 1868. He could now realize more than ever before his gospel of wealth.

Taking an active part in British politics, indeed helping to shape its course, had been Carnegie's primary intent in writing *Triumphant Democracy*. But if the land of his birth was not immediately accessible to him, he could still keep resounding the book's message, particularly on

American shores. This was nowhere more evident than in his address to the Nineteenth Century Club of New York in early December 1887. With his marriage in late April 1887 and with the resettlement of his domestic life in a new home in New York City, he was able to resume his usual enthusiasm, conviction, and proselytizing. Entitled "Triumphant Democracy," the address was Carnegie's answer to the fears about the security of the American republic that had been raised in Josiah Strong's popular book, *Our Country*, which had appeared two years earlier. As secretary of the Congregational Home Missionary Society for Ohio and other states, Reverend Strong warned that the nation was imperiled by seven major threats, including urbanism, Mormonism, intemperance, Romanism, unrestricted mass immigration, socialism, and wealth. Calling Reverend Strong's view "pessimistic," Carnegie undertook to refute it with his own "optimistic" view.

Facts and figures, particularly those of the recent census, he said, indicated that three of the cited threats were not increasing: indeed, in the context of the rapidly growing nation, some of them were *relatively* decreasing. Intemperance was regrettable, of course, but the data showed that the per capita consumption was declining; he scoffed at the "threat" of Mormonism; urbanism, said the figures, was not growing; in terms of the diverse numbers and practitioners of other religions, Catholicism was hardly a peril; immigrants were a comparatively small part of the burgeoning American population; and immigration was "one of the chief sources of the Republic's wealth and progress." But what safeguarded the United States against all of the ostensible threats, said Carnegie, was that it was a democracy, a polity in which the evils that may arise "will beat in vain and leave no impression upon the immortal principle which they assail."

Two of Reverend Strong's list of "evils" elicited Carnegie's longest comments: socialism and wealth. "Socialism is not an American danger. It is not indigenous to the soil of Triumphant Democracy. It does not flourish in the Republic." American workers and their leaders "are not socialistic. Why should they be? Many of them have their own homes and in small sums they have laid away in the savings banks of this country over one billion dollars." Those to whom the socialist appeal is made do not listen because "they have achieved their present condition of comfort through their own effort and are intense individualists. It is only those at the bottom that favor revolution and these, mainly in our large cities, are few in number, ignorant and disreputable in character, and despised by the majority of their fellows." Socialism was a various and specious doctrine. It appealed to the dregs of society and taught dependence rather than independence. "There is not in America today, a skilled, industrious workman of good habits, able and willing to perform a fair day's work, and of good character from past character, who cannot earn sufficient to keep his family, educate his children, and save a competence for his old age." As a doctrine, socialism drew Carnegie's impassioned ire. It could not stand against the doctrine of democracy triumphant.

About the issue of wealth, Carnegie had already thought much, done much, and written much. His famous essay on wealth was to come two years later, but he already anticipated it in his earlier writings, in his letters to his cousin Dod, in his 1868 memorandum, in the libraries he had helped build, and, as we have already noted, in *Triumphant Democracy*.

In his address to the Nineteenth Century Club, he repeated his maxim that "he who dies rich, dies disgraced." The very rich ought to disburse their wealth. They should not leave it to their children. They should not give it to charity, lest they create an unproductive kind of dependence. The very rich man ought to administer his wealth wisely during his lifetime. Libraries elicited his particular administration, but other possibilities existed. The key answer to wealth was democracy. "All over, whenever Democracy reigns, we begin to see the reflex action of wealth—accumulation giving place to beneficent distribution."

Indeed, the answer to all the dangers that Reverend Strong feared was "benign, divine Democracy." Carnegie offered his own experience. He had been born in a state run by kings and aristocrats and ruled with injustice. Indeed, it was his "proud privilege" to say that "my grandfathers were renowned Radicals in those corrupt days." But in the last half-century Britain had been responding to the American model, to hear "the message from Philadelphia," from "this blessed land of Liberty," indeed from this "ideal state." "That the condition of the masses has been improved just in proportion to the infusion of Democracy in England is a truism which passes almost indisputed."[3]

Reverend Strong and Andrew Carnegie were two sides of the same American coin. A committed evangelist, the minister wished to warn the republic about the ways in which it was being undermined. The wells of American democracy were being poisoned by sources, many of them foreign, that were flooding into the United States. Carnegie's gospel was, as he put it, optimistic. The government "of the people, by the people, and for the people" was its own antidote to any dangers the good reverend had noted. Both men were, in fact, evangelists. And both were strong Pan-Anglians. True, Josiah Strong was a devout Protestant and Carnegie's beliefs rested on a Spencerian secularism. For the rest, however, both believed that Anglo-Saxon principles and institutions were properly destined to spread their dominion throughout the world.

Remarkably enough, though the British political world was no longer the immediately relevant market for Carnegie's message about America, Carnegie kept up the message. As Britain changed, so did what Carnegie said. His theme was always the same: the United States offered a useful model for Britain. In successive articles that he wrote for major reviews, he kept up his argument, always adapting it to the issues of the day.

Even as the massive volume was in the bindery, there were always the monthly reviews to repeat and update his urgent gospel. In "Democracy in England," which appeared in the January 1886 issue of the *North American Review*, Carnegie hailed the recent electoral reforms in Great Britain. The "record of [England's] recent legislation shows only a copying of our institutions."[4] England was moving toward republican practice. She had earlier set the pattern for her colonies, and indeed for the Western world. But new problems were emerging and England had to change her guiding principles. As things still stood, "instead of standing forth a model, she has become a warning. No state would think of adopting throne, hereditary chamber, primogeniture and entail, union of church and state, or any other of the remains of feudal institutions with which England is afflicted."[5] All these would yield to the principle of political democracy that had gained ascendancy in England. True enough, England was step-by-step adopting key features of the American model. But English politics should be seen in a larger context: "In all this we see the unceasing movement of the various divisions of the English-speaking race throughout the world to assimilate their political institutions, each division taking that which the others have proved to be best. . . . The world is soon to see this community of language, religion, and political forms merge into the great Anglo-Saxon democracy."[6]

The American model, said Carnegie, could offer valuable instruction to Britain in perhaps the most critical issue they were facing in the mid-1880s: Irish Home Rule. Many prominent Liberals, led by Joseph Chamberlain and John Bright, broke with Gladstone over his plan for giving the Irish Home Rulers, led by Charles Parnell, the essence of what they were insisting on. The Liberal Unionists, as they were called, differed with Gladstone on several basic points. In a notable address to the

Glasgow Junior Liberal Association that Carnegie delivered in September 1887, he argued that the United States was based on the principle of home rule, one that, judiciously adjusted to meet the United Kingdom's particular circumstances, could guide Britain in resolving its turbulent domestic conflict. To those British leaders who cried, "We do not want to Americanize our institutions," he had a ready answer: "Why not? The Americans have taken from you everything they could lay their hands on. They have taken your Constitution and bettered it; they have taken your literature, your laws, they have taken your language."[7] Again, why resist the course of the future? The English-speaking race throughout the world will have the same political institutions; the English-speaking peoples everywhere are inevitably being assimilated.[8] For virtually every problem Britain had, for virtually every crisis it faced, Carnegie offered an essentially similar solution: adopt the American principle of governance, go the way of the democracy triumphant. It did not escape him that he was reformulating the elements of his model. Britain had already achieved political equality, but it feasibly blended it with aristocracy. The model Carnegie increasingly offered was one based on the association of English-speaking peoples. It seemed to him a reasonable sequitur that the English language brought its own history and that its history embraced a commonality of institutions.

As new nations and new alliances were changing the alignments of European power during the 1880s, British leaders sought to meet the challenges they saw in a radically altered continental order. Their logical response was to reverse the course of several decades, the quasi-official policy of Little Englandism, and to revive Britain's links with the different parts of her scattered empire. Out of this reversal came two of the most prominent associations of the time: the Imperial Federation League, founded in 1884, and the United Empire League, founded in 1891. The idea of imperial federation was, as one of its supporters put it, to "use all our energies to promote the union and political consolidation of the Great Britain which still owns one flag and acknowledges one sovereign."[9] The purpose of the United Empire League was to promote trade among the constituent members of the empire by offering them tariff advantages and thereby encourageing intra-imperial trade.

But where did the democracy triumphant fit into this new concept of British empire? And what would Carnegie say about the two new British imperial associations? In his essay on "Imperial Federation," which appeared in 1891, Carnegie appraised both leagues. Citing facts and figures on the matter of intra-imperial trade, he tried to show how specious was the proposal of the United Empire: Britain had "nothing to gain by any change in fiscal relations between herself and the colonies." Heavily engaged in world trade as she was, Britain would "jeopardize the control of the markets of the world."[10] The bond of sentiment offered by the Imperial Federation League also engaged Carnegie, but he was concerned that the federationists were egregiously omitting the United States of America from their league. In doing so, they were ignoring the majority of the English-speaking race.[11] What the federationists had to do was to expand the concept of their league. They had to conjure up "a much grander mission," one that would move from a Britain-centered alliance to a race alliance embracing all the English-speaking peoples of the world.[12] They had to entertain the proposal of John Richard Green, one of England's most popular historians, that the English-speaking peoples' "future home is to be found along the banks of the Hudson and the Mississippi."[13] Race alliance, argued Carnegie, would yield many material and commercial benefits, but most important was that it would usher in an era of peace. Populous and productive as it was, and always expanding its capacity, the United States could be excluded from the plans of Britain's changing world only at great loss. Again, the United States offered a ready model for the institutions that would structure the new age.[14]

In September 1891, just before his departure for the United States, responding to a reporter's questions, Carnegie reiterated his by now standard comments about Britain and America.[15] The site of the interview was Cluny Castle, a vast, magnificent eleven-thousand-acre estate in the Scottish highlands that Carnegie had been renting for several years. Were the Socialists a growing body in America as they were getting to be in Britain? "No," said Carnegie, "they are not. There is no ground under Republican institutions for Socialism to grow. Every man has the same chance; he has the privilege that every other man has, and this is the sure preventive of Socialistic ideas." What about the conditions of labor in the United States, about which the newspapers were regularly reporting? "I have no pity for the man who is discontented because he has to labour, because I believe this is the best state for man. . . . There is no comparison between the lot of the skilled workman and the heir to an hereditary title, who is very likely to lead an unhappy, wicked life. Inherited wealth is oftener a curse than a blessing." As to unskilled labor: "he lacks the necessary qualities; educational, physical, and moral. The common labourer is a common labourer because he is common."

The great inducement in America is for men to own their own homes. "The reason the United States is such a conservative country—and it is the most conservative country in the world—is because five to six millions of its citizens own the soil, their own homes. You cannot preach Socialism to these people."

What about the contrasts between wealth and poverty in the republic—are they just as great as those you find in Great Britain? There are indeed contrasts, agreed Carnegie, "but the laws give no man rank and wealth. We have no hereditary privileges. . . . We have no blackguard princes, dukes. . . . The native American is the most self-respecting man in the world, and hence he naturally respects the rights and merits of others." Were there no scandals and corruption in the United States? Yes, there were some, Carnegie granted, but the evildoers were "chiefly foreigners, emigrants from your own country to the foreign city of New York." And again Carnegie returned to the fundamental point he had stressed in *Triumphant Democracy*. "The American has no fundamental questions to settle now. All are settled, and no one advocates a change. . . . The system is perfect." And then the most basic 'articles of faith of the star-spangled Scottish-American: "In our new country we have perfection of institutions. There is not a party in America dissatisfied with the political institutions; no man rises to ask that any of these should change; no man suggests an improvement; we have only the proper administration of perfect institutions to look after. There are other modes of bribery than money. Your bribes flow from your monarchical institutions, making ranks, one above another. . . . No true man should wear a privilege not accorded to all his fellows."

The interviewer persisted with questions about the conditions of labor in Britain and America, particularly the issue of the eight-hour day. Carnegie seemed to be wavering on the need for legislation mandating a shorter workday. Fierce competition between industries and nations would seem to preclude the possibility of regulation, all the more so in industries like steelmaking, where twelve-hour days and seven-day work weeks were dictated by the competitive costs of manufacturing. On the other hand, granted the steelmaster, "we shall have more and more occasion for the State to legislate on behalf of the workers." For all that, "state interference should not be resorted to unless it is clear that a case is made out for its necessity."

But even as he was speaking to his interviewer, Carnegie must have pulsated with full consciousness that the terms of his company's contract with the Amalgamated Association of Steelworkers at his Homestead

Conclusion 163

works was coming up for renewal. The grand lessee of the feudal Cluny Castle estate was sailing westward for a battle that would have made Robert the Bruce flinch, if not quite fail.

In that spring of 1892 the two eminent Scotsmen—Gladstone and Carnegie—were facing formidable problems. The Liberal prime minister who resumed power—for two years as it turned out—was, at eighty-three, remarkably vigorous, a master of debate, still a hewer of wood and wanting, as he had been for many years, "to pacify Ireland." His new ministry included John Morley, a long-time friend of Carnegie's, as Irish secretary, as well as Henry Labouchere, a radical M.P. and another close acquaintance of the American industrialist. In 1892, Carnegie was the unquestioned controller of his steel company, and though not yet sixty, seeking no less than Gladstone to finish an important part of his life's work—amassing wealth—so that he could get on with the no less important part of it—giving that wealth away and entering ever more zestfully the lively streams of British politics. The Chartist of Dunfermline, laird of Cluny Castle, would in a few years purchase Skibo Castle, an even more eminent domain, all his own.

Gladstone's "Newcastle Programme" had as its centerpiece a new plan for Irish Home Rule: Ireland would now send members to the imperial parliament at Westminster, to vote there only on issues pertaining to Ireland or the empire. His new Irish bill, Gladstone hoped, would answer the fears of those Liberals who, having been disaffected by his 1886 Irish Home Rule bill, could now return to a restored Liberal Party. The open debate over the Second Home Rule Bill in the Commons went on

for over eighty-five sessions. But despite Gladstone's best efforts, the bill was finally vetoed by the House of Lords on September 8, 1893. In the spring of 1892, the looming issue for Carnegie was Homestead and renewing the contract with the skilled ironworkers of the Amalgamated Association. Far from following the model of his great Liberal model in London, Carnegie approached Homestead apprehensively, as much worried about the hard-fisted temperament of Henry Clay Frick, the chairman of Carnegie Brothers and Company, as about the demands of the union. Gladstone stood powerfully and always self-righteously arguing his cause in the well of the Commons, but Carnegie secreted himself in Rannoch Lodge, south of Cluny Castle and an unusual, unpretentious residence for a multimillionaire to whom conspicuous habitation was a compelling art. He had reason to be secluded. For Gladstone, the defeat of his bill by the House of Lords was regrettable, of course, but he was confident that the Lords were not the Lord, and his standing before the Lord was ultimately what mattered. For Carnegie, who feared the possible, Homestead realized the worst. Chartism, his reputation, his high standing among Britain's workers, his philanthropies, his Scottish heritage: all were suddenly lost and, so it seemed, beyond redemption.

Homestead seemed to contradict *Triumphant Democracy*. Indeed, to his many of his contemporaries, the battle at Carnegie's steel plant made a mockery of the book he had published six years before. Homestead revived the Anglo-American evaluation of Carnegie that with great liveliness had entered the transatlantic reviews of 1886 when his massive acclamation of American principles and institutions first appeared.

The English newspapers were particularly critical of Homestead. The *Sheffield Daily Telegraph* proposed a fitting sequel by "the man of the people, the great protector of tariffs and Pinkertons," a book entitled *The Tyrannies of Democracy*.[16] The *Times* of London remembered how *Triumphant Democracy* sought to instruct Britain in managing Irish Home Rule: "Every country, however fortunate, will always have its hands full of it if it attends to its own affairs." And, even though Frick might have caused the debacle at Homestead, using "a private police force is a thing that should neither be permitted nor required in a civilized community."[17] Indeed, he was denounced by the *London Echo*, which had once been part of his newspaper chain.[18] The *London Financial Observer* added its own indictment of "this Scotch-Yankee plutocrat meandering through Scotland in a four-in-hand."[19] *St. James's Gazette*, the bastion of Conservatism, shouted its own Toryism at the spread-eaglism of the "star-spangled Scotchman," the "iron master, millionaire, philanthropist, and free lecturer to the inhabitants of Great Britain." Homestead, it said, was a "civil war" in which "the maintenance of 'order' has been left to a hired band of private mercenaries." The "effete old country" had yet something to instruct and that was "the lesson of liberty. . . . Freedom can only exist where all rights are safely secured. Mr. Andrew Carnegie has preached to us upon 'Triumphant Democracy,' he has lectured us upon the rights and duties of wealth." The bloodshed at Homestead showed grimly that it was all "a wholesome piece of satire."[20]

Again, the Scottish press seemed to be doubly sensitive and doubly critical. The *Edinburgh Dispatch* said that, despite the intensity of labor disputes in Britain, they had never been as intense as those at Homestead, and we "may well be thankful that neither our capitalists nor our labourers have any inclination to imitate the methods which prevail in the land of 'Triumphant Democracy.'"[21] To which the newspaper of the steelmaster's native city, the *Dunfermline Journal*, added its regretful voice: yes, the workers should not have taken over the steel mill, but they had "a perfect right to refuse to submit to a reduction" of their wages.[22]

An additional dimension of the widespread public reaction to Homestead was offered by James Howard Bridge, who had been so helpful to Carnegie in preparing the manuscript of *Triumphant Democracy*. Having been privy to its workings, Bridge brought out a very informed account of *The Inside Story of the Carnegie Steel Company* in 1903, a decade after Homestead and a decade and a half after *Triumphant Democracy*. Newspapers everywhere, Bridge wrote, underscored the discrepancy between Carnegie's "idealistic utterances" and the actualities of Homestead. They now found in his practical philanthropy nothing but the expression of an unmitigated egotism. Does he praise unionism in Glasgow but violate it in the United States? Wrote Bridge: "Municipal bodies, workmen's unions, political clubs, vied with preachers, lecturers, and editors in England and America in fierce denunciation of one whose acts, it was said, conform so little to his verbal utterances."[23] Opinion in the United States was widely outraged by Homestead. Perhaps none was so fierce as the writer for the *St. Louis Post-Dispatch*.

> Three months ago Andrew Carnegie was a man to be envied. Today he is an object of mingled pity and contempt. In the estimation of nine-tenths of the thinking people on both sides of the ocean he has not only given the lie to all his antecedents but confessed himself a moral coward. One would naturally suppose that if he had a grain of consistency, not to say decency in his composition, he would favor rather than oppose the organization of trades-unions among his own working people at Homestead. . . . But what does Carnegie do? Runs off to Scotland out of harm's way to await the issue of the battle he was too pusillanimous to share. A single word from him might have saved the bloodshed— but that word was never spoken. . . . America can well spare Mr. Carnegie. Ten thousand Carnegie Public Libraries would not compensate the country for the direct evils resulting from the Homestead lockout. Say what you will of Frick, he is a brave man. Say what you will of Carnegie, he is a coward.[24]

Thus the transatlantic colloquy about *Triumphant Democracy* continued, but in a transmuted form. Events had outrun the Scotsman's Anglo-American vision, as indeed they had changed his earlier prominence in British politics. Homestead undercut Carnegie's role even further. He immediately felt the impact of Homestead. The events "burst upon him like a thunderbolt from a clear sky. They had such a depressing effect upon him that he had to lay his book aside and resort to the lochs and moors, fishing from morning to night."[25]

Just as soon as he came back to the United States in January 1893, Carnegie went directly to Pittsburgh. He knew he had to speak to the workers in his mills: what Frick and Homestead had torn asunder, he must now try convincingly to join. In a carefully prepared speech, he declared that his purpose was "to bury the past" and to banish it "as a horrid dream." Improbable though they may have seemed, but quite necessary for the success of the Carnegie Steel Company, his words on the surface seemed to support Frick while at the same time disavow his own power and capacity "in the management of the business."[26] Remarkably enough, he was at the same time sustaining his part of the transatlantic dialogue—he was hard at work on a revised edition of *Triumphant Democracy*.

The most important feature of the new edition was its concluding chapter, "A Look Ahead," in which Carnegie undertook to answer those in Britain who were arguing for imperial federation as a means of countering the customs unions that were being forged by the enlarged new nations on the European continent. The British movements for imperial federation were animating the ideas Carnegie presented in "A Look Ahead," which reiterated the sanguine view of the republic's growth that he had projected in the original version seven years before.[27]

Taking careful note of the British problems of the day, Carnegie did more than outbid his British federationists. He offered yet once again his solution for what seemed to be the almost insoluble Irish Home Rule question. If European states were becoming larger and more nationalist, Carnegie's proposal of a Greater America seemed almost insuperable. The federal republic of the United States, he said, was being enlarged decade by decade by the ready entrance of additional states. The way therefore lay open to the constituent states of the United Kingdom: to England, Scotland, Wales, and of course to Ireland. Except for the English principle of monarchy, they all shared institutions that were virtually similar to the United States. But, and here Carnegie was outflanking the imperial federationists, the U.S. open access of commerce, industry, and finance—the greatest *Zollverein* in the world—would vastly enrich an economically troubled Britain. True enough, there were some problems and impediments in the way of the merger, but the prospect, said Carnegie, was an enticing one, offering far more advantages than disadvantages, which he carefully enumerated and discussed. One might accuse him of being utopian, he granted. One might accuse him of being a dreamer of dreams. Still, he was certain that the future would see "The Re-United States," "the British-American Union."[28]

In late summer of 1898, Carnegie returned rather sharply to the basics of his Americanism. The Spanish-American War may have impressed his friend John Hay, McKinley's secretary of state, as "a splendid little war," because of its short duration and its offer—in the acquisition of Spain's widespread empire—of potentially great territorial gains. But in those very gains Carnegie found a threat to the ideals he had made his creed all his life. Acquiring distant possessions, he believed, would undermine the higher causes for which the United States had always stood. The republic had fought for two great causes: independence and union.[29] Let us not now subvert our fundamental ideas. "It has hitherto been [our] glorious mission to establish upon secure foundations *Triumphant Democracy*, and the world now understands government of the people, for the people, and by the people."[30] By imposing "in other lands the rule of the foreigner over the people" America would become a triumphant despot.[31] Carnegie pleaded with American leaders to avoid the European model of empire and wars. The republic "stands apart, pursuing her own great mission, and *teaching all nations by example*."[32]

By the treaty of Paris of December 1898, the United States took over Spain's scattered possessions. In November 1898, a small group of America's most prominent intellectuals founded the anti-imperialist league, including in their number such figures as E. L. Godkin, Mark Twain, William James, Jane Addams, and Carl Schurz. Carnegie joined their company, supporting them both with thousands of dollars and with his powerful voice. In the *North American Review*, he warned against becoming involved in European imperialism, which could only lead to costly establishments and costly wars. The republic should be the friend of all nations, the ally of none. More than that: the imperial idea was at bottom wrong. The American Civil War had underscored Lincoln's declaration that "no man is good enough to govern another without that man's consent. . . . This is the leading principle, the sheet-rock of American republicanism."[33] He wondered in particular about the threat America's new possessions might pose for her relations with Britain. Carnegie pointedly raised the danger of an Anglo-American diplomacy that would bode ill for the United States. The republic should not become "the cat's paw of Britain, in order that we may grasp the phantom of imperialism."[34] He nowhere wanted a diplomatic alliance of Britain and America. He surely wished to retain the Anglo-American affinity, "the alliance of hearts" that he had long argued for.[35] This was to be the race alliance of the English-speaking peoples he had long been celebrating. For Carnegie, American imperialism contradicted the singular virtue of the American republic. No less indeed, in challenging the American principle, it challenged the rationale of his own life.

FOR ALL THE RELATIVE SIMPLICITY of its theme, Andrew Carnegie's *Triumphant Democracy* leaves the reader pondering its many essences, the multiple facets of its importance. As an analysis of American politics and sociology, how does it compare with other major analyses of American life? To what extent are the tenets of political equality and a gospel of wealth two sides of the same doctrine? How much was he writing about triumphant democracy or the saga of Carnegie triumphant? In contemplating his magnum opus, what do we know about Andrew Carnegie: his psyche, the mainsprings of his individuality; and indeed how far should a historian, working from recorded sources, presume to know, and venture to infer? Assaying Carnegie and *Triumphant Democracy* at a greater distance, what are the enduring legacy of the great industrialist and the message of his book?

How does *Triumphant Democracy* compare with other books on the United States written by foreigners? It was an essay on American institutions, by a native-born Scotsman, for the edification of British leaders. During all of its history, especially in the period between 1776 and 1914, the United States attracted foreigners to its shores, always looking for instruction for their own countries. Virtually all came with set agendas, and, depending on what conclusions they wished to arrive at, drew positive or negative portraits of the transatlantic republic. The most influential of these books were Alexis de Tocqueville's *Democracy in America* (1835 and 1840) and James Bryce's *The American Commonwealth* (1888). But there were others, of a lesser magnitude perhaps, but noteworthy nonetheless: among these were the American portraits by Harriet Martineau, Michel Chevalier, Francis Grund, and, later, Hugo Munsterberg. The other books were travelogues and, however famous the author, of no lasting distinction.[36] Tocqueville started with profound questions and he cast his vision far and wide, but there could be no question at all that he was writing for Orleanist France. Bryce was at once a superb lawyer, a very competent historian, a longtime member of Parliament, and an astounding master of facts and what they signified, but his magisterial tome was written to answer the practical questions that America raised for the 1880s generation of mid-Victorian British leaders. Because Tocqueville and Bryce posed their findings more in terms of searching questions than of insistent answers, their books have endured. Carnegie came with a ready answer. And therefore his book seemed to matter only so long as his times did not outlast his argument. And, of course, they did. But as Joseph Frazier Wall, one of Carnegie's principal biographers reminds us, his book "is valid for the historian today. . . . It remains one of the most important documents of America's Gilded Age."[37]

A document of its age, *Triumphant Democracy* was as well, as Harold C. Livesay has explained, a wide-ranging study of American entrepreneurship and the nation's economic growth. While sounding the virtues of democracy against those of aristocracy, Carnegie also sounded the needs of a renewed affinity between America and Britain. Above all, his book was a study of Andrew Carnegie: in effect, an autobiography. It was not accidental that the five decades during which the democracy had become triumphant were precisely the decades of Carnegie's own life. He, like Whitman, sang of himself in also singing of America. In the United States he had found the Chartist republic. His own triumph realized all that the Chartists of the 1840s, and particularly those of Scotland, had fought for. The libraries of his teens, in which his voracious reading had educated him, the Union's struggle for the republic, his own mastery of steelmaking, his rise to fabulous wealth—where else than in the United States would this have been possible, and what more than the story of his life and success testified to the realization of Chartist ideals? There was one more thing: in a republic of political equality, great wealth brought great responsibility. Carnegie's gospel of wealth, as his *Triumphant Democracy* makes clear, was basically a gospel of democracy.

How far had political equality—the essential feature of America's triumphant democracy—necessarily dictated Carnegie's gospel of wealth? How much did his gospel of wealth enhance the importance of his gospel of democracy? The questions are insistent. Could a highly notable writer on American society have achieved great fame without having practiced great philanthropy? Conversely, could a major American philanthropist have been famous without having explained his philanthropy in a major analysis of American institutions? The brief answer is that major philanthropy and major books are separable. But the remarkable fact about Carnegie is that he did both. And more than that: he saw one as a dimension of the other. *Triumphant Democracy* announced the gospel of wealth three years before Carnegie's famous 1889 essay on "Wealth." But the idea of distributing his vast fortune had been inherent in his view of himself and the social order decades before he wrote either one. It could be found in his memorandum of 1868, in which he said that "the amassing of money is one of the worst species of idolatry" and hoped to devote himself to "public matters especially those connected with education & the improvement of the poorer classes."[38]

Triumphant Democracy had clearly laid out the centrality of education in the republic and it was only fitting that Carnegie devoted the bulk of his wealth to the dissemination of knowledge. The devotion of the Scots to education is proverbial. Like so many Americans, Carnegie saw education—basic, but not necessarily higher—as the great equalizer. Joseph Frazier Wall summarizes it this way: "If one defines education in the broadest sense possible, which would include libraries as a form of popular, undirected public education, then one can say that the great bulk of Carnegie's fortune—over 80 percent—was to go for educational purposes: libraries, colleges and universities, institutions to promote scientific research and the diffusion of knowledge, and individual grants and pensions to college teachers."[39] This vast sum totaled nearly $300,000,000.[40] That philanthropy triumphant comprised a facet of democracy triumphant was clear enough to Carnegie, and surely his money underscored the message of his book. But both emanated from a few other sources as well: his Chartist origins, his social ambitions, and no less imperatively, the driving force of his driven individuality.

Triumphant Democracy was a passionate republican argument by its Scottish-American author at a particular moment in American and British history. But the embattled bitterness between capital and labor in the United States would dull its edge. Republicanism in Britain would before long be drowned out in the celebratory tributes to an old, enshrined queen. Remarkably, as he aged along with the queen, Carnegie joined the salutations. In 1897, he joined the hundreds of thousands who witnessed the grand procession acclaiming the Diamond Jubilee of Victoria's reign. He wrote these enraptured words for the *North American Review*.

"The Queen" means everything that touches and thrills the patriotic chord. That both as a woman and a sovereign, she has deserved the unique tribute paid her goes without saying: the wildest radical, or even republican, will concur in this. . . . Washington, Tell, Wallace, Bruce, Lincoln, Queen Victoria or Margaret are the stuff of which heroes or saints are made.[41]

The list arrests one's attention. With one exception, the heroes are Americans and Scots, the saints are two women: the Queen, whom Carnegie had earlier maligned, and his mother Margaret, whom he always venerated. He had gone beyond wanting to dethrone Victoria; he yet again enthroned his mother.

Carnegie's republicanism bound his book's chapters and enlivened his message. And yet Carnegie himself responded to motives that may, in some way, make his acts and words seem contradictory. Was it simple irony that made him, by spending his prodigious funds, Laird of Skibo (as he had been at Cluny) and Laird of the Dunfermline glen and estate of Pittencrief? Why had he earlier taken those boisterous, ostentatious carriage trips from Brighton to Inverness? When Carnegie balked at providing his funds to make the Scottish universities tuition-free, Lord Thomas Shaw of Dunfermline offered what was very likely the true reason: "the danger [to the plan] was in Carnegie himself, who naturally wanted to be associated with men of power, and who always had a real weakness towards the aristocrat. In later life, poor man, this led him astray."[42] A more severe critique was entered by a friend's son, who had closely watched the steelmaster's philanthropy. It was "social advertising and flattery" that had purchased Carnegie, said John Bigelow's son. "No wonder that he felt himself infallible when Lords temporal and spiritual courted him and hung upon his words. They wanted his money, and flattery alone could wring it from him."[43]

Did Carnegie act out of apparently conflicting motives? Yes. Did the passage of time change these motives and explain the apparent conflicts? Again, yes. In any event, do these contradictions minimize the importance of *Triumphant Democracy*? The answer is no. He was not confined by the consistency of a small mind, as Emerson had advised, not did he fear contradictions, as Whitman had admitted about himself.

One big contradiction he could not readily either ignore or overcome was the deadly war between the union and the strikebreakers at Carnegie's

Homestead steel plant on July 6, 1892. Anyone contemplating the importance of *Triumphant Democracy* must also contemplate the importance of Homestead. In Carnegie's life, they appear to stand as antipodes. In many respects they were. Deep in the recesses of his Scottish homeland at the time of the wars on the Monongahela, Carnegie understood at once that he was party to what was probably the worst deed of his life. Secreted at Rannoch Lodge, inaccessible to his usual lines of communication, he was like Adam hiding from the presence of a reproving and wrathful God. Carnegie had worried about Frick's belligerent temper and his confrontational style. He had also worried about open conflict. The news from Homestead was dreadful, and it immediately flooded both sides of the Atlantic. It weighed heavily on Carnegie's conscience because it sharply injured his transatlantic image. With the American presidential election in the immediate future, the Republican leadership was blaming him for imperiling Harrison's chances against Cleveland. Gladstone's Liberal Party, the homestead of his British friends and therefore Carnegie's natural habitat, had just resumed office. The war at his steelworks could not have happened at a worse time.

Years later, after he had sold his steel works to J. P. Morgan, writing in the very private confines of the memories he would record from time to time, he protested that, while he was himself sympathetic to his workers, the view of it "throughout the country was naturally the reverse, owing to the Homestead riot. The Carnegie Works meant to the public Mr. Carnegie's war upon labor's just earnings."[44] The public image of Carnegie, of all benevolences, counted for little. "Nothing I have ever had to meet in all my life, before or since, wounded me so deeply. No pangs remain of any wounds received in my business career save that of Homestead."[45] Yet for all his wounds—it was a humiliation if not quite a crucifixion—he insisted that the relatively few men (as he self-reassuredly numbered them) who led the strike "were outrageously wrong." Perhaps his most famous aphorism could now be reversed. Perhaps it was no less true that he who dies disgraced dies without riches.

Homestead signified the precise point of convergence of his trinitarian faith: his passion for success and money, his driven ego, his Chartist creed. If these constituted his identity, then Homestead threatened to rob him of it. That is why he could never forgive Frick, and after Homestead looked tirelessly to get rid of him as from a guilt-ridden conscience. That is why he sublimated all his energies into that destructive and creative enterprise of horizontal and vertical integration that constituted Carnegie's unique brand of capitalism. That is why after Homestead he was driven to make so much money that he could sell out at the highest price that his benevolences could then pay for. The sale to J. P. Morgan was an event, hardly an accident, waiting—indeed needing—to happen. There was yet a neo-Chartist life, one of philanthropy, or more significantly of atonement.

To Carnegie and his generation, Britain and the United States were Anglo-Saxon nations, and had, in the dim mist of earlier centuries, grown up in the German forests. *Triumphant Democracy* preached race alliance. The phrase resonates in his writings no less than that "political equality" he intoned throughout his masterpiece. How are we to explain the great late nineteenth-century vogue of Anglo-Saxonism? English historians had, in the mid-Victorian decades, dug into their pre-Norman records to come up with a picture of the freedoms their forebears had practiced before the Norman conquest. What possibly prompted their inquiry was the push for collectivism against, as they perceived it, Anglo-Saxon liberty. In the United States, the Anglo-Saxon past served intellectuals, and historians among them, as a bulwark against the massive incursions of foreigners of different stocks bringing with them their babel of tongues and illiberal institutions.

For Scots coming to the United States, it was particularly important to stress the English-speaking community to which they all belonged. Carnegie's resplendent touring coaches in England and Scotland and the vast sums he spent on English politics and Scottish institutions of learning were an answer, in a way, to the servitude James Boswell had given Samuel Johnson: they also serve themselves who serve their masters. *Triumphant Democracy* is noteworthy for its celebration of Scottish invention and entrepreneurship in America. It is no less noteworthy for preaching race alliance. For Carnegie and his Pan-Anglian confreres, the United States and Britain had regrettably been divided for far too long. It was time for them to resume their community of language, politics, literature, history, and mores. Carnegie wanted nothing so much as to reconnect England's offspring with the mother country. The words "mother country" were charged with meaning for Carnegie for so many reasons, and most important because he could never forget Dunfermline, to which he always returned, and because Margaret Morrison Carnegie was a daily living motive throughout his life.

How much did Carnegie's character and persona enter into the shaping of *Triumphant Democracy*? He was, as so many other details of his life testify, ebullient, self-proclaiming, self-promoting, often oblivious of facts that stood in his way, vainglorious, indeed, no small braggart. It matters of course how one perceives Carnegie himself. Was he a robber baron? How would he then regard his barony? Was he a captain of industry? Does such a captain demean his industry? Was he a master of capital? With the historiography of the later twentieth century, writers of the American past changed their premises. In *The World of Andrew Carnegie, 1865–1901,* Louis M. Hacker suggested that the better way to judge Carnegie's achievement was in terms of the mores of his age and the entrepreneurship that his age acclaimed. By these terms, what the steelmaster had wrought was not merely prodigious, but valid and justifiable. No less than that, looking at the land where he had succeeded so astoundingly, he saw it in the large and embraced its premises as equitable. And in carrying on his endless argument with England—which, so he felt, had demeaned his Scottish family and himself—he put aside whatever nagging questions he may have had about the United States. In judging Carnegie—and his book, of course—a later age, and indeed many of his contemporaries, found not merely warts and all, but *warts as all.* To that judgment, the most warranted answer is that, as his biographers have approached him, Carnegie lived by the premises of his sharply changing new business age and of its fiercely competitive managers of industry. It helps to understand Carnegie, though nowhere to justify, to remember that he was a manager of steelmaking rather than an active participant, more often from a distance, than in immediate proximity. Whatever doubts Carnegie had about himself, his conduct, his treatment of his partners and his workers, in his quasi-Lutheran self-probing, were answered by Spencer and Darwin and by his own enormous success, displayed in his Dunfermline and Chartist ways. That is as far as the historian should sensibly venture in pondering the question of *Triumphant Democracy* as a product of Carnegie's character and psyche.

For those looking for the psychological mainsprings of Andrew Carnegie's great success, the driving elements would seem to be all there. He always had to prove himself: he saw life as an endless competition— he knew that about himself. His father had failed in the old country; he was to be "the man of the family," its only true breadwinner. He was the firstborn: his immediate competing alternate was his only sibling, his young brother Thomas, who, by contrast, was shy, retiring, uncompetitive. He was utterly devoted to his mother, a strong, untiring woman, to whom he was bound by what a later generation might regard as an unseemly connection. His mother did not approve of Louise Whitfield, whom he was courting and whom he did not marry until very shortly after his mother's death.

Freud or Jung or their disciples or cohorts could be called on to offer clues about the proclaimer of *Triumphant Democracy* or the lord of the manor at Cluny Castle. He was rather short, five feet two inches by some accounts, five feet four by others: he compensated for his marked physical shortness by rising tall where he could. He always sought the company of highly educated men, not only to better himself but with whom he could form personally advantageous connections. And he sought the company of men of power, which he could hope to exert by knowing them or by helping pay for their political causes. He was an alien in a new land, yet linked by tongue, though marked by brogue: he was driven by the ambition of a young, adaptable, ambitious, freshly arrived alien. What made Andy run? If *Triumphant Democracy* was indeed his incarnation, his persona, the many reasons might help a venturesome Carnegie psychobiographer explain its message, its massive volume, its great success.

At the urging of his friends on both sides of the Atlantic, Carnegie started writing his memoirs some time after he had retired from the business of steel and the business of philanthropy. As his widow recalled, he would retire for a few weeks each summer to their bungalow in the moors near Skibo Castle to jot down his recollection of "those early times, and as he wrote he lived them all over again." It all ended when war came to Europe in early August 1914 and Carnegie returned home, brokenhearted and physically sick, never to go back to Skibo or again to try writing his life.[46] His memoirs were posthumously collected and published as his *Autobiography* in 1920, the year after he died. Serviceable as they are, the memoirs are only a fragment of Carnegie's personal story. No less helpful in many ways was his *Triumphant Democracy*. The book's subtitle is *Fifty Years' March of the Republic*, and Carnegie was exactly fifty years old when the book appeared. Why had he dated the start of the republic's march in 1830 and why did its phenomenal rise virtually coincide with Carnegie's own rise in the United States? Yet it was, more than that, a highly personal argument with impassioned statements from Carnegie's republican creed about the insults and abasements of English aristocracy. What bound the statistics into a unified book was what Carnegie had to say about the access to opportunity and wealth that he had himself pursued. He laid particular stress on the Scottish contribution to the

American achievement. As he wrote it up in *Triumphant Democracy*, and indeed as several of his reviewers noted, the book could as well have been called *Triumphant Carnegie*.

Triumphant Democracy represented Carnegie in motion. The Chartism he had been raised in served him as a program of action more than a deep-seated creed. That creed he found in Herbert Spencer and his "faith in progress through evolution toward perfection." His faith became, as he put it, "the truth of evolution. 'All is well since all grows better' became my motto, my true source of comfort."[47] He saw that faith realized by his own success and the phenomenal material progress of the United States.

A book of its times, its life was coeval with Carnegie's public life. That life began to diminish when the close friends he had made among the Gladstonian Liberals in Britain lost office. It may not have been by chance for a man of Carnegie's driving ambition, that his political activities were soon translated into philanthropy. The enormous wealth he disbursed soon gave him the influence that his more limited preachment of democracy in Britain never achieved. Carnegie himself was crushed by the outbreak, in August 1914, of a war that soon enveloped the whole Western world. His friend Matthew Arnold's sustaining phrase of "sweetness and light" now became a hollow mockery, and as for the maxim he had taken from his greatest mentor, Herbert Spencer, it now seemed that all was bad because all had grown worse. The Spencerian faith he had built as a sanctuary was savagely torn down. Carnegie survived the Great War by a year, dying at the very time that the victors were not merely dividing the spoils but almost irredeemably spoiling the new world they were vengefully patching together.

Yet remarkably, through the agency of the monies he had entrusted to institutions, the good that Carnegie did lived after him: it was not interred with his bones. One cannot turn far, especially in the American and Scottish worlds, without meeting the good works his monies endowed, particularly in the broad fields of education and research, and in the larger European world, for the cause of settling disputes among nations, the Carnegie Endowment for International Peace, which he announced in November 1910 with a trust of ten million dollars.[48] In protean forms, big and small, the Carnegie legacy lives on: in the hundreds of public libraries, in the Carnegie Institution of New York, in the teachers' pension funds, in the Carnegie Institution of Washington, in the Hague Court (Tribunal) of International Peace, in the Carnegie Institute of Pittsburgh, and in New York's Carnegie Hall, to cite some of the most familiar.

His good works live on. But what is remarkable about *Triumphant Democracy* is that so too do his informing ideas. He often said that the great republic would grow insuperably in population and wealth. In 1893, when he brought out the revised edition of *Triumphant Democracy*, he ventured confidently that the future would see a "Re-United States" featuring a "British-American Union." In issues of power and international affairs, subsequent events fulfilled his prediction. America joined Britain in the Great War and far more decisively in the war against Hitler. When the Soviet Union fought its erstwhile partners for world dominion in the years after World War II, once again the United States and Britain allied as the building blocks of the North Atlantic Treaty Organization.

Differ though they might on particular issues, the kindred polities stood together. The personal associations of their respective leaders bound successive decades: Roosevelt and Churchill, Kennedy and Macmillan, Reagan and Thatcher, Bush and Blair; the kindred polities went their particular ways together. Carnegie's race alliance of the principal English-speaking nations held sway during the twentieth century. The roles of metropolis and colony changed, as he had always said they would, but the institutions they shared bound them strongly. In that affinity of institutions, it was important that the aristocracy Carnegie had so much denounced, whose great prominence in British society and politics had moved him to write his book, was very significantly decimated by its mortal wounds in the Great War and much further weakened by the impact of depressions and continuous social change. In terms of privilege and wealth distinctions, Britain had largely outdemocratized the republic. The Laird of Skibo, however predictive and evolutionary his mindset, could scarcely have imagined what the monarchy would become a century after *Triumphant Democracy*.

CARNEGIE'S DEDICATION of *Triumphant Democracy* deserves special attention. The passionate sentiments seem at first to push credibility. But a careful reading of his words clears away the haze that might otherwise becloud what he is about to say in his analysis of America's great material and cultural advance. His massive book of facts and figures makes one accept finally that the sentiments are quintessential Carnegie that he meant every word in his inscription.

An offertory to the United States, it is also a song of himself. Only slightly below the surface of his words, he identifies his own progress with that of the republic and particularly, as he saw it, the triumph of the

Union's ideal of equality over the Confederacy's ideal of inequality. He reproves his motherland for what she had denied him. But he reproves no less the indigenous American who cannot grasp the celebration of America by the immigrant—made into a new man by his new land. In their wider range, his words sum up more than a century of the relationship between British aristocracy and American democracy.

These are the carefully chosen words of the dedication of *Triumphant Democracy*.

<blockquote>
To The
BELOVED REPUBLIC
under whose equal laws I am
made the equal of any man, although denied
political equality by my native land,
I DEDICATE THIS BOOK
with an intensity of gratitude
and admiration which the native-born citizen
can neither feel nor understand.

ANDREW CARNEGIE
</blockquote>

Notes

INTRODUCTION

1. The word "civism" is used throughout this book in its traditional sense, the principles of good citizenship. It encompasses all the duties and responsibilities essential to being a good citizen.

2. Bernard Alderson, *Andrew Carnegie: The Man and His Work* (New York: Doubleday, Page & Co., 1902), 105–06.

CHAPTER 1

1. Joseph Frazier Wall, *Andrew Carnegie* (New York: Oxford University Press, 1970), 358–60.

2. Burton J. Hendrick, *The Life of Andrew Carnegie* (New York: Doubleday, Doran & Co., 1932), 1: 256–59.

N. B.: I started my research on this book by twice canvassing the papers of Andrew Carnegie in the Manuscript Division of the Library of Congress; the papers are organized in 300 containers. It is my tribute to Hendrick's comprehensive, prize-winning two-volume biography that, for the years I was researching, I found no noteworthy letter or memorandum of Carnegie's that had not already appeared in his biography. I have therefore depended on Hendrick for citing these important Carnegie sources. I have similarly referenced the Carnegie sources cited in Joseph F. Wall's magisterial work on Carnegie, which appeared forty years after Hendrick's.

3. Andrew Carnegie, *Autobiography of Andrew Carnegie*, ed. John C. Van Dyke (Boston: Houghton Mifflin, 1920), 2; Hendrick, *Life of Carnegie*, 1:11–15.

4. Carnegie, *Autobiography*, 9.

5. Ibid., 9–10.

6. Cited in Hendrick, *Life of Carnegie* 1:72–77; italics added.

7. Ibid., 119–20; emphasis is Carnegie's.

8. Ibid., 146–47.
9. Ibid., 238.
10. Ibid., chaps. 9–12, passim.
11. Ibid., 286.
12. Ibid., 230–36.
13. Cited in Wall, *Andrew Carnegie*, 417.
14. Hendrick, *Life of Carnegie*, 1:275–76.
15. Wall, *Andrew Carnegie*, 417.
16. Ibid., 436–37.
17. Ibid., 224–25.
18. Ibid.
19. Hendrick, *Life of Carnegie*, 1:265–66.
20. Wall, *Andrew Carnegie*, 436–38.

Chapter 2

1. Andrew Carnegie, *Triumphant Democracy* (New York: Charles Scribner's Sons, 1886), 1.
2. Ibid., 364.
3. Ibid., 365.
4. Ibid., 19.
5. Ibid., Preface, v.
6. Ibid., 20.
7. Ibid., 364.
8. Ibid., 500.
9. Ibid., 11.
10. Ibid., 11.
11. Ibid., 25.
12. Burton J. Hendrick, *The Life of Andrew Carnegie* (New York: Doubleday, Doran & Co., 1932), 1:26.
13. Carnegie, *Triumphant Democracy*, 27–28.
14. Ibid., 119–20.
15. Ibid., 121.
16. Hendrick, *Life of Carnegie*, 1:9.

17. Ibid., 1:92.
18. Ibid., 1:95.
19. Ibid., 1:84.
20. Ibid., 1:58.
21. Ibid., Preface, 1:ix.
22. Carnegie, *Triumphant Democracy*, 84–85.
23. Ibid., 34.
24. Ibid., 138.
25. Hendrick, *Life of Carnegie*, 1:144.
26. Carnegie, *Triumphant Democracy*, 204–05.
27. Ibid., 217.
28. Ibid., 218.
29. Ibid., 296. The italics are Carnegie's.
30. Ibid., 469–70.
31. Ibid., 447–48.
32. Ibid., 139ff.
33. Ibid., 135.
34. Ibid., 316.
35. Ibid., 323.
36. Ibid., chaps.14–15, passim.
37. Ibid., 339.
38. Ibid., 361.
39. Ibid., 363.
40. Carnegie, *Triumphant Democracy*, 95–96.
41. Ibid., 95.
42. Ibid., 153.
43. Ibid., 158–60.
44. Ibid., 161.
45. Ibid., 443–44.
46. Joseph Frazier Wall, *Andrew Carnegie* (New York: Oxford University Press, 1970), 428–29.
47. Hendrick, *Life of Carnegie*, 80–81.
48. Carnegie, *Triumphant Democracy*, 367.
49. Ibid., 367.

50. Ibid., 135.

51. Ibid.,148.

52. Ibid.

53. Ibid., 118.

54. Ibid., 391.

55. John Morley, *The Life of William Ewart Gladstone* (New York & London: Macmillan, 1903), 3:173–74.

56. Carnegie, *Triumphant Democracy*, 369–70.

57. Ibid., 392.

58. Ibid., 490.

59. Ibid.

60. Ibid., 477–78.

61. Ibid., 451.

Chapter 3

1. Bernard Bailyn, *The Ideological Origins of the American Revolution* (Cambridge: Harvard University Press:1967), 47. Italics added.

2. Ibid., 83. Bailyn ascribed many of his ideas to the seminal work of Caroline Robbins, *The Eighteenth-Century Commonwealthman* (Cambridge: Harvard University Press, 1959). But in tracing the emergence of the antithesis of ideals between establishment Britain and radical America, and notable too with Bailyn's works, are the magisterial volumes of Gordon Wood, *The Creation of the American Republic, 1776–1789* (Chapel Hill: University of North Carolina Press, 1969), and *The Radicalism of the American Revolution* (New York: Alfred A. Knopf, 1992). Several other books invite attention: Robert Middlekauff, *The Glorious Cause* (New York: Oxford University Press, 1982); Edward Countryman, *The American Revolution* (New York: Hill & Wang, 1985); Theodore Draper, *A Struggle for Power* (New York: Random House, 1996); and Marc Egnal, *A Mighty Empire: The Origins of the American Revolution* (Ithaca: Cornell University Press, 1988).

3. See Jane L. Mesick, *The English Traveler in America, 1785–1835* (New York: Columbia University Press, 1922), 301ff.

4. Perhaps the best single collection of these pamphlets is Bernard Bailyn, ed., *Pamphlets of American Revolution* (Cambridge: Harvard University Press,1965). Out of more than 400 pamphlets, he decided that 72 merited republication. See also the impressive and compendious collection of Merrill Jensen, *Tracts of the American Revolution, 1763–1776* (Indianapolis: Bobbs-Merrill, 1967).

5. Linda Colley, *Britons: Forging the Nation, 1707–1837* (New Haven: Yale University Press, 1992).

6. Adam Sisman, *Boswell's Presumptuous Task: The Making of the Life of Dr. Johnson* (New York: Farrar, Straus & Giroux, 2000) is a very fine analysis not only of the shaping of Boswell's life of Johnson but, no less remarkably, of the Anglo-Scottish connection in the later eighteenth century.

7. The breach between Franklin and his son has been treated by Edmund S. Morgan, *Benjamin Franklin* (New Haven: Yale University Press, 2002); see 223–24.

8. The best single treatment of this subject is by Mary Beth Norton, *The British Americans: The Loyalist Exiles in England, 1774–1789* (Boston: Little, Brown: 1972).

9. Frank Thistlethwaite, *The Great Experiment* (Cambridge: Harvard University Press, 1955), chap. 1.

10. John Bartlet Brebner, *North Atlantic Triangle* (New Haven: Yale University Press, 1945), passim.

11. Gordon Wood, *Creation of the American Republic*, 103.

12. Ibid., 47–48, 91–93.

13. Evarts Boutel Greene, *The Revolutionary Generation, 1763–1790* (New York: Macmillan Co.,1943), 386–95.

14. John Bach McMaster, *A History of the People of the United States, from the Revolution to the Civil War* (New York: D. Appleton & Co., 1914), 5: 287.

15. Alexis de Tocqueville, *Democracy in America*, trans. George Lawrence (Garden City: Doubleday & Co., 1966), 438, 442.

16. F. O. Matthiessen, *The American Renaissance* (New York: Oxford University Press, 1941), 678.

17. Washington Irving, "English Writers on America," in *The Sketch Book of Geoffrey Crayon, Gent.* (New York: New American Library, 1961), 61, 63–64.

18. Brooks Atkinson, ed., *The Complete Essays and Other Writings of Ralph Waldo Emerson* (New York: Modern Library, 1950), 540–51.

19. Joseph J. Ellis, *Founding Brothers: The Revolutionary Generation* (New York: Alfred A. Knopf, 2001), 187–95.

20. The best exploration of this theme is Gordon Wood, *The Radicalism of the American Revolution* (New York: Alfred A. Knopf, 1992).

21. See David Hackett Fischer, *The Revolution of American Conservatism: The Federalist Party in the Era of Jeffersonian Democracy* (New York: Harper & Row, 1965).

22. Louis Hartz, *The Liberal Tradition in America* (New York: Harcourt, Brace & World, 1955).

23. Atkinson, *Complete Essays of Ralph Waldo Emerson*, 686, 614.

24. See W. B. Cairns, *British Criticism of American Writings: 1783–1833* (Madison: University of Wisconsin, 1922).

25. Cited in Robert E. Spiller, *The American in England during the First Half Century of Independence* (New York: Henry Holt & Co., 1926), 310.

26. H. C. Allen, *Great Britain and the United States* (New York: St. Martin's Press, 1952), 108.

27. Max Berger, *The British Traveler in America, 1836–1860* (New York: Columbia University Press, 1943), 101–02.

28. Quoted in Spiller, *American in England*, 293.

29. John Stuart Mill, *Essays on Politics and Culture*, ed. Gertrude Himmelfarb (Gloucester: Peter Smith, 1973), 174. And again: "Every [English] book of travels in America has been a party pamphlet . . . and been pressed into the service of one party or of the other." Ibid., 215.

30. Frances Trollope, *Domestic Manners of the Americans, 1832*, ed. Pamela Nevile-Sington (Bury St. Edmunds: Penguin Classics, 1997),118, 122, 254–56.

31. Among the more prominent ones were those of John Pierpont and Noah Webster.

32. By far the best book on the subject is Ruth Miller Elson, *Guardians of Tradition: American Schoolbooks of the Nineteenth Century* (Lincoln: University of Nebraska, 1964). See especially chaps. 5 and 6.

33. Very fine examples may be found in Alexander Mackay, *The Western World, or Travels in the United States in 1846–47* (London, 1850), cited in Allan Nevins, ed., *America through British Eyes* (New York: Oxford University Press, 1948), 241–62.

34. This idea appears prominently in such books are Richard Hofstadter, *The Paranoid Style in American Politics, and Other Essays* (Cambridge: Harvard University Press, 1996) and also in his *The Age of Reform* (New York: Alfred A. Knopf, 1955); Lee Benson, *The Concept of Jacksonian Democracy: New York as a Test Case* (Princeton: Princeton University Press, 1961); John Higham, *Strangers in the Land: Patterns of American Nativism, 1860–1925*, 1963 reprint (Westport, CT: Greenwood Press, 1980); Robert Wiebe, *The Search for Order, 1877–1920* (New York: Hill & Wang, 1967). An important collection of essays is Richard O. Curry and Thomas N. Brown, eds. *Conspiracy: The Fear of Subversion in American History* (New York: Holt, Rinehart & Winston, 1972).

35. Robert Kelley, *The Transatlantic Persuasion: The Liberal-Democratic Mind in the Age of Gladstone* (New York: Alfred A. Knopf, 1969), xix.

36. Allen, *Great Britain and the United States*, 164.

37. Daniel J. Boorstin, *The Americans: The National Experience* (New York: Vintage Books, 1965), 389–90.

38. George W. Pierson, *Tocqueville and Beaumont in America* (New York: Oxford University Press, 1938), 183.

39. Francis J. Grund, *The Americans*, 1837 (New York: Johnson Reprint Corporation, 1968), 58.

40. Ibid., 57.

41. Henry T. Tuckerman, *America and Her Commentators*, 1864 (New York: American Antiquarian Press, 1961), 286–87.

42. Ibid., 410.

43. Ibid., 291.

44. Fischer, *Revolution of American Conservatism*, xi–xx.

45. Washington Irving, "Essay on Campbell," 1810, cited in Spiller, *American in England*, 276.

46. Henry Adams, *The Education of Henry Adams* (New York: Modern Library, 1931), 19.

47. R. W. B. Lewis, *The American Adam: Innocence, Tragedy, and Tradition in the Nineteenth Century* (Chicago: University of Chicago Press: 1955), chaps. 6, 7.

48. Cushing Strout, *The American Image of the Old World* (New York: Harper & Row, 1963), 77, and chap. 5, passim.

49. Ibid., 100–03.

50. Cited in Spiller, *American in England*, 327.

51. R. R. Palmer *The Age of the Democratic Revolution: The Challenge* (Princeton: Princeton University Press, 1959–64), 282.

52. Elie Halevy, *England in 1815*, E. I. Watkin and D. A. Barker, trans. (New York: Barnes & Noble, 1968), part 3, chap. 1.

53. J. P. Mayer, ed., *Journeys to England and Ireland* (New Haven: Yale University Press, 1958), 67.

54. Ibid., 75. Said Tocqueville: "The French wish not to have superiors. The English wish to have inferiors. The Frenchman constantly raises his eyes above him anxiously. The Englishman lowers his beneath him with satisfaction. On both sides there is pride, but it is understood in a different way."

55. Ibid., 86–87.

56. See G. D. Lillibridge, *Beacon of Freedom: The Impact of American Freedom upon Great Britain, 1830–1870* (Philadelphia: University of Pennsylvania Press, 1955).

57. This is the working idea of Frank Thistlethwaite's *The Anglo-American Connection* (Philadelphia: University of Pennsylvania Press, 1959), an idea that, it is fair to say, Dr. Thistlethwaite does modify.

58. Thistlethwaite, *Anglo-American Connection,* and David Paul Crook, *American Democracy in English Politics, 1815–1850* (Oxford: Clarendon Press, 1965).

59. Crook, *American Democracy in English Politics*, 70.

60. Thistlethwaite, *Anglo-American Connection,* 165.

61. Berger, *British Traveler in America, 1836–1860*, 183.

62. Thistlethwaite, *Anglo-American Connection,* 167–69.

63. Ibid., 43.

64. Herman Ausubel, *John Bright, Victorian Reformer* (New York: John Wiley & Sons, 1966), 49.

65. Cited in Thistlethwaite, *Anglo-American Connection*, 43.

66. Ibid., 43.

67. Crook, *American Democracy in English Politics*, 35–51.

68. Cited in Lillibridge, *Beacon of Freedom*, 49.

69. Ibid., 45.

70. Ibid., chaps. 1, 2.

71. Burton J. Hendrick, *The Life of Andrew Carnegie* (New York: Doubleday, Doran & Co., 1932), 1:79–80.

72. Wall, *Andrew Carnegie*, 47ff. See also Joseph Frazier Wall, "Andrew Carnegie: Child of Chartism," *History* 4 (May 1961), 153–66.

73. Hendrick, *Life of Carnegie*, 1:74.

74. Strout, *American Image of the Old World*, 50–57.

75. G. M. Young, *Victorian England, Portrait of an Age* (London: Oxford University Press, 1936), 77–78.

Chapter 4

1. For a brief and very illuminating comment on the transforming British aristocracy, see "The End of the Patrician Polity," in David Cannadine, *The Decline and Fall of the British Aristocracy* (New York: Anchor Books, 1992), 37–54.

2. Barbara Miller Solomon, *Ancestors and Immigrants* (Cambridge: Harvard University Press, 1956), 13.

3. Edward C. Kirkland, ed., *The Gospel of Wealth and Other Timely Essays* (Cambridge: Harvard University Press, 1962), 197.

4. John Bartlet Brebner, *The North Atlantic Triangle* (New Haven: Yale University Press, 1943), chaps. 10–11.

5. Ernest May, *Imperial Democracy: The Emergence of America as a Great Power* (New York: Harcourt, Brace & World, 1961), 7–10.

6. Milton Plesur, *America's Outward Thrust* (DeKalb: Northern Illinois University Press, 1971), 134.

7. Cushing Strout, *The American Image of the Old World* (New York: Harper & Row, 1963), 148.

8. Rowland Berthoff, *British Immigrants in Industrial America, 1790–1950* (Cambridge: Harvard University Press, 1953), 194.

9. John A. Garraty, *The New Commonwealth, 1877–1890* (New York: Harper & Row, 1968), 284–86.

10. Ibid., 108.

11. Kirkland, ed., *Gospel of Wealth*, 200–01.

12. James Muirhead, *America, the Land of Contrasts: A Briton's View of His American Kin* (London: John Lane, 1902), 75.

13. Ibid., 78.

14. Berthoff, *British Immigrants in Industrial America*, 131.

15. James Bryce, *The American Commonwealth*, 2nd ed., revised (London: Macmillan & Co., 1891), 2:410.

16. Bryce, *American Commonwealth*, 2:654.

17. Charles Wentworth Dilke, *Greater Britain: A Record of Travel in English-Speaking Countries during 1866 and 1867* (London: Macmillan & Co., 1868), 217.

18. Kirkland, ed., *Gospel of Wealth*, 197ff.

19. Bryce, *American Commonwealth*, 2:410–11.

20. Ibid., 2:650–51.

21. Muirhead, *Land of Contrasts*, 78–79.

22. Howard Mumford Jones, *The Age of Energy* (New York: Viking, 1971), 263–65.

23. Ibid., 143.

24. William Maxwell Evarts, "Oration," cited in *Popular Culture and Industrialism 1865–1890*, Henry Nash Smith, ed. (Garden City: Anchor Books, 1967), 14.

25. James M. McPherson, *Battle Cry of Freedom* (New York: Oxford University Press, 1988) is an excellent one-volume history of the Civil War. See in particular chaps. 14, 16, 20, 28, and the epilogue. The epilogue, pp. 853–62, surveys the nature and cost of the war.

26. W. D. Rubinstein, *Britain's Century* (London: Arnold, 1998), 136.

27. K. Theodore Hoppen, *The Mid-Victorian Generation 1846–1886* (New York: Oxford University Press, 1998), 230.

28. Henry M. Pelling, *America and the British Left* (New York: New York University Press, 1957), 8.

29. Ibid., 7–8.

30. Cited in Pelling, *America and the British Left*, 18.

31. Rubinstein, *Britain's Century*, 137.

32. Hoppen, *Mid-Victorian Generation*, 231.

33. It was not by chance that the powerful chopper of oaks and chairman of his board became a popular icon during the years of his third ministry: "Gladstone personified

mid-Victorian progress and piety." See Hoppen, *Mid-Victorian Generation*, 638–41. See also Jonathan Perry, *The Rise and Fall of Liberal Government in Victorian Britain* (New Haven: Yale University Press, 1993), 247–73, which deals with Gladstone's Liberalism and its critics.

34. Pelling, *America and the British Left*, 30–48, discusses these years at great length.

35. Rubinstein, *Britain's Century*, 196–98.

36. Hoppen, *Mid-Victorian Generation*, 640.

37. Ibid.

38. Pelling, *America and the British Left*, 17.

39. Ibid., 24–25.

40. Adam Badeau, *Aristocracy in England* (New York, 1886), cited in H. S. Commager, *Britain Through American Eyes* (New York: McGraw-Hill, 1974), 478.

41. Cited in Pelling, *America and the British Left*, 45.

42. Cited in Burton J. Hendrick, *The Life of Andrew Carnegie* (New York: Doubleday, Doran & Co., 1932), 1:74.

43. Cited in H. C. Allen, *Great Britain and the United States* (New York: St. Martin's Press, 1952), 102–04. Allen says that he has taken his figures from a few sources, including J. B. Brebner, *North Atlantic Triangle* and the U.S. Bureau of the Census, *Historical Statistics of the United States*.

44. Hoppen, *Mid-Victorian Generation*, 651.

45. Ibid.

46. Ibid., 641.

47. Ibid., 639.

48. Michael Kammen, *A Machine that Would Go of Itself: The Constitution in American Culture* (New York: St. Martin's Press, 1994), 162.

49. Bryce, *American Commonwealth*, 2:658.

50. Ibid., ix.

51. Henry Maine, *Popular Government* (London: Murray, 1885), 207–11, 218, xi.

52. W. E. H. Lecky, *Democracy and Liberty* (New York: Longmans, Green, 1896), 1:286, 465. See also Benjamin E. Lippincott, *Victorian Critics of Democracy* (Minneapolis: University of Minneapolis Press, 1938).

53. Albert Venn Dicey, *Lectures Introductory to the Study of the Law of the Constitution* (London: Macmillan & Co., 1885).

54. Ibid., 157–65.

55. Bryce, *American Commonwealth*, 2: 344.

56. Ibid., 2: 479.

57. Ibid., 2:450.

58. See Bradford Perkins, *The Great Rapprochment* (New York: Atheneum, 1968).

59. Richard L. Rapson, *Britons View America* (Seattle: University of Washington Press, 1971), 22.

60. Frank Thistlethwaite, *The Anglo-American Connection in the Early Nineteenth Century* (Philadelphia: University of Pennsylvania Press, 1959), 176.

61. A very helpful guide to religion as the mainspring of his life may be found in David W. Bebbington, *William Ewart Gladstone: Faith and Politics in Victorian Britain* (Grand Rapids: William B. Eerdmans, 1993), especially chaps. 1–3, 9, 10, and 12.

CHAPTER 5

1. R. C. K. Ensor, *England 1870–1914* (Oxford: Clarendon Press, 1936), 103. His figures are taken from Michael G. Mulhall, *Dictionary of Statistics* (London: Routledge, 1899).

2. See Asa Briggs, *The Age of Improvement* (New York: D. McKay, 1962), 48–49.

3. For the most comprehensive guide to the nineteenth-century English press, see John S. North, ed., *The Waterloo Directory of English Newspapers and Periodicals 1800–1900* (Waterloo, ON: North Waterloo Academic Press, 1997).

4. The reviews cited in this chapter and the next are to be found in the Andrew Carnegie Papers, Manuscripts Division, Library of Congress, Washington, DC.

5. *Spectator*, May 29, 1886.

6. *St. James' Gazette*, May 29, 1886.

7. *Saturday Review*, September 18, 1886.

8. *Academy*, August 7, 1886.

9. *St. James' Gazette*, May 29, 1886.

10. *Somerset County Herald*, June 5, 1886.

11. *Academy*, August 7, 1886.

12. *Saturday Review*, September 18, 1886.

13. Ibid.

14. *St. James's Gazette*, May 29, 1886; emphasis added.

15. *Saturday Review*, September 18, 1886; emphasis added.

16. *London State*, May 27, 1886.

17. *Spectator*, May 29, 1886.

18. *Salisbury Journal*, June 16, 1886.

19. *Somerset County Herald*, June 5, 1886.

20. *North-Eastern Weekly Gazette*, May 20, 1886.

21. *Reynolds of London*, May 23, 1886.
22. *London Echo*, May 13, 1886.
23. *London State*, May 27, 1886.
24. *Academy*, August 7, 1886.
25. *Saturday Review*, September 18, 1886.
26. *Economist*, May 22, 1886.
27. *Civil Service Gazette*, May 15, 1886.
28. *Globe*, May 13, 1886.
29. *London Sunday Chronicle*, May 9, 1886.
30. Ibid.
31. *Globe*, May 13, 1886.
32. *Court and Society*, September 16, 1886.
33. *St. James' Gazette*, May 29, 1886.
34. *Somerset County Herald*, June 5, 1886.
35. *Salisbury Journal*, June 26, 1886.
36. *Edinburgh Scotsman*, June 15, 1886.
37. *Glasgow Herald*, July 14, 1886.
38. *Dunfermline Saturday Press*, May 22, 1886.
39. Ibid.
40. *Elgin Courant*, May 18, 1886.

Chapter 6

1. These included, among many others, Henry George, William Dean Howells, William Graham Sumner, Josiah Strong, Mark Twain, Edward Bellamy, and Henry Adams.

2. John A. Garraty, *The New Commonwealth, 1877–1890* (New York: Harper Torchbooks, 1968), 166–68.

3. Cited in Ibid., 185.

4. See N. W. Ayer and Sons, *American Newspaper Annual* (Philadelphia: N. W. Ayer & Sons, 1886).

5. The phrase is from Robert Wiebe, *The Search for Order, 1877–1920* (New York: Hill & Wang, 1967).

6. See *The National Cyclopedia of American Biography* (New York: J. T. White), which appeared serially during the late nineteenth and early twentieth centuries.

7. *Albany* [NY] *Times,* May 1, 1886. The reviews cited in this chapter are to be found in the Andrew Carnegie Papers, Manuscripts Division, Library of Congress, Washington, DC.

8. *New Haven News,* June 12, 1886.

9. *New York Critic,* May 8, 1886.

10. *New York Independent,* June 3, 1886.

11. *Rome* [NY] *Sentinel,* April 14, 1886.

12. *San Francisco Argonaut,* June 5, 1886.

13. *San Francisco Post,* May 1, 1886.

14. *Rochester* [NY] *Post-Express,* May 25, 1886.

15. *New York Star,* June 27, 1886.

16. *Indianapolis Journal,* May 8, 1886.

17. *Boston Commercial Bulletin,* May 29, 1886.

18. *Troy* [NY] *Times,* April 30, 1886.

19. *Springfield* [MA] *Union,* June 14, 1886.

20. *Chicago Evening Herald,* June 5, 1886.

21. *Davenport* [IA] *Democrat,* May 23, 1886.

22. S. B. Elkin, letter to Carnegie, May 16, 1886. Andrew Carnegie Papers, Manuscripts Division, Library of Congress, Washington, DC.

23. Letter, f:1393, Carnegie Papers; emphasis added.

24. L. S. Metcalf, letter to Carnegie, f:1393, Carnegie Papers, emphasis added.

25. W. T. Hornaday, letter to Carnegie, May 5, 1886, Carnegie Papers.

26. W. Phelps, letter to Carnegie, 1487ff. Carnegie Papers.

27. John Forrest Dillon, letter to Carnegie, 1479ff., Carnegie Papers.

28. *Newark* [NJ] *Advertiser,* May 5, 1886.

29. *Chicago Herald,* May 16, 1886.

30. *Boston Traveller,* April 21, 1886; *Brooklyn Times,* May 1, 1886.

31. *Boston Pilot,* May 1, 1886.

32. *Chicago Dial,* May 1886.

33. *Boston Pilot,* May 1, 1886.

34. *Newburyport* [MA] *Herald,* June 12, 1886.

35. *Chicago Evening Herald,* June 5, 1886.

36. *Philadelphia Ledger,* May 3, 1886.

37. *Springfield* [MA] *Union,* June 14, 1886.

38. *New Haven News,* June 12, 1886.

39. *Washington Post*, June 27, 1886.
40. *Brooklyn Times*, May 1, 1886.
41. *Chicago Herald*, May 16, 1886.
42. *Chicago Journal*, May 1, 1886.
43. *Philadelphia Bulletin*, April 23, 1886.
44. *Boston Commercial Bulletin*, May 29, 1886.
45. *Boston Beacon*, April 14, 1886; emphasis added.
46. Henry George, undated letter, Carnegie Papers.
47. *Boston Gazette*, April 14, 1886.
48. *Brooklyn Times*, May 22, 1886.
49. *Rome* [NY] *Sentinel*, May 24, 1886.
50. *Chicago Dial*, May 1886.
51. *Dallas News*, April 25, 1886.
52. *The Nation*, June 3, 1886.
53. *New York Graphic*, May 1, 1886.
54. *New York Star*, June 27, 1886.
55. *Philadelphia Record*, June 26, 1886.
56. *New York Star*, June 27, 1886.
57. *The Nation*, June 3, 1886.
58. *Chicago News*, May 25, 1886.
59. *Boston Courier*, April 15, 1886.
60. *Newark* [NJ] *Daily Advertiser*, May 15, 1886.
61. *Dallas News*, April 15, 1886.
62. *New York Graphic*, May 1, 1886.

Chapter 7

1. Charles Wentworth Dilke, *Greater Britain: A Record of Travel in English-Speaking Countries during 1866–1867* (London: Macmillan & Co., 1868). For a biography of the radical Liberal, see David Nicholls, *The Lost Prime Minister: A Life of Charles Dilke* (London: Hambledon Press, 1995).

2. Particularly valuable on the literature dealing with the context of the Pan-Anglian persuasion is David A. Lincove and Gary R. Treadway, *The Anglo-American Relationship: An Annotated Bibliography of Scholarship, 1945–1985* (Westport, CT: Greenwood

Press, 1988). The many writings that examine this context are cited in references 1–427 and 1196–1299.

3. Carnegie used these phrases almost interchangeably in *Triumphant Democracy*.

4. L. P. Curtis, Jr., *Anglo-Saxons and Celts: A Study of Anti-Irish Prejudice in Victorian England* (New York: New York University Press, 1968), 19–21.

5. Richard H. Heindel, *The American Impact on Great Britain, 1898–1914: A Study of the United States in World History* (Philadelphia: University of Pennsylvania Press, 1940), 128.

6. John R. Dos Passos, *The Anglo-Saxon Century and the Unification of the English-Speaking Peoples* (New York: G. P. Putnam's Sons, 1903), 213.

7. Ibid., 216.

8. See George Macaulay Trevelyan, *The Life of John Bright* (Boston: Houghton Mifflin, 1913), in particular, chap. 14. Also Herman Ausubel, *John Bright, Victorian Reformer* (New York: John Wiley & Sons, 1966), 139.

9. Ibid.

10. Heindel, *American Impact*, 130–31.

11. Ibid., 131.

12. Cited in H. C. Allen, *Great Britain and the United States: A History of Anglo-American Relations* (New York: St. Martin's Press, 1952), 19.

13. Some of the noteworthy books on the Pan-Anglian connection are George Louis Beer, *The English-Speaking Peoples* (New York: Macmillan Co., 1918); Sinclair Kennedy, *The Pan-Angles* (New York: Longmans, Green & Co., 1914); James Muirhead, *The Land of Contrasts: A Briton's View of his American Kin* (London: John Lane, 1902); Archibald R. Coloquhoun, *Greater America* (London: Harper & Brothers, 1904); William T. Stead, *The Americanization of the World* (London: H. Markley, 1901).

14. Dilke, *Greater Britain*, vii.

15. Ibid., 223, 572, 573.

16. Ibid., 555, 556, 571, 573.

17. Ibid., 573.

18. Ibid., 229, vii, 199.

19. Ibid., 219–21.

20. Dos Passos, *The Anglo-Saxon Century*, vii.

21. Ibid., x, 89, 69–98.

22. Ibid., 101–41.

23. Ibid., 69.

24. Ibid., xi.

25. Curtis, *Anglo-Saxons and Celts*, 7–12, 74–76, 89.

26. Edward N. Saveth, *American Historians and European Immigrants, 1875–1925* (New York: Columbia University Press, 1948), 19.

27. Cited in A. S. Eisenstadt, *Charles McLean Andrews: A Study in American Historical Writings* (New York: Columbia University Press, 1956), 12–13.

28. Ibid., 6, 124, 128, 129, 143–52.

29. See Michael Kraus and Davis D. Joyce, *The Writing of American History* (Norman: University of Oklahoma Press, 1985). See also G. O. Trevelyan, *The American Revolution*, 14 vols. (London: Longmans, Green, 1880–1914).

30. On the imperial school see John Higham, *History: Professional Scholarship in America* (Baltimore: Johns Hopkins University Press, updated 1989), 161–65, and A. S. Eisenstadt, *Charles McLean Andrews*, chap. 7.

31. Moses Coit Tyler, *The Literary History of the American Revolution, 1763–1783* (New York: G. P. Putnam's Sons, 1897), 1:303.

32. Ibid., 1:313–15.

33. Ibid., 1:498–99.

34. Ibid., 1:ix.

35. Ibid., 1:x.

36. See Stanley Elkins and Eric McKitrick, "The Founding Fathers: Young Men of the Revolution," *Political Science Quarterly*, 76 (June 1961), 181–216. They have further drawn on and enriched these ideas in their magisterial volume *The Age of Federalism: The Early American Republic 1788–1800* (New York: Oxford University Press, 1993), 23–26.

37. Robert Kelley, *The Transatlantic Persuasion: The Liberal-Democratic Mind in the Age of Gladstone* (New York: Alfred A. Knopf, 1969), xix, 408.

38. Allan Nevins, *America through British Eyes* (New York: Oxford University Press, 1948).

39. Henry Steele Commager, *Britain through American Eyes* (New York: McGraw-Hill, 1974).

40. Richard L. Rapson, *Britons View America: Travel Commentary 1860–1935* (Seattle: University of Washington Press, 1971).

41. For an analysis of how Americans, including American Pan-Angles, viewed Britain during the later Victorian age, see A. S. Eisenstadt, "The Special Relationship: Britain through American Eyes," *The Massachusetts Review*, 18 (Winter 1977), 824–43.

42. Re Freeman see Curtis, *Anglo-Saxons and Celts*. Re Morley, see H. A. L. Fisher, *James Bryce* (New York: Macmillan, 1927), 1:50.

43. Edmund Ions, *James Bryce and American Democracy, 1870–1922* (London: Macmillan & Co., 1968), 24–26. See also Fisher, *James Bryce*.

44. See James Bryce, *The American Commonwealth*, 2nd ed., revised (London: Macmillan & Co., 1891), 1:vii–ix. The best single book on Bryce's tireless pursuit of U.S. life and institutions is Edmund Ions, *James Bryce and American Democracy*. Directly rele-

vant here are chaps. 4–10. Less helpful on this subject is H. A. L. Fisher's conventional life and letters biography: *James Bryce* in 2 volumes.

45. John Higham, *Strangers in the Land: Patterns of American Nativism, 1860–1925*, 1963 reprint (Westport, CT: Greenwood Press, 1980), 36–40.

46. Robert Wiebe, *The Search for Order, 1877–1920* (New York: Hill & Wang, 1967), chaps. 2, 3.

47. Ibid., 51.

48. Carl Schurz, quoted in Richard Hofstadter, *Anti-Intellectualism in American Life* (New York: Alfred A. Knopf, 1963), 178, 174.

49. For insightful suggestions about many of the American Pan-Angles see John Tomisch, *A Genteel Endeavor: American Culture and Politics in the Gilded Age* (Stanford: Stanford University Press, 1971), particularly chaps. 1, 4, 8, and 9; also Geoffrey Blodgett, *The Gentle Reformers: Massachusetts Democrats in the Cleveland Era* (Cambridge: Harvard University Press, 1966).

50. See Allan Nevins, *The Emergence of Modern America* (New York: Macmillan Co., 1927), 178–202.

51. Cited in Hofstadter, *Anti-Intellectualism*, 179.

52. Ibid., 182–85.

53. Barbara Miller Solomon, *Ancestors and Immigrants* (Cambridge: Harvard University Press, 1956), 60.

54. Ibid., 58, 67, 64.

55. See: Max Beloff, "The Special Relationship: An Anglo-American Myth," in *A Century of Conflict 1850–1950,* Martin Gilbert, ed. (New York: Atheneum, 1967), 151–71.

56. Bradford Perkins, *The Great Rapprochement: England and the United States 1895–1914* (New York: Atheneum, 1968), 150–53.

57. Ibid., 151.

58. Ibid., 153.

59. Ibid., 59–61.

60. Ibid., 54.

61. Bernard Crick, ed., *Essays on Reform: 1967, A Centenary Tribute* (London: Oxford University Press, 1967), 8.

62. W. L. Guttsman, ed., *A Plea for Democracy* (London: MacGibbon & Kee, 1967), 140–47.

63. Andrew Carnegie, *Triumphant Democracy* (New York: Charles Scribner's Sons, 1886), 12, 23, 27, 28, 120.

64. Ibid., 18, 20, 496, 45.

65. Ibid., 492–93.

66. Ibid., 492–93, 496.

67. Ibid., 509, v, 508–09.

68. Bernard Alderson, *Andrew Carnegie: The Man and His Work* (New York: Doubleday, Page & Co., 1902), 105–08.

Chapter 8

1. Burton J. Hendrick, *The Life of Andrew Carnegie* (New York: Doubleday, Doran & Co., 1931) 1:254.

2. William Serrin, *Homestead* (New York: Vintage Books, 1993), 68–95; Joseph Frazier Wall, *Andrew Carnegie* (New York: Oxford University Press, 1970), 537–82.

3. Andrew Carnegie, "Triumphant Democracy," Address, December 8, 1887 (New York: Burgoyne Printing), 30, 14–15, 23, 9–10.

4. Edward C. Kirkland, ed., *The Gospel of Wealth and Other Timely Essays* (Cambridge: Harvard University Press, 1962), 168.

5. Ibid., 169.

6. Ibid., 173.

7. Ibid., 194–95.

8. Ibid., 196.

9. Carnegie, "Imperial Federation," *Nineteenth Century*, 30 (September 1891), reprinted in Kirkland, *Gospel of Wealth*, 220.

10. Ibid., 215.

11. Ibid., 221.

12. Ibid., 231.

13. Ibid., 229.

14. Ibid., 236–37.

15. The reporter was from the *Aberdeen Northern Daily News*. The interview was published as a pamphlet: *Mr. Andrew Carnegie on Socialism, Labour, and Home Rule* (Aberdeen: Northern Newspaper Company, 1892).

16. Cited in Wall, *Andrew Carnegie*, 571.

17. Ibid.

18. James Howard Bridge, *The Inside Story of the Carnegie Steel Company* (New York: Aldine Book Co., 1903), 237.

19. Ibid.

20. Wall, *Andrew Carnegie*, 572.

21. Ibid., 571.

22. Ibid.

23. Bridge, *Inside Story*, 232–33.

24. Ibid., 234.

25. Ibid.

26. Wall, *Andrew Carnegie*, 577.

27. Andrew Carnegie, "A Look Ahead" was separately published in *North American Review*, 156 (June 1893), 685–710.

28. Ibid., 710.

29. Andrew Carnegie, "Distant Possessions: The Parting of the Ways" in Kirkland, *Gospel of Wealth*, 124.

30. Ibid., 130.

31. Ibid., 123.

32. Ibid., 132; emphasis added.

33. Andrew Carnegie "Americanism versus Imperialism," *North American Review* (January and March 1899), reprinted in Kirkland, *The Gospel of Wealth*, 164.

34. Ibid., 146.

35. Ibid., 141.

36. A helpful contemporary survey of the literature of the changing foreign view of the United States is John Graham Brooks, *As Others See Us* (New York: Macmillan Co., 1908).

37. Wall, *Andrew Carnegie*, 445.

38. Ibid., 225.

39. Ibid., 832.

40. Ibid.

41. Ibid., 686–87.

42. Cited in Wall, *Andrew Carnegie*, 840.

43. Ibid., 822.

44. Andrew Carnegie, *Autobiography of Andrew Carnegie*, ed. John C. Van Dyke (New York: Houghton Mifflin, 1920), 234.

45. Ibid., 232.

46. Ibid.

47. Wall, *Andrew Carnegie*, 365; Hendrick, *Life of Carnegie*, 1:238–39.

48. Wall, *Andrew Carnegie*, 898.

A Brief Note on Sources

WHAT WERE THE SUBSTANCE and importance of Andrew Carnegie's *Triumphant Democracy?* The sources I have consulted in trying to answer this question appear in the notes I have cited in my chapters. I have situated myself at the intersecting point of Carnegie and the place of his book in the British-American relationship. Because the literature on this subject is so vast, I have tapped only a fraction of it that relates directly to my interest. Strict limitations of space have restricted my bibliographical citations.

As to the manuscript materials I have used, my principal source has been the collection of the Andrew Carnegie Papers in the Manuscripts Division of the Library of Congress. These are to be found in some 300 containers, of which the first twenty-four background the years through 1893, when the revised edition of *Triumphant Democracy* appeared. It was helpful that the materials of the Carnegie Papers had been so thoroughly canvassed by Burton J. Hendrick, the first of Carnegie's principal biographers. Under Hendrick's guidance, Doubleday, Doran, which published the biography, also reissued all of Carnegie's writings. For my account of Carnegie's road to *Triumphant Democracy,* I have also depended on Joseph Frazier Wall's biography, which won the 1970 Bancroft award.

Other books about Carnegie are noteworthy: Harold C. Livesay, *Andrew Carnegie and the Rise of Big Business* (Boston: Little, Brown, 1975); Louis M. Hacker, *The World of Andrew Carnegie, 1865–1901* (Philadelphia: J. B. Lippincott, 1968); Peter Krass, *Carnegie* (Hoboken: John Wiley & Sons, 2002); James A. Mackay, *Little Boss: Life of Andrew Carnegie* (Edinburgh: Mainstream, 1997), and David Nasaw, *Andrew Carnegie* (New York: The Penguin Press, 2006).

My use of contemporary sources has been extensive (as indicated by my notes). Given the center of my interest and theme, however, my use of manuscript materials has been limited. I have consulted the papers of

James Bryce at the Bodleian Library at Oxford, of Albert Shaw at the New York Public Library, and of William Gladstone at what was then the British Museum in London.

I first encountered the idea of the Pan-Anglian persuasion when I studied the life and contributions of Charles McLean Andrews, one of America's most distinguished writers on colonial history. His papers and library were then at his home at 424 St. Ronan Street in New Haven. They were later transferred to the Sterling Memorial Library of Yale University; they contain 100 boxes of his manuscript materials. Professor Andrews' Pan-Anglianism was judicious and highly informed. His collection is a treasure of Pan-Anglian historiography.

In addition to the books cited in the notes, the following have been particularly helpful.

Cannadine, David. *The Decline and Fall of the British Aristocracy.* New Haven: Yale University Press, 1990.

Colley, Linda. *Britons: Forging the Nation, 1707–1837.* New Haven: Yale University Press, 1992.

Crook, David Paul. *The North, the South, and the Powers, 1861–1865.* New York: John Wiley & Sons, 1974.

Erickson, Charlotte. *Invisible Immigrants: Adaptation of English and Scottish Immigrants in Nineteenth-Century America.* London: Weidenfeld and Nicolson, 1972.

Hobsbawm, Eric. *The Age of Empire 1875–1914.* New York: Pantheon, 1987.

Kammen, Michael. *A Machine that Would Go of Itself: The Constitution in American Culture.* New York: St. Martin's Press, 1994.

Lease, Benjamin. *Anglo-American Encounters: England and the Rise of American Literature.* Cambridge: Cambridge University Press, 1981.

Wood, Gordon S. *The Americanization of Benjamin Franklin.* New York: Penguin Books, 2004.

Index

Academy, 76, 77, 79, 84
Adams, Charles Francis, Jr., 129
Adams, Henry, 46, 129, 135, 139
Albany Times (NY), 103
Anglo-American:
   dialogue, 10, 90, 94, 100, 108–09, 114, 116
   diplomatic exchanges, 52, 69
   historical context, 33–34, 41–43, 45–46, 55–56, 59, 126, 136, 142–44, 177 (*see also* Civil War)
   intellectual relationship, 35–37, 44, 45, 46, 132
   kinship, 60, 70, 91, 141 (*see also* Pan-Anglianism)
Anglo-American League, 144
Anglophiles, 45–47, 58–60, 140–41
Anglophobia, 43, 56–58
Anglo-Saxonism, 59, 60, 122, 124–26, 128, 141, 148, 173
Anglo-Saxon race, 18–19, 71, 118–21, 148, 151, 161, 168
Atlantic Monthly, 131
Atlantic Union, 143

Benthamites, 3, 39, 49, 50–52
Blaine, James G., 97, 101, 102, 110, 112
Boer War, 57, 122, 144
Boston Beacon, 110

Boston Brahmins, 46, 76, 108, 135, 140
Boston Commercial Bulletin, 108
Boston Courier, 113
Boston Gazette, 111
Boston Pilot, 106, 107
Bradlaugh, Charles, 12
Bridge, James Howard, 165
Bright, John, 12, 16, 50, 52, 59, 63, 64, 65, 70, 118, 131, 156, 159
Brooklyn Times, 108, 111
Bryce, James, 15, 16, 44, 58–59, 68–69, 70, 97, 99, 101, 115, 129, 131, 132, 133, 134, 135, 136, 143, 144, 146, 150, 152, 169
Burke, Edmund, 34, 126, 147

Canada, 34, 57, 142
Carnegie, Andrew (*see also Triumphant Democracy*):
   An American Four-in-Hand in Britain, 8, 164
   "As Others See Us," 7, 9
   and British system, 17, 19, 152–53
   Carnegie Endowment for International Peace, 176
   "Democracy in England," 159
   and education, importance of, 10, 22–23, 26–27, 170, 176

Carnegie, Andrew (*continued*)
  Glasgow Junior Liberal Association, address to, 160
  gospel of wealth, 6, 158, 169
  and Greater America, 166
  and home rule, 26, 76, 160, 166
  and immigration, 149, 157
  and imperialism, 167–68
  "Imperial Federation," 160
  influences on, 3–7, 52, 134
  marriage, 8, 156, 175
  newspaper ownership, 3, 6, 9, 12, 20, 25, 65, 75, 77, 83, 86, 87, 114, 156, 164
  opinions toward, 84–85, 91, 92, 101, 111, 113–14, 164, 174
  Pan-Anglicanism, 120, 129, 131, 134, 148–53, 173
  personal memorandum, 6, 9, 12, 137, 158, 170
  philanthropy, 10, 23, 27, 137, 169, 176
  and protective tariff, 88–89, 112, 114, 164
  and religion, 24
  Round the World, 18
  and Spanish-American War, 167–68
  star-spangled Scotchman, 3, 79, 89, 164
  "Triumphant Democracy" address, 157, 162
  U.S. political ties, 95, 101
  U.S. prosperity (reasons for), 17–20
  and U.S. Socialism, 157–58, 162
  "Wealth," 170
Chamberlain, Joseph, 12, 26, 64, 70, 72, 93, 118, 119, 131, 144, 158
Chamberlain, Lord Randolph, 93
Charter, The, 51
Chartism, 2, 3–4, 32, 39, 48, 51, 52, 53, 64, 66, 156
Chicago Dial, 107, 111

Chicago Evening Herald, 104, 107
Chicago Herald, 108
Chicago Journal, 108
Chicago News, 109, 113
Churchill, Randolph, 26, 144
Civil Service Gazette, 85
Civil War (U.S.), 6, 11, 55, 56, 62, 70, 102, 104, 119, 120, 129, 136, 144
  and slavery, 55, 63, 128, 147
Cobbitt, William, 3
Cobden, Richard, 50, 52, 156
Conservative Party, 2, 26, 67, 70, 114
Court and Society, 86

Dallas News, 111, 114
Davenport Democrat (IA), 104
Dicey, Albert Venn, 20, 66, 68, 129, 131, 133, 134
Dilke, Charles, 12, 25, 58, 64, 70, 117, 119–21 123
Dos Passos, John R., 119, 121–24
Dunfermline Journal, 165
Dunfermline Saturday Press, 89, 90

Economist, 76, 85
Edinburgh Dispatch, 164
Edinburgh Review, 44
Edinburgh Scotsman, 89, 90
Edinburgh Scottish Reformer, 90
Elgin Courant, 91, 92
Elkin, S. B., 105
Emerson, Ralph Waldo, 36, 38, 44, 46, 110, 135, 138
English-speaking peoples, 117, 129, 160–61, 168
equality, 23, 66, 77, 81, 100
  Carnegie and, 4, 10, 16, 18, 19–21, 26–27, 80, 87

Fiske, John, 125, 135, 141
Fortnightly Review, 7

Index

Forum, 105, 131
Freeman, Edward Augustus, 76, 124–25, 132, 133, 148, 150
Frick, Henry Clay, 163, 166, 172

George, Henry, 95–96, 98, 110, 138
Gladstone, William Evert, 2, 8, 9, 12, 21, 62, 63, 70–72, 74–75, 119, 126, 145, 158
Glasgow Herald, 89, 90, 91
Globe, 76, 80, 85, 86
Godkin, E. L., 99, 102, 109, 111, 113, 136, 167
Graphic, 76, 112
Great Britain
  reform, 25, 31–32, 37, 39, 41, 47–51, 53, 64, 66, 74, 147
Grund, Francis J., 43, 48, 168

Harper's Weekly, 139
Haymarket Square, 80, 96, 98
home rule (*see also* Irish Home Rule), 60, 65, 74
Homestead Steel Mill, 156, 162–66, 172
Hornaday, William Temple, 95, 105

Imperial Federation League, 160
Independent, 131
Irish-Americans, 38, 40, 57, 60, 65, 97, 131, 138, 140, 145
Irish Home Rule, 10, 13, 26, 57, 60, 70, 74–75, 93–94, 155, 159, 163
  Tennyson and, 66–67
Irving, Washington, 36, 40, 44, 46, 110, 135, 148

James, Henry, 119
July 4th celebrations, 43, 44, 61, 107

Labour Party, 156
Lauder, George, Jr. (Dod), 4–6, 52, 66, 158
Lechy, W. E. H., 66, 68
Liberal Party, 2, 25, 67, 70–72, 75, 138
Liberalism and Scotland, 89
London Echo, 83, 164
London Financial Observer, 164
London State, 81, 84
London Sunday Chronicle, 86

Macaulay, Thomas Babington, 67, 126, 139, 143
Maine, Henry, 16, 68, 76,
Manchester Liberals, 49–50, 52
Mill, John Stuart, 39, 40, 138
Money, 78
Morley, John, 7, 12, 16, 25, 64, 76, 129, 131, 133, 150
Muirhead, James, 58, 59

Nation, The, 111, 113, 131, 139
Newark Advertiser (NJ), 106
New Haven News, 103, 107
New York Critic, 103
New York Evening Post, 139
New York Graphic, 111, 114
New York Independent, 103
New York Star, 103, 109, 112–13
New York Tribune, 139
North American Review, 71, 131, 139, 159, 167, 170
North-Eastern Weekly Gazette, 83

Pall Mall Gazette, 7
Pan-Anglianism, 11, 110, 117–18, 124–25, 128–33, 144–50, 173
  Andrew Carnegie and, *see* Carnegie, Andrew
  in Great Britain, 76, 129, 132–34, 146
  historiography, 124–28, 150
  in the United States, 60, 110, 121–24, 134–41, 145

Philadelphia Bulletin, 108
Philadelphia Ledger, 107
Philadelphia Record, 109, 112
Pilgrim Society, 143

radicals (British), 3, 39, 48, 51, 64, 70, 83
Reynolds of London, 83
Reynolds's Newspaper, 64, 65
Rochester Post-Express, 103
Rome Sentinel (NY), 103, 111

Salisbury Journal, 82, 85, 87
Salisbury, Lord (Marquess), 2, 12, 67, 114, 144
San Francisco Argonaut, 103
Saturday Review, 76, 78, 80, 81, 84
Scottish Enlightenment, 88
Scribner's, 131
Sheffield Daily Telegraph, 164
Somerset County Herald, 79, 82, 87
Spanish-American War, 122, 144, 167–68
Spectator, 76, 78, 82
Spencer, Herbert, 7, 10, 20, 66, 131, 138, 159, 174, 176
Springfield Union (MA), 107
St. James's Gazette, 76, 78, 81, 86, 164
St. Louis Post-Dispatch, 165
Storey-Carnegie chain, 83, 86, 87 (*see also* Andrew Carnegie: newspaper ownership)
Storey, Samuel, 25 (*see also* Storey-Carnegie chain)
Strong, Josiah, 97, 140, 157–59

Times (London), 164
Tocqueville, Alexis de, 15–16, 24, 36, 38, 39, 40, 41, 44, 47, 48, 56, 65, 67, 69, 146, 168, 169
Tory, 39, 70, 81, 86, 93, 155, 164

Trevelyan, George Otto, 126–27, 129, 133, 143
Triumphant Democracy, 23, 33, 48, 52, 69, 71, 75–76, 100, 115–16, 145, 177–78
  conservative shift in, 66
  and criticism of Carnegie, 113–14
  English reaction: 76–83
  and Homestead, 164–65, 172
  importance of, 9, 109, 115–16, 152, 168–71
  misrepresentations and errors in, 78, 90, 100, 109
  and Pan-Anglicanism, 11, 122, 148–53
  reasons for writing, 2–3, 9, 15, 114, 150
  revised edition, 122, 166, 177
  Scottish reaction, 87–93
  themes, 1–2, 9, 10, 15–20, 59, 76–77
  transatlantic debate, 95, 108, 115
  United States: reaction in, 98–102, 104, 110–15; and unrest in, 96, 100–01, 114
Trollope, Francis, 40–41, 48

United Empire League, 160
United States:
  civic education in, 42, 45, 57–58, 143
  as model for Great Britain, 19, 31–32, 37–39, 47, 48–51, 56, 65, 67–69, 74, 77, 86–87, 90, 146
  reformers in, 136, 139
  unrest in, 96–98, 99, 109–10, 145

Washington Post, 107
Westminster Review, 50
Whigs, 38–39, 52, 64, 126, 147